UNEARTHING
NEW ZEALAND

UNEARTHING NEW ZEALAND

Michael Trotter and Beverley McCulloch

Contributors:
John Wilson, Simon Best, Mike Bradstock, Nigel Prickett,
Geoffrey Thornton, Neville Ritchie, Jack Diamond & Bruce Hayward.

A Bookmakers Book

General Editors: *Michael Trotter, Beverley McCulloch and Phillip Ridge*
Reconstructions and illustrations: *Geoffrey Cox, Gainor Jackson*
Maps and diagrams: *Julie O'Brien and Caroline Philips*
Art Director: *Phillip Ridge/Bookmakers*

Thanks also to Graeme Leather, Gordon Maitland, Harry Morton, Roger Neich, and Ian Snowden for their help in production.

Edited, designed and produced by
Bookmakers Design and Production Ltd.
PO Box 67-074, Mt Eden, Auckland

Photographic and illustration credits

The producers of *Unearthing New Zealand* are indebted to the following individuals, institutions and organisations for their invaluable assistance:

Alexander Turnbull Library (ATL); *Andris Apse Ltd; Anthropology Department, University of Auckland* (AD/ UA); *Auckland Art Gallery; Auckland Institute and Museum* (AIM); *Auckland Public Library* (APL); *Simon Best; Binsted's Studio; Alastair Buist; Colin Burrows; Canterbury Museum* (CM); *John Coster; Janet Davidson; Jack Diamond; Hawke's Bay Art Gallery and Museum* (HBAG & M); *Hocken Library; Gainor Jackson; Warren Jacobs* (WJ); *R. & M. Lane; David Larnach; Rod Morris; National Museum* (NM); *Julie O'Brien; Polynesian Voyaging Society; Nigel Prickett; Neville Ritchie; Geoffrey Thornton; Michael Trotter and Beverley McCulloch and Vivian Ward.*

Where abbreviations appear after a name, those abbreviations are used in the book when crediting photographs or works of art.

Unless otherwise credited, photographs appearing in this book belong to the collection of the authors. Similarly, unless otherwise credited, all colour illustrations and maps are copyright to the producers, Bookmakers Design & Production Ltd.

Title page: A unique stone pectoral pendant from Okains Bay, Banks Peninsula. Dating to the earliest period of Maori settlement in New Zealand, it is 178 millimetres wide, with two fish carved in low relief. When worn, this pendant would have been lashed to a cord by its three suspension holes. It is reminiscent of pearl-shell pectoral ornaments that were worn by the inhabitants of some tropical Pacific islands, and the fish may be a traditional rendering of the bonito which was important in Eastern Polynesian economies. (Photograph by Warren Jacobs)

Right: Canine teeth of the Polynesian dog, kuri, were often drilled and used as personal ornaments. They were probably worn individually as ear or neck pendants.

Published by the Government Printing Office/Publishing
Private Bag, Wellington.

ISBN 0-477-01457-7

© various. Michael Trotter and Beverley McCulloch (text: pp. 7-99).
This selection © Bookmakers Design and Production Ltd.

First Published 1989

Typeset by Saba Graphics Ltd, Christchurch

Printed by Toppan Printing Co. Pty. Ltd, Singapore

Contents

We gratefully acknowledge everyone who knowingly or unknowingly assisted with the writing of this book, particularly: our scientific colleagues — both in New Zealand and overseas — whose research and knowledge provided an indispensable resource; the staff of Canterbury Museum — especially Claudia Reid, Julie O'Brien and Lyn Peck; and finally, but perhaps most importantly, all those people of the prehistoric and historic past who, in their living, left us a record of their lives.

About the authors

MICHAEL TROTTER is director of Canterbury Museum, Christchurch. Educated at Canterbury University, where he took a degree in geography, his early training as an archaeologist was under Dr H. D. Skinner of Otago Museum. In July 1965 he took up the position of archaeologist at Canterbury Museum (the first appointment of a professional archaeologist to any New Zealand museum), a position he held until being appointed director in 1983. He has published more than 80 archaeological papers and books, a number co-authored with Beverley McCulloch.

BEVERLEY McCULLOCH originally studied geology at Canterbury University, and is a qualified teacher. Besides teaching, she has worked as an artist for the DSIR, and as an archaeologist for both the Historic Places Trust and Canterbury Museum, where she is currently employed as liaison officer and curator-in-charge of subfossil birds. Her great interest is in educational writing at a popular level — presenting accurate and up-to-date scientific and historical information to the public in an accessible and readable way.

About the contributors

SIMON BEST is a contract archaeologist, whose current projects include the first Auckland gaol, an early Auckland brickworks and pottery, an 1800-year-old Fijian burial ground, an adze quarry in American Samoa, and the initial archaeology of Tokolau. He is also currently researching the influence of stray sea-going crocodiles on the folklore of the Maori, and the onset of wife strangulation in Fiji.

MIKE BRADSTOCK's involvement with shipwrecks stems from a lifelong interest in diving and maritime history. He has dived on many New Zealand shipwrecks and has taken part in searches for others. Formerly a marine biologist with the Ministry of Agriculture and Fisheries, he currently works in publishing in Auckland.

JACK DIAMOND has devoted much of his spare time to researching the history of the western districts of Auckland. He is a recognised authority on the history and archaeology of that area and has published books and many articles. He was a long-serving field officer for the Auckland Regional Committee of the Historic Places Trust and is a member of the New Zealand Archaeological Association.

BRUCE HAYWARD is a micropalaeontologist at the New Zealand Geological Survey, Lower Hutt. He became interested in relics of the kauri timber and gum industries while doing fieldwork in the Kauaeranga Valley, Coromandel and Waitakere Ranges. He has collaborated with Jack Diamond on a number of booklets, scientific papers and archaeological reports and has also had published a variety of books of his own, such as the kauri industry in the Kauaeranga Valley, the kauri gum industry and a book on building stones and their uses.

NIGEL PRICKETT received his archaeological training at Otago and Auckland Universities, and during two years at the Taranaki Museum, New Plymouth. He is now E. Earle Vaile Archaeologist at the Auckland Museum. In the early 1970s he was involved with the Otago University Palliser Bay archaeological programme during which time he excavated the Moikau Valley Maori dwelling dating to the late twelfth century. A survey of fortifications in Taranaki was part of a wider interest in the archaeology of that region.

NEVILLE RITCHIE graduated from the University of Otago and has been involved in archaeology since 1968 when he was involved in salvage excavations on the site of the future Tiwai Point aluminium smelter. In 1977 he was appointed project archaeologist on the Clutha power project, a position he held for 10 years until the completion of the archaeological programme in 1987. During his time in Cromwell he developed a special interest in the archaeology of historic sites (European and Chinese). More recently he has been involved in the archaeology and conservation work on Scott's and Shackleton's base huts in Antarctica, and documentation of early mining sites in the Coromandel. Dr Ritchie is married with two children and lives in Hamilton, where he is employed as regional archaeologist (Waikato) by the Department of Conservation.

GEOFFREY THORNTON retired from the position of assistant government architect in 1980. He has been on the board of the Historic Places Trust since 1971 and its deputy chairman since 1979. He has been chairman of the Trust's Buildings Classification Subcommittee since 1977. A keen photographer, he wrote and illustrated a key book in arousing interest in New Zealand's industrial past, *New Zealand's Industrial Heritage* (1982).

JOHN WILSON is a Canterbury historian and journalist. He studied history at Canterbury University and Harvard University, from which he graduated with a PhD in Chinese history. Since his return to New Zealand in 1974 he has worked on the staff of *The Press*, Christchurch, and as publications officer of the Historic Places Trust, 1982-84. He continues to edit the Trust's quarterly magazine from his 120-year-old farmhouse at Springston on the Canterbury plains.

Introduction/Digging up the Past

FROM about the middle of the nineteenth century until archaeological research showed otherwise in the 1950s, there was a widespread popular belief that New Zealand had in the past been inhabited by two different races of non-European peoples. It was commonly thought that the 'Maoris', the Polynesians who inhabited the country at the time the first Europeans arrived in the late eighteenth century, had been preceded by a darker skinned, more primitive race, possibly with Melanesian affinities. In later decades these supposedly earlier people were often referred to as 'Morioris'. The most popular version of events held that the Morioris had been supplanted by the arrival of the truly Polynesian Maoris, who arrived in a 'Great Fleet' of named canoes from their island homeland of Hawaiki. They had been told of New Zealand's existence by an early pioneer explorer, Kupe, who had returned home after a voyage of discovery.

In retrospect, such ideas were understandable. They were due largely to the inappropriate application of a two-stage European model of prehistory that was fashionable in the 1850s and 60s, and which resulted in the misinterpretation of archaeological evidence from New Zealand, compounded by the uncritical acceptance of Maori oral 'traditions', some of which were written down for the first time more than 100 years after European contact.

The history of archaeology in New Zealand can be said to begin with Walter Mantell's investigation of a site, which he named Awamoa, in North Otago in 1852. Mantell had dug up archaeological remains (at Waingongoro in Taranaki) even earlier, as had others in both the North and South Islands, but none of these were serious attempts to obtain information from evidence preserved in the ground — which is the essence of archaeology.

The Awamoa site comprised a deposit of bones, burnt stones and flaked artifacts in a matrix of sandy soil buried beneath about 30 centimetres of alluvial deposit. Although cautious in his interpretations, Mantell obtained a considerable amount of information about the early Awamoa people from the archaeological evidence. Midden bones and shells indicated that they had eaten a variety of foods, although they probably did not include human flesh in their diet. The sharp-edged flakes of stone they used as knives were of a material obtained some distance away, possibly inland Otago, but there was a marked absence of the polished stone and bone artifacts known to have been used by the Maoris. Food was cooked using heated stones in earthen ovens. Of most importance to Mantell were the broken bones and eggshells of at least two species of moa, providing '. . . unmistakeable proof of the co-existence of man with the Moa'.

The date of the extinction of these giant flightless birds — and whether or not they had still been alive when the first humans arrived here — was to be the single biggest question to exercise the minds of investigators for some decades.

Although some enthusiastic scientists were later to suggest that 20 or even upwards of 40 different moa species once existed, most investigators today believe that there were only 13 or fewer species, ranging in height from one to three metres. Their former existence was first made known to the world by a trader, Joel Polack, in 1838 — he had found and recognised some moa bones in about 1834. These had come from the base of Hikurangi Mountain in the East Cape area and Polack was told by the local natives that these very large birds had existed

in times long past . . . whose probable tameness, or want of volitary powers, caused them to be early extirpated by a people driven by both hunger and superstition . . . to rid themselves of their presence.

As more and more moa bones were found by the early European explorers, traders and missionaries from the 1840s onwards, further questions were raised: How long ago had the moa become extinct? And had it ever lived contemporaneously with man? Hence Mantell's findings at Awamoa were of considerable importance since they appeared to provide clear evidence that man had hunted moas.

Mantell stressed that he had no fixed ideas on the moas' antiquity, but he could not doubt that they had been hunted and exterminated by man. Some of Mantell's colleagues believed that the extinction of the moas occurred about the same time as that of the megafauna of Europe — such as the mammoth and the woolly rhinoceros — and, therefore, dated back many thousands of years; others thought that the apparent freshness of some of the remains indicated that moas had lived until comparatively recent times.

The moa bones at Awamoa were of

medium-sized species, suggesting that the largest varieties had already become extinct in the district by the time the moa hunters camped there, but the bones and eggshell left Mantell in no doubt that smaller species had been hunted and eaten. In an 1853 newspaper report of his Awamoa investigation, he dryly speculated that a ball of baked clay which he found in the site was most likely the work

> . . . *of some ingenious young savage, stopped on the threshold of the invention of pottery by a vindictive tibia thrown at his head by his enraged parent, with a concise order to go egg-hunting, and not waste time in that way.*

Forty kilometres north-west of Awamoa, Mantell also found some prehistoric rock drawings on an overhanging limestone cliff-face up the Waitaki River, becoming the first European to record the existence of this art form. In an early discussion of the site, he maintained that these drawings included a 'rudely depicted likeness of a moa', although he thought that moa extinction occurred within a very short time of man's arrival in the country — as indicated by the almost total lack of Maori traditions relating to these birds.

Other sites were discovered in both the North and South Islands during the 1850s — most notably an extensive moa-hunter encampment at Redcliffs near Christchurch and a human burial with an associated moa egg and adze heads at Kaikoura — but it was not until 1869 that any significant progress was made in archaeological research. That year was marked by the arrival on the archaeological scene of a German geologist, Julius Haast, the founder and first director of the Canterbury Museum. This was the beginning of some of the most important and influential archaeology ever to be done in New Zealand.

Haast's initial investigations were of a large site near the mouth of the Rakaia River in Canterbury. The Rakaia site comprised principally a series of oven hollows, each containing layers of stones, many of which were broken into angular fragments by the heat of cooking fires. Inside the hollows were broken bones, many of them moa, and flake knives, and there were also heaps of these nearby. Haast believed that here at Rakaia was evidence of two separate periods of prehistoric occupation. Over part of the site were the large ovens, moa bones and flaked stone tools, while elsewhere were smoothly polished stone tools including some made of nephrite (greenstone), which he identified as coming from a later 'Maori' occupation. It was largely on the basis of his work here that Haast proposed that a period of moa-hunter occupation had preceded the Maori occupation of New Zealand. The terms *palaeolithic* and *neolithic* had come into use during the previous decade to describe major divisions of the prehistoric stone-working cultures in Europe, and Haast now applied them here to his moa hunters and Maoris respectively. In accordance with the European model, he considered that the latter had achieved greater technological skill in that they used abrasive methods in the grinding and shaping of stone tools.

Bones of at least five different species of moas were identified from the Rakaia moa-

Hunting for moa bones became a popular and even fashionable pursuit last century. These boatered and skirted women and their friends are digging for bones in a beach swamp near Riverton in Southland.

CM Coll.

hunter middens. Most of the leg bones had been broken, and the ends often appeared to have been scraped out as if to remove the marrow. Skulls too had been broken open, presumably to remove the brains. No bones showed any signs of dog tooth marks, although dog bones were not uncommon in the midden, and this suggested to Haast that the dog was a feral animal. Other food remains left by the moa hunters included bones of eight or nine other species of birds, a whale, two kinds of seals, and shells of freshwater and marine shellfish.

Although Haast found only flaked and chipped stone tools among the moa-hunter middens and ovens, these were made from a variety of materials. Some cut-marked bones were also found, but none was considered to be a manufactured object.

The Rakaia evidence seemed to confirm and add to Mantell's findings at Awamoa — moas had been hunted and eaten by a people whose material culture (a term used for human activities involving material things) was more primitive than that of the Maoris at the time of European settlement. It was not clear how long ago they had lived, but possible parallels with the European palaeolithic era and its megafauna, and the finding of polished stone implements at a depth of about 4.3 metres below the surface on the West Coast, suggested to Haast that man had been in New Zealand for some considerable time. Without more sophisticated tools, he reasoned, the moa hunters could not have built canoes and must, therefore, have been 'autochthones' (derived from the Greek, meaning 'sprung from the land'). This in turn suggested the former existence of a continent in the Pacific basin

where 'now the boundless ocean rolls'.

Haast enquired about Maori traditions relating to moas, and concluded from their general absence that the moas had been exterminated before the present Maori race came to New Zealand.

Although some of Haast's detailed ideas on the culture of the moa hunters were soon to change, his original basic concept of a division of prehistory into two cultural periods has persisted, in spite of later research, in one form or another to the present day.

Yet opposition soon emerged to Haast's suggestions of the great age and the palaeolithic culture of the moa hunters. Some of his colleagues even produced evidence from other sites of polished stone implements being found alongside the remains of moas that had apparently been cooked and eaten. However, work at the mouth of the Shag River in Otago revealed, at least according to Haast, only flaked stone implements in the moa-hunter middens. As at Rakaia, it appeared to him that there had been two distinct occupations of the site; deposits of moa and seal bones being distinctly separated from a later Maori midden of shells. The presence of some ovens 60 centimetres below high-water level in the tidal estuary provided further evidence for Haast of the antiquity of the

The great British anatomist Sir Richard Owen was the first scientist to describe formally moas, giving them the name *Dinornis*, meaning 'the Terrible Bird'. He is shown here with an early reconstruction of a moa skeleton.

The term *Maori*, to describe a native New Zealander, did not come into use until the late 1830s, and is now used to refer to all the prehistoric Polynesian settlers and their descendants in New Zealand. Other terms include *moa hunter* for the early Maoris in whose economy the hunting and utilisation of moas had some importance, and occasionally *archaic* and *classic* to refer to early and late culture respectively. The term *Moriori* refers only to a native of the Chatham Islands and is of even later origin.

The Shag River mouth site (right) in North Otago as it is today. A number of early workers investigated this 700-year-old moa-hunter site which yielded enormous quantities of moa bones and artifacts.

It was the discovery of this polished stone adze head (below right) in the lowest deposits of Moa-bone Point Cave that led to the recognition that the moa hunters, during the first centuries of human occupation of New Zealand, had quite a highly developed 'neolithic' stone tool technology.

Canterbury Museum, Christchurch, 1872 (below). When first displayed in museums, the reconstructed moa skeletons were often mounted at such an angle that the birds appeared taller than they actually were — as if they always moved with their heads erect.

moa hunters; he believed that this could be due only to gradual subsidence of the land over thousands of years.

Again, however, there were dissenting opinions. Frederick Hutton, who like Haast was a geologist, visited the Shag River site about the same time, and according to him moa bones were always associated with shell middens and with a whole range of artifacts; he could see no reason to believe that the moa remains were of any great age. (A few years later, in 1891, he estimated that the moas had been exterminated only 300 or 400 years ago in the South Island and about a century earlier than that in the North.) Hutton believed that the presence of oven stones below high-water mark resulted from their being washed out of a bank that had been undercut by the river. He employed B. S. Booth to explore the site for three months in 1875, and many of his published conclusions were based solely upon Booth's observations — a fact that Haast was quick to point out. Booth reported a greater proportion of broken moa bones at the Shag River site than had Haast and concluded that the bones had been broken open to extract marrow and hence that moas were not particularly abundant. He also found two pieces of bone that appeared to have been gnawed by dogs, which he believed indicated a domesticated breed — also contrary to Haast's ideas.

Eventually the argument about the moa-hunting people not possessing polished stone implements was quashed by Haast's own research at Moa-bone Point Cave near Christchurch. Moa bones had been known since

at least 1849 to occur in this area, and in 1872 Haast employed two men to dig the stratified floor deposits of the cave in an attempt to obtain further indisputable information about the moa hunters.

Once again Haast thought the distinction between the contents of the 'moa hunter' and the 'Maori' deposits was quite clear, and that there was a layer of sterile sand separating them. Moa bones occurred only rarely in the Maori shell beds and there were few shells among the moa bones of the lower dirt-bed. As at Rakaia, no bones from the moa-hunter level appeared to have been gnawed by dogs. Both Maori and moa-hunter deposits contained a variety of artifacts made of wood, bone and stone. More importantly, however, some of the moa-hunter stone implements were polished. Although Haast still maintained his position on the great antiquity of his moa hunters (he was too much of a scientist to guess at their age in years), he was at last forced to conclude that their material culture was not significantly inferior to that of the later Maoris, and that they were in fact 'neolithic'.

Haast did not immediately publish these findings, and nearly two years later a paper by one of his workmen, Alexander McKay, was read to the Wellington Philosophical Institute. It described the stratified floor deposits with a moa-hunter level being overlaid by a later shell deposit, and, of course, the presence of polished stone implements in the lower level. Haast was furious at this unauthorised presentation of data by a 'paid employee' and quickly had a report of

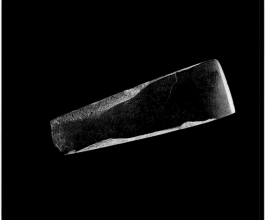

his own published to pre-empt the publication of McKay's account.

Further complexities emerged with the discovery of rock drawings in Weka Pass, North Canterbury, in 1876. Haast, whose recent Austrian knighthood recognising his work made him Julius *Ritter von* Haast, was again in the forefront of the investigation and ensuing controversy. The Weka Pass rock shelter (now usually called Timpendean), contained a large area of black and red drawings, none of which resembled any Maori artwork known at that time. Haast noted that 'paintings of similar character' could be found in other places, including those at Takiroa described earlier by Mantell, but maintained that none were like those at Weka Pass. From their imagined likeness to the works of other cultures, diverse theories were proposed, ascribing them to shipwrecked Tamil mariners, to the 'somewhat mythical Ngapuhi' and even to Buddhist missionaries! The matter was still not resolved at the time of Haast's death in 1887.

Throughout the nineteenth century a number of other people helped, or tried to help, throw light on the prehistoric occupation of New Zealand. Traditional references to the settlement of the country were collected by European travellers in the 1830s and 40s, and major contributions were made by Edward Shortland and George Grey in the 1850s. During the Haast era several missionaries — especially William Colenso, Richard Taylor, James Stack and Johann Wohlers — published traditions they had collected, and John White produced an immense

seven-volume compilation of traditional histories, the first in 1887. Pragmatist William Maskell and 'biblical archaeologist' Mackenzie Cameron were also to leave their mark, but it was mainly the geologists of the nineteenth century, even if they couldn't always agree with each other, who produced sound archaeological evidence of the pre-European occupation of this country, and it was their theories that formed the foundations of our knowledge of New Zealand's prehistory.

By the turn of the century it was generally accepted that New Zealand had been settled for about 1000 years; Haast's notions of greater antiquity were by now quietly dismissed. Interestingly, little account had been taken of the Maori people or the innumerable village sites in the North Island as a potential source of information. Most research was still being conducted in the South Island where there were relatively few Maoris living. It is likely that the much greater Maori population in the north actually provided a barrier to scientific enquiry, particularly since the northern land wars had been fought only a few decades before.

During the first half of the twentieth century, the role of studying the pre-European Maoris was largely taken over by traditionalists and ethnologists. A growing obsession with the interpretation of Maori traditions was led primarily by two men, Percy Smith and Elsdon Best. Smith was the founder and some time president of the Polynesian Society — formed in 1892 to promote the study of the anthropology, ethnology, philology, history and antiquities of the Polynesian races — and he edited its

Plan and section of Moa-bone Point Cave, Christchurch, which was first occupied over 600 years ago.

Archaeologist Jack Golson (below) explaining the complex but disturbed stratigraphy in Moa-bone Point Cave during the first official excavations carried out by the New Zealand Archaeological Association in January 1958. The cave had initially been excavated by Julius Haast in 1872 and contained evidence of occupation dating back to the moa hunters.

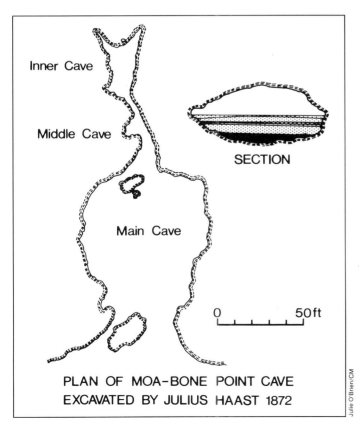

Inner Cave

Middle Cave

SECTION

Main Cave

0   50 ft

Julie O'Brien/CM

PLAN OF MOA-BONE POINT CAVE
EXCAVATED BY JULIUS HAAST 1872

quarterly journal until his death in 1922. Best had spent some years among the Tuhoe tribe in the Urewera country until being appointed to the staff of the Dominion (now National) Museum in 1910; he followed Smith, first as president, then as editor, of the Polynesian Society's journal until his death in 1931.

Both men obtained much of their information about traditions from 'an ancient and learned Maori chief' known as Whatahoro, who in turn had learned most of what he knew some decades earlier at a wharewananga, or school of learning, conducted principally by one Te Matorohanga during the 1860s. Whatahoro, who received both money and kudos for the information he gave, ably answered nearly all the questions put to him, and often gave precise descriptions of events that had occurred many hundreds of years before. Where the traditional record fell short, this canny informant was quite adept at using his imagination. As a member of the Polynesian Society he had ready access to publications on traditional histories, particularly those by Percy Smith himself, and he confirmed and enlarged upon information that had been obtained from other sources, much to Smith's delight. Smith published two volumes of this 'information' in 1913 and 1915, and Best produced his version in 1916.

Together with George Grey's earlier folklore, these provided the basis for a standardised story of the discovery of New Zealand at about AD 950, its initial settlement by an 'inferior' race (often referred to as 'Morioris'), and the subsequent arrival of the Polynesians. This fabricated story became so soundly established that it was taught in schools, was accepted by scholars, and gave rise to several

Kennett Watkins, *The legend of the voyage to New Zealand*, 1912. This painting, depicting the arrival of the Maoris to New Zealand, is perhaps more realistic than many of its genre. Although it depicts a 'Great Fleet', the double canoes shown, the type of sail, and their numerous occupants, are at least based on early observations of Polynesian sailors and their craft.

myths of New Zealand's past which persist even to this day. It was at this time that the concept of a 'Great Fleet' of canoes, bringing the Maori people to New Zealand in the fourteenth century, became firmly established as fact in the mind of both Maori and European.

In the fourteenth century . . . a number of voyaging canoes set out on Kupe's sailing directions with the definite object of colonising the land that lay to the south. Most of the voyagers made their landfall in the Bay of Plenty. . . . The newcomers came into conflict with the first settlers . . . the earlier settlers were absorbed into the more dominant groups of later comers.

So wrote Peter Buck (Te Rangi Hiroa), who was later to be knighted as a pre-eminent Maori anthropologist and authority on Maori culture. Although undoubtedly a scholar in his own right, he relied heavily on the work of Smith and Best for much of his information.

Smith and Best had synthesised a prehistory that appealed to romantic notions, and at the same time confounded the armchair critic with its air of 'scientific' authenticity; their credibility was such that their publications influenced ethnologists for decades to come. Probably no one was more taken in by the 'traditional histories' than the two stalwarts themselves, and because of their prestigious positions, it was difficult for any opposing voice to get a hearing while they lived.

One voice that would not be silenced was that of ethnologist Henry Devenish Skinner. Skinner's forte was to become the study of comparative art forms and artifacts, and he can be credited with having established a new era in

the research of New Zealand's prehistory. In later years Skinner was criticised by fellow ethnologist Roger Duff for his single-minded determination to dismiss the Whatahoro myths, yet the myths survived not only their progenitors but Skinner and Duff as well at a popular level.

In Skinner is reflected a paradox of archaeology at that time — the beginnings of a scientific methodology entwined with notions that were essentially mythological and, therefore, not based on historic fact. If at once he ridiculed certain aspects of the Whatahoro myths, he still regarded as inviolable the concept of a 'Great Fleet' in the fourteenth century. Instead, what he sought to disprove was the notion that the Morioris of the Chatham Islands were a remnant inferior Melanesian race driven from New Zealand by the arrival of warlike Polynesians, as supposedly traditional histories claimed. In the course of his research he visited the Chatham

Islands in 1919, getting there by stowing away in the hold of a steamer because the Marine Department forbade the carriage of passengers. Not surprisingly, Best did not accept the demolition of his traditional history and is said to have referred disparagingly to 'Skinner's quaint theory'.

However, Skinner was not deterred; he encouraged and later employed David Teviotdale to excavate archaeological sites, mostly in Otago, but also in Canterbury, Marlborough and even in the North Island. Teviotdale's main mission was to collect artifacts which Skinner could use in his comparative studies. On the basis of information from the Shag River mouth site, particularly that obtained by Teviotdale, Skinner described in 1924 what he believed to be the essential characteristics of the material culture of the people who had hunted moas in that region. He found that their culture did not differ significantly from that of the Otago Maoris in times immediately preceding the arrival of the Europeans — if anything, their craftsmanship actually appeared to be of a *higher* standard. On a wider field, Skinner noted that Maori material culture, particularly the decorative art, most closely resembled that of the Marquesas Islands, although there were some Melanesian similarities.

Elsewhere in New Zealand, more information was gradually being accumulated by other investigators. An American antiquarian studied rock drawings in North Otago and South Canterbury, Maori canals were mapped near Blenheim, there was some argument as to the

Dittmer's illustration *The Coming of the Maori* (left) reflected the unashamed romanticism of early twentieth-century notions about the prehistoric Maoris. Note the canoe decorated in a carving style developed only after the Polynesian arrival in New Zealand.

Victorians (below) revelled in gory depictions of Salome receiving John the Baptist's head on a plate. This engraving by Danvin, *A native showing a young girl the head of her father*, is typical of early ideas of the savagery of the New Zealand Maori which yet somehow titillated nineteenth-century sensibilities.

purpose of pits in the Marlborough Sounds, modified soils were studied near Nelson, ancient drains were described at Kataia, and a classic paper was published on the Korekore pa site near Auckland. And of special importance in the development of archaeological methodology, a young man who had worked as a volunteer assistant for Teviotdale started conducting his own research into South Otago archaeological sites. This was Leslie Lockerbie and what distinguished him from his contemporaries was his attention to recording details — he first mapped the site, then measured the exact location of every artifact and significant bone he excavated; he took particular notice of stratigraphy and of variations in the nature of the deposit he was investigating.

Then in 1939 a double-column report in the *Marlborough Express* announced that a schoolboy, Jimmy Eyles, had dug up a human skeleton with an associated moa egg, a bone necklace and possibly an adze head, at the mouth of the Wairau River in Marlborough. Although the discovery did not attract much attention at the time, it was later to prove to be one of the most significant archaeological discoveries of the twentieth century. Having been paid handsomely for his find, Jim Eyles again took up his shovel in 1942 and dug up another skeleton. This time the Canterbury Museum's ethnologist, Roger Duff, was sent up to make an on-the-spot assessment of the site, and so commenced a project which culminated in the 1950s with Duff's definitive publication, *The Moa-hunter Period of Maori Culture*.

The Wairau Bar site, as it is usually known, covered an area of six to eight hectares, much of

which had been ploughed for agricultural purposes before Eyles's and Duff's investigations, and quantities of shells, bones and artifacts had been turned up and lay on the surface. Duff assumed that the site had been occupied for a single, possibly lengthy, period during which there had been no cultural change. Moa bones, both in the middens and the graves, indicated that moa hunting had been important to the occupants' economy, and Duff took the site to be representative of occupation in New Zealand at that time. Duff was particularly interested in the typology of adze heads — he classified them according to their shape — and in the large distinctive necklaces found around the necks of many of the Wairau Bar burials he excavated.

As a student of H. D. Skinner, Duff largely followed the same lines in his investigations, and while his field methods were vastly superior to those of Teviotdale, they lacked the sophistication of Lockerbie's techniques, with the result that many of his conclusions are questioned today. Nevertheless, that his fairly solid book on New Zealand prehistory could go into three editions says something of the effect of the 'Duff phenomenon' — no single person since Julius von Haast had had a greater impact on New Zealand archaeological thinking. He achieved this by presenting a two-period synthesis of prehistory that took the most acceptable of the orthodox 'traditions', interwove them with the evidence of archaeology and provided a series of diagnostic criteria by which the two periods could be distinguished.

One of the most prehistorically significant aspects of the Wairau research was Duff's findings with regard to the physical

David Teviotdale (below right), seen here at Little Papanui, second from the right, carried out many excavations for H. D. Skinner during the 1920s and 1930s. His methods were basically crude and the shovels and spades that were used are prominent in this photograph.

A moa leg (below), with gizzard stones alongside, excavated at Tautuku, South Otago, in 1956. Les Lockerbie carried out important investigations in this area, pioneering the use of archaeological radiocarbon dating in New Zealand.

characteristics of the 'Moa-hunter' people. Although he still accepted the concept of two separate colonisations of New Zealand (the end papers of his book depict *'Major Landfalls of Canoes of Fleet of 1350 A.D.'*), Duff was able to show very clearly that the 'Moa-hunters' were Polynesians, physically identical with the Maori people, and that there was no evidence of any other race ever having occupied New Zealand in prehistoric times. Despite this, however, the myth of the Melanesian Moriois continued to persist — as it does to this day.

The other important feature of Duff's theories was his use of the term 'Moa hunter' to describe a distinct stage of Maori culture, whereas previous researchers, such as Haast, employed 'moa-hunter' simply to denote a person who hunted moas.

During the 1950s several developments occurred which were to have a far-reaching impact on archaeological research here in New

Zealand. The decade started with the development overseas of radiocarbon dating. This allowed researchers for the first time to gauge accurately the age of prehistoric occupational remains. This is done by measuring the residual radioactivity of a carbon isotope which is present in known quantities in a living animal or plant but which reduces at a fixed rate after death. It allows the calculation of the years that have passed since the death of the organism; thus, for example, a piece of moa bone or some shells left after a meal can be analysed to determine how long ago that meal was eaten. In New Zealand radiocarbon dating was pioneered by Leslie Lockerbie, who successfully documented a chronological sequence of economic and cultural change in South Otago.

By 1954 sufficient interest in archaeology had been promoted — largely by Duff's book and by Jack Golson, an English archaeologist appointed to the University of Auckland — that

H. D. Skinner identified close similarities in Maori art and artifact morphology with those not only of Polynesia but also other areas around the rim of Oceania. Faced with trying to determine Maori origins without the benefit of the information now available, much importance was placed upon such similarities, the assumption being that the designs were related rather than having evolved independently. One of Skinner's suggestions was that crocodilian features which appear in Maori pendants (as in this end of a rei puta) and carvings may have resulted from 'traditional memories' of crocodiles in some far off homeland that was not Polynesia. Recently, Auckland-based researcher Simon Best has provided an alternative theory: that large salt-water crocodiles could have crossed the ocean from Australia to New Zealand some time in the past, giving rise to the taniwha of Maori art and tradition.

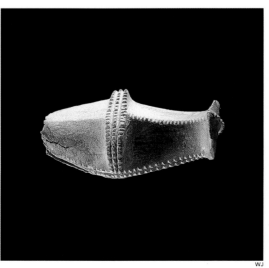

This unique early pendant from a Kaikoura site is recorded by Ngai Tahu tradition as being one of three brought to New Zealand from Hawaiki, the homeland. Made from whale ivory, its shape and decoration are both early Eastern Polynesian features.

the New Zealand Archaeological Association was formed; it held its first conference two years later in 1956. One of its most important achievements was a national scheme for recording archaeological sites; it also produced a quarterly *Newsletter* (now called *Archaeology in New Zealand*) and later started to publish an annual *Journal of Archaeology*. The New Zealand Historic Places Trust was also established in 1954 and, although it was, at least initially, mainly concerned with preserving and marking historic sites, it did as early as 1956 commence investigating and recording prehistoric rock drawings that were to be destroyed by hydro-electric dams on the Waikato and Waitaki Rivers. The Trust has since played an ever-increasing role in New Zealand archaeology, particularly since 1975 when legislation was passed protecting all archaeological sites.

And then in the midst of all this activity and enthusiasm a civil servant, Andrew Sharp, dropped a bombshell, the effects of which were to resound around the Pacific for years. In essence, Sharp cast serious doubts on some of the cherished beliefs and 'traditions' which had not been questioned since being universally accepted some decades earlier. In particular, he challenged the idea of deliberate voyaging between the Pacific Islands and New Zealand (and with it the concept of a 'Great Fleet'). He suggested instead that the Maoris and their moa-hunting ancestors had originated from one or more canoes which accidentally discovered the country; the widely accepted canoe traditions, he proposed, were relatively late developments. That an unknown amateur should so convincingly challenge the beliefs of two generations of ethnologists and traditionalists — acknowledged authorities such as Percy Smith, Elsdon Best, H. D. Skinner, Peter Buck and Roger Duff — not to mention the Maori race, was quite unthinkable. Skinner refused to review Sharp's book; Golson gathered together the views of a number of experts in related fields, not all of whom disagreed with the heretic. Sharp responded to his critics with another book.

In retrospect, Sharp's theories represented a watershed in archaeological thinking, preparing the ground for an essentially more scientific approach to the study of our prehistory. Further impetus was given in the late 1950s by Jack Golson, Roger Green and others who demonstrated the existence of moa-hunter sites on the Coromandel Peninsula and around Auckland. It was largely because of the character of these northern sites that Golson proposed replacing the term *Moa-hunter* with *Archaic*, on the grounds that people who were Moa-hunters in a cultural sense may not have actually hunted moas; he also proposed that the term *Classic* be

Believing that Moa-bone Point Cave had been completely dug out by Haast's workmen 70 years earlier, Roger Duff dug adjacent shelters in the early 1940s. It was later found that although much disturbed, the main cave deposits still contained many fragile artifacts.

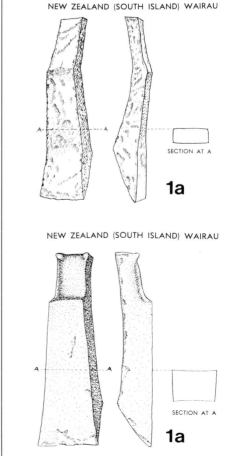

NEW ZEALAND (SOUTH ISLAND) WAIRAU

SECTION AT A

1a

NEW ZEALAND (SOUTH ISLAND) WAIRAU

SECTION AT A

1a

CM Coll.

used to describe Maori culture as it was at the time of the first European visitors. The distinction was important since it further refined the notion of a continuum of Polynesian occupation and, although there have been difficulties with these terms, both are still in fairly common use today. At the same time Golson suggested a more flexible framework on which archaeological data could be ordered — in effect, subdivisions of his Archaic and Classic. This concept was shortly used to good effect by his American colleague Roger Green in a review of the prehistory of the Auckland region, and by a number of others thereafter.

One effect of Green's work was to reinforce the swing away from studies of artifacts to a more careful attention to stratigraphic details in the field. Within the main layers of archaeological deposit, sub-layers can often be defined — 'lenses', intrusions and other variations which have been produced by the human occupation of a site. A hole or pit that was dug into the ground some centuries ago may have become filled in, but the archaeologist can still recognise it from the colour, texture or compactness of the fill material. With careful excavation it may even be possible to recognise the marks made by the implements used to dig the hole and other signs or stains may indicate what the hole was used for.

Once archaeologists started looking for them, a bewildering array of subsurface pits of all shapes and sizes, a proliferation of post holes of all dimensions, and a variety of drains, hollows, stone walls and underground chambers were uncovered, particularly in the North Island. Earlier workers such as Duff had largely ignored these features in their search for portable artifacts. Pits had been known as a feature of the archaeological landscape since the end of the nineteenth century, and the larger rectangular ones had generally been thought of as the remains of dwellings, while smaller, particularly rounded or bell-shaped pits, had been thought of as for storage.

In 1965 anthropologist Les Groube presented (though never formally published) a carefully and cleverly constructed argument that even the larger pits were actually storage pits for storing kumaras. Groube may well have been arguing for the sake of academic exercise, but the effect among most archaeologists was dramatic. Subsurface structures that had been accepted as the remains of dwellings were suddenly redefined as storage pits, even in sites where kumara storage was most unlikely. One archaeologist even went as far as to say that Groube had

. . . dealt the death blow to the underground house or pit dwelling and established in its

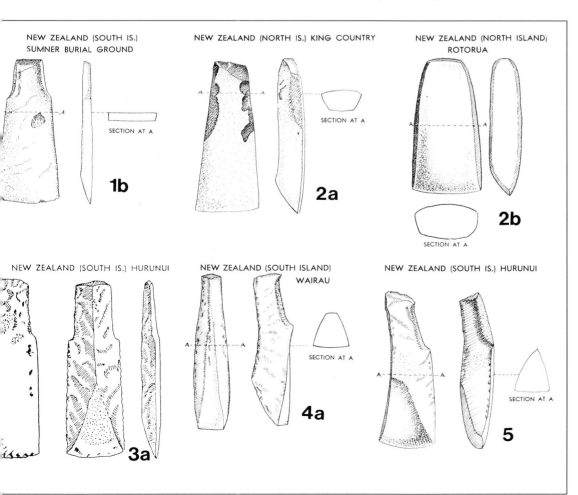

NEW ZEALAND (SOUTH IS.) SUMNER BURIAL GROUND

SECTION AT A

1b

NEW ZEALAND (NORTH IS.) KING COUNTRY

SECTION AT A

2a

NEW ZEALAND (NORTH ISLAND) ROTORUA

SECTION AT A

2b

SECTION AT A

NEW ZEALAND (SOUTH IS.) HURUNUI

3a

NEW ZEALAND (SOUTH ISLAND) WAIRAU

SECTION AT A

4a

NEW ZEALAND (SOUTH IS.) HURUNUI

SECTION AT A

5

The more common types of Duff's classification of Maori adze heads: (1a) quadrangular section with tang (the reduced area to facilitate binding to a handle); (1a) quadrangular section with tang and knobs on the poll; (1b) quadrangular section with 'spade shouldered' tang; (2a) quadrangular section without tang; (2b) rounded quadrangular section without tang; (3a) triangular section with tang; (4a) 'hog backed' triangular section with apex to front; (5) 'side hafted', tang on one side only.

17

place the kumara storage pit as an essential component of Maori settlement and economy.

While the negative aspect of this was unfortunate — there is undoubted evidence of 'pit dwellings', particularly in the South Island — Groube's argument did draw attention to the possibility of horticulture having been practised from the very earliest times, as some pits had been found on indisputably early sites.

Closely linked with horticulture was the question of climate; warmer temperatures in the past would have helped ensure the survival of kumaras and other plants brought from tropical Pacific islands. Since at least 1948 some botanists had been suggesting — mostly on the evidence of the forests reverting to grasslands on the east coast of the South Island — that average temperatures in New Zealand had been cooling over the past 700–800 years. This, in turn, had been incorporated by some archaeologists in their reconstructions of prehistory. In 1962, however, these views were challenged by geographer Kenneth Cumberland who suggested instead that the forests had been largely destroyed by man-made fires. Today this aspect of Cumberland's views has been largely accepted by prehistorians, as has the even more radical

Many prehistorians were not amused when Andrew Sharp scoffed at their fondly held beliefs on the abilities of Polynesians to navigate over long distances of ocean.

Source: Andrew Sharp, *Ancient Voyagers in Polynesia*

FIG. 4. Courses by following Migratory Birds

Courses by following migratory birds give no clue to lateral displacement because migratory birds are not affected by currents at night but surface craft are. The diagram represents prehistoric navigators looking for migratory birds at night.

notion of 'prehistoric overkill' to explain the wholesale extinction of much of New Zealand's fauna in prehistoric times.

By the late 1960s the traditionalist version of New Zealand's prehistory was in complete tatters. Anthropology professor Ralph Piddington had pointed out that even genuine Maori traditions should not be thought of as historic records but were rather more comparable to Arthurian legends. Similarly, Andrew Sharp had highlighted the problems with many of the traditions' most cherished beliefs, and had even suggested that the Hawaiki from which the traditional canoes were supposed to have come may not have been in the far Pacific at all but in the Hauraki Gulf in the North Island. However, it was left to David Simmons, then ethnologist at Auckland Museum, to show that long-accepted stories of the Polynesian discovery and settlement of New Zealand did not represent authentic Maori tradition. Simmons published his first exposé of the so-called traditions in 1969 and subsequently in his book *The Great New Zealand Myth* in 1976. His ideas were widely accepted by the archaeological community although they did nothing to improve relations with the Maori people, many of whom had by now incorporated aspects of the Percy Smith stories into their traditional histories. Today the pendulum has swung back a little, and a more tolerant, more understanding attitude prevails. Margaret Orbell has gently chided Simmons and his adherents, suggesting that they are still looking for factual history in what is essentially mythology.

During the 1960s most archaeological field work was carried out by groups of volunteers under the auspices of research institutions, and often directed by professional archaeologists. Existing groups in Auckland, Canterbury and North Otago were active, and new groups were formed in Wellington and Otago; archaeologists were appointed for the first time to the staff of the Canterbury and Auckland Museums. Such appointments were significant because until well into the 1970s the backbone of archaeological

(Continued on page 22)

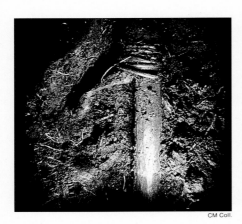

CM Coll.

Radiocarbon dating involves measuring the residual radioactivity of the carbon 14 isotope in a sample of plant or animal material. As this radioactivity decays at a known rate since the death of the plant or animal, it is possible to calculate how long ago that death took place. In reporting radiocarbon dates certain conventions are used. A date of 501 ± 67 yrs BP, for example, means that the sample tested gave a result that has two chances in three of being within 67 years of 501 years Before Present — 'Present' is taken as AD 1950. The date may need modification according to the 'half-life' of carbon 14 used, and may also need secular correction to convert it from 'radiocarbon years' to an approximation of calendar years. Two main factors that affect the accuracy of radiocarbon dating are the 'standard' used and contamination. The 'standard' is a modern sample of the same or similar species collected before the widespread atomic bomb testing which started in the 1950s — standards from different parts of the country can give different results. Contamination takes many forms ranging from atmospheric contamination of bone carbonate to the absorption of organic material from the ground by charcoal.

THE FYFFE SITE AND MODERN ARCHAEOLOGY

THE archaeological site usually referred to as Fyffe's is situated on the northern side of Avoca Point, Kaikoura Peninsula. It is one of the oldest known in New Zealand and was first occupied by the earliest Maoris about 900 years ago. Archaeological excavations to salvage information from this site, before it was largely destroyed by building operations, were carried out by Canterbury Museum from 1982 to 1987.

The story of the occupation of Fyffe's can be derived from the evidence gathered during those excavations. In both acquiring and interpreting that evidence a number of diverse techniques and disciplines were employed — probably the most important being geology. An understanding of the general geology of the area was needed; this included recognising that the whole site had been lifted by tectonism shortly before man's arrival, a knowledge of the limestone-mudstone stratigraphy, and of the manner in which the local 'Amuri' limestone reacts to weathering, both above and below water.

Two branches of geology — palaeontology (the study of fossils) and sedimentology (the study of sediments) — were important in analysing the original beach sand. Its high content of fragile but unbroken shells from minute organisms indicated that it had been deposited in a calm environment such as a lagoon rather than on a wave-battered, open beach. The details of the site stratigraphy from the beach upwards were also studied, with a cross-section from hill to beach fortuitously revealed in a sewer trench cut to the back of the housing subdivision. And besides interpreting the general history of the site, geology was important for the identification of the materials

utilised in the manufacture of stone tools. This gave information of the use — sometimes experimental — of local rocks and also indicated contact with other areas.

The actual 'archaeological' techniques involved ranged from a general theodolite survey of the site, recording the exact contour of the surface and the laying out of an excavation grid, to the excavations themselves involving fine tools such as trowels, brushes and fine blowers. (At one stage a household vacuum cleaner was used to clear dust from an excavated grid square so that the rock formation at the bottom could be clearly studied!) In excavating, a team of up to 16 people, mostly volunteers, carefully removed 1000 years of deposit a layer at a time — in some places this deposit reached a thickness of up to a metre above the original beach sand. And everything was recorded meticulously.

The science of nuclear physics played its role with the radiocarbon dating of the site, and chemistry allowed an analysis of the garden soils. Zoology was, of course, vital to the identification of animal remains used as food — fish, reptile, bird and mammal bones, a wide variety of marine shells — and also materials from which some artifacts were manufactured: bone, shell and ivory. Further work is expected to tell us more about butchering techniques and if certain species were favoured among those available. Ecological studies of the animal remains also will tell something of the environment at the time the site was occupied. Much of this information will be subjected to statistical analysis to discover even more about the quantity and distribution of both faunal and artifactual material from the site.

A section through the stone wall of the kumara garden (below) and down through the moa-hunter level to the original sandy beach. Some early European whaling relics were found on the top surface of the wall, deposited eight centuries after the earliest remains of human activity.

Excavating the section through the garden wall (right) revealed the large stones used to delineate the line of the wall. These were undoubtedly cleared off the garden area first as they would have had to have been individually lifted and placed in position.

Some preliminary ethnological work has been done on the artifacts — particularly comparing them to those recovered from other sites of similar age both within and outside New Zealand. More detailed analyses will take several years. Nevertheless, an interim analysis of the information obtained reveals the following story.

When people first came to Avoca Point they found an embayed sandy beach sheltered from the south by a

At Kaikoura they hunted and ate moas and a variety of other birds as well as seals. They collected shellfish from the rocks of the peninsula and caught fish — particularly barracouta. They used the larger moa bones to make fish hooks, ornaments and other artifacts, moa eggs for water containers, and bones, shells and teeth of several other species for implements and decorations. They also experimented with local rocks for both tools and fire stones for cooking. For all of their artifact manufacture they used techniques developed by their recent ancestors in the Pacific Islands to the north.

Prehuman era

Geoffrey Cox/BM

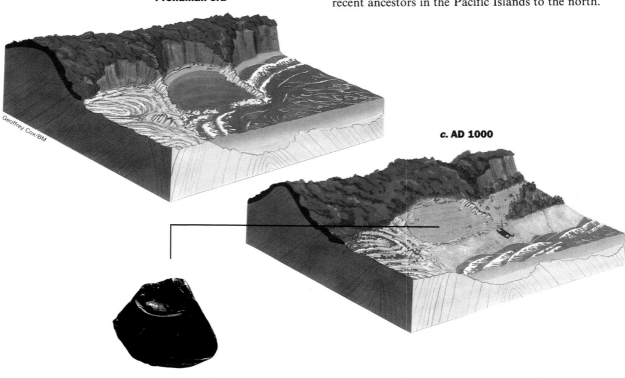

c. **AD 1000**

This large piece of obsidian or volcanic glass recovered from the early level at Fyffes had been brought to the site from Mayor Island in the north as raw material from which to strike flake knives.

Diagrammatic representation of the series of events which resulted in the formation of the archaeological site at Avoca Point, Kaikoura, which is commonly referred to as Fyffes.

steep ridge. Additional shelter was provided by folded and tilted limestone which jutted from the base of the hill in natural walls and mounds. The beach had originally formed the floor of a small marine lagoon, protected from the full force of waves from the north by a barrier or bar of folded limestone across the mouth of the bay. Subsequent uplift of Kaikoura Peninsula, as a result of tectonic activity, left the lagoon floor high and dry.

The sandy beach was an attractive place for the early people, sheltered and warm, with abundant food resources of both the sea and the land close to hand, a ready supply of timber, and also stone materials — especially flint which formed nodules in the limestone and could be found washed out on the beach. The site was used as a camp rather than a permanent village by moa-hunter Maoris who brought with them tools of obsidian from the North Island and possibly some argillite from Nelson. They also brought Polynesian dogs or kuri.

There is no archaeological evidence as to the clothes they wore or the shelters they used. Nor do we know what plant foods they ate. We do know they buried their dead with some ceremony, along with grave offerings.

However, this pleasant sandy beach was not to remain a desirable place forever. Within a short time of its exposure, the surrounding limestone, also exposed by uplift, began to weather, breaking off in sharp rubbly chunks. And although the original rock barrier across the mouth of the bay now formed the base for a shingly beach ridge, a certain amount of sea and storm-deposited material still reached the inner beach area. Over the centuries the sand became covered with a layer of limestone rubble, uncomfortable to live on and as yet not covered by soil or vegetation.

But it was still visited from time to time by the descendants of the early people. On at least one occasion a craftsman seated on the beach ridge making fine and beautiful fish hooks from the bone of a mollymawk or albatross lost two of his finished works when they fell down into the rubble beneath.

Eventually, however, vegetation formed over the rubble; this, along with material derived from the erosion of mudstone from the hill above, in turn produced a soil which eventually trickled down to fill the spaces between the limestone pieces and formed a surface layer, although it still contained a proportion of rubbly bits. And in places some of the folded limestone still projected from below to break the level surface.

At this stage in the site's history, possibly 3-400 years ago, a later group of Maoris used the area for gardening, almost certainly for growing kumaras. They cleared the soil of larger pieces of rock, piling them on to, and extending, natural limestone ridges to the east and west of the selected area, as well as on to the beach ridge in front, to the north. With the hill behind, the whole garden area was now enclosed in sheltering boundaries.

This was the final phase of Maori occupation of the Fyffe site. In 1770 James Cook and his men sailed past Kaikoura Peninsula, giving it the name 'Lookers On',

because of the Maoris who watched them and who sailed out to see them at closer quarters. Then in 1842, the prehistoric era came to an end with the establishment of Robert Fyffe's shore whaling station, Waiopuka, close by on the southern side of Avoca Point. Robert's cousin, George Fyffe, who succeeded him, built a house adjacent to the old kumara garden, and it is from him that the site has got its present name. While preparing building foundations he uncovered evidence of the earliest Maori occupation, including a moa-hunter burial with adze heads and a complete, moa-egg liquid container.

The whalers, too, left archaeological evidence of their occupation scattered across the site, including early coins and hand-made buttons, carved from whale bone.

After George Fyffe's death in 1867 the main area of the site remained grassed and largely undisturbed — known in recent years as 'George Low's cow paddock' — until on Low's death in 1980 it was sold for building sections. The presence of a very early Maori site had been confirmed by archaeological excavations carried out in 1973, from which radiocarbon dates were obtained indicating a first occupation about 900 years ago. This had suggested it was one of New Zealand's oldest known sites, and the subsequent operations to retrieve information before it was destroyed were of great importance.

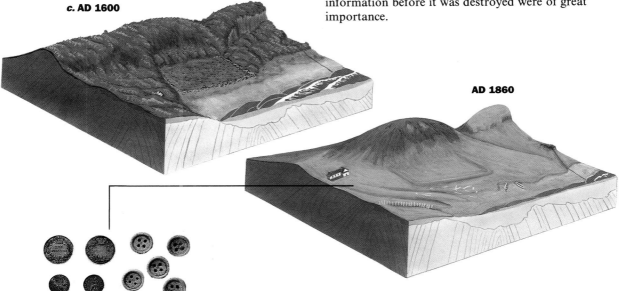

c. AD 1600

AD 1860

Early coins — dating back to 1834 — and hand carved whale bone buttons indicate the arrival of the first Europeans, the whalers of George Fyffe's Waiopuka station, at Kaikoura.

Looking across to the Fyffe site (George Fyffe's house, centre) with a beach of Amuri limestone and remnants of native scrub in the foreground. Modern houses (to the left of the scrub) now cover much of the moa-hunter site and later kumara garden.

research in New Zealand was the dedicated amateur who if not a professional archaeologist *per se* at least applied basic archaeological techniques to their research.

One of the most important research projects of the 1970s was a series of interrelated investigations on the Wairarapa coast of the North Island. Helen and Foss Leach of the Otago University's Anthropology Department, who organised the project, believed that there was an urgent need for studies of prehistory in New Zealand to be undertaken on a regional basis; they chose the Wairarapa area because the archaeological sites there were relatively well preserved — there had been little disturbance from curio hunting, development work, farming or erosion along that section of the coast. The project covered many aspects of the prehistory of this area — housing, agriculture, fishing, ecology, climate, the physical attributes of the people themselves — in an attempt to provide a more complete, composite picture of how the people lived and the environmental and cultural influences that affected their lives. Research of this nature represented a major shift in emphasis and the published volume of the findings that resulted ranks as one of the major publications of its kind, inspiring other large-scale projects that have now been carried out elsewhere, and are being planned for the future.

Since legislation was passed in 1975 to protect all archaeological sites more and more field investigations have been carried out as commercial salvage operations. This has, in turn, given rise to the development of contract

archaeology where professional archaeologists are contracted to excavate and research specific sites. There is now a new urgency to record and investigate sites threatened by commercial developments in the cities, horticultural enterprises in the country or by large hydro-electric projects.

Archaeology today is very different from that of the last century or even a few decades ago. We have moved a long way from Haast's 'autochthones' and the 'Great Fleet' of Percy Smith's traditions, and now have a more complete understanding of this country's prehistory. The methodology has also changed, becoming at once more sophisticated and its emphasis shifting from a preoccupation with artifacts and the *things* of the past, to the people and the environment in which they lived. Archaeology today embraces a range of disciplines and uses a wide spectrum of sophisticated techniques and equipment. The study of human skeletal remains, for example, until recently added little to our real knowledge of the prehistoric Maoris. It was generally accepted, at least by prehistorians, that these remains conformed to a Polynesian type but beyond that they divulged little. It has only been since the research of people like Philip Houghton of the Otago Medical School, who has made a detailed study of Maori skeletal material housed in museums and universities, that we now have a more comprehensive understanding of the health, diseases, stature, age at death, and various physical characteristics of the people themselves.

Wilfred Shawcross (below right) excavating at Mount Camel, Houhora. At the time of the first excavations in 1965-66 the site was considered to be 'the northernmost of those which are related to Wairau Bar'.

Archaeological techniques (below) have changed radically from those used only 40 years ago. Here soil samples are being taken for laboratory analysis from a section cut into a defensive wall at Takahanga Pa, Kaikoura.

It is now even possible to estimate how many childbirths were experienced by a woman who died, say, 500 years ago!

The detective work of the modern investigator calls on a variety of disciplines. Today's archaeologists are at once prehistorians and antiquarians, surveyors, geologists, botanists, ethnologists; they pioneer zoological studies; they study soils, volcanic ash deposits, and geomorphology; they borrow ideas from other disciplines, and give back new ideas, data and theories. They experiment with techniques that are only newly developed and even undeveloped, and sometimes the increase in knowledge is not always in proportion to the time and resources expended. Occasionally, they will go down cul-de-sacs of research to produce conclusions that are untenable. The present-day archaeologist is often able to discuss radio isotopes learnedly yet is human enough to select radiocarbon dates subjectively. And yet despite anomalies and failures, all this is indicative of a developing and vigorous discipline.

One of the most exciting recent developments has been how archaeological research has now extended to include aspects of the European period, supplementing and giving new meaning to the historical record. Investigations of the archaeological remains of dwellings, industries, farming facilities and burials of the last 100–200 years have provided valuable information not recorded in contemporary documentation. Whereas written history usually records only major events and the broad sweep of political and social change, archaeology can document in detail the impedimenta of everyday life, often providing insight into how people lived, even the personal — or private — detail of an individual's life. What written history can only describe, archaeology can reach out and touch. The recent excavation of a nineteenth century European cemetery in Christchurch, for example, not only yielded details of Victorian burial customs, coffin construction and ornamentation, but also the health problems of a small nineteenth-century community, the familiar ailments that plague ordinary people. In such ways archaeologists are unearthing aspects of our more recent past hitherto ignored or unrecorded.

Nevertheless, where written history exists, researchers with a European cultural background — and particularly those researching European cultural history — continue to use written records as their primary source of information. For this reason, 'dirt' archaeology relating to the historic period has not been carried out extensively in New Zealand. There have been few systematic excavations, for example, of the early whaling and mission stations, while marine archaeology and the excavation of wreck sites is virtually nonexistent. Our understanding of the early development of our major cities and towns remains similarly incomplete — the evidence either destroyed or buried under layers of successive developments. And even where excavations have been undertaken, the results are usually 'written in' to the existing historic record. So long as this bias persists, important aspects of our recent history will remain untold.

Michael Trotter (left) examining the remains of palisading on a small hill-top pa overlooking a garden complex at Clarence Bridge, Marlborough.

When in 1989 the 137-year-old Pegasus Press building in Christchurch (below) was shifted from its foundations, archaeologists carried out salvage excavations, which yielded information on the history of the building, the people who lived in it, and even nineteenth-century butchering practices.

I. Origin of the Maoris

The Polynesians

*I*T has long been convenient to divide the islands of the Pacific into three main groups: Micronesia, Melanesia and Polynesia. These are not simply geographic divisions, but have become established largely on the basis of the similarities in the physical appearance, languages and material culture of the people living in each group. Polynesia is a large, roughly triangular area with Hawaii in the north, Easter Island in the east and New Zealand in the south.

More than two centuries ago Sir Joseph Banks and his companions on the *Endeavour* noted that the language spoken throughout what today we call Polynesia was 'precisely the same at least in fundamentals', and such observations have been confirmed by modern linguistic studies. Some artifacts strongly resemble those from islands thousands of kilometres distant. The people also have a distinct 'family likeness', and even some of their myths and traditions are much the same.

We must remember, however, that the Pacific divisions have been drawn up on relatively modern observations. Any such groupings of Oceanic islands would undoubtedly be quite different if we used the languages or material culture of, say, 2000 years ago.

The apparent uniformity within Polynesia has made it all the more puzzling that the origin of Polynesian cultural traits, indeed of the people themselves, could not clearly be traced outside that area. Botanists have shown that many of the plants grown by Polynesians were brought in from the west, yet one of these plants, the sweet potato or kumara (*Ipomoea batatas*), undoubtedly comes from the east. Ethnologists have drawn attention to comparable art and artifact forms in both South-East Asia and the Americas, but there are too many gaps in the trail or their evidence is swamped by conflicting data from elsewhere for their studies to indicate unequivocal origins. For example, Roger Duff believed that the distinctive tanged quadrangular adze head came from South-East Asia but was unable to explain convincingly how it got through Micronesia (or Melanesia for that matter) without leaving some trace in the material culture of the people living there. Thor Heyerdahl, on the other hand, was a strong proponent of the idea of settlement from South America, and made a much-publicised raft trip from Peru to the Tuamotu Islands in 1947 to show that such voyaging was possible. But as one reviewer put it: 'His theory was patiently suffered and quietly discredited . . .'

Simply stated, the answer to most of these problems is that much of what distinguishes Polynesians originated in the central Pacific, in and around the western edge of the Polynesian 'triangle'.

Recent archaeological research traces the origin of the Polynesians to Melanesia, and one of the most important clues has been a distinctive type of pottery known as Lapita ware (named after a locality in New Caledonia). Lapita ware has been found in early sites from the Melanesian Admiralty Islands (above Papua New Guinea) in the west to the Polynesian Tongan and Samoan islands in the central Pacific. Generally, all that is found are sherds of broken cooking pots and bowls, rather than complete utensils, made of a sand-tempered pottery that was fired in open fires. Many of the bowls were decorated, often coloured red, with geometric and other designs stamped or incised into the outer surface — a 'dentate-stamped' design being a particularly distinctive indication of Lapita pottery. The people who made Lapita ware lived from about 3500 to 2500 years ago, and undoubtedly possessed some of the attributes that allowed the later widespread settlement of the Pacific. They were, for example, highly skilled sailors — we know this by their rapid spread throughout the islands on which Lapita pottery is found. Other than this, however, we know very little about the people themselves. Islands further to the east were at this time uninhabited.

In Fiji, which borders Melanesia and Polynesia, Lapita ware eventually gave way to plainer types of pottery, and in the western Polynesian islands of Tonga and Samoa it disappeared altogether about 2000 years ago, probably prior to the settlement of the remainder of Polynesia, particularly the eastern area.

With pottery having been used so widely throughout the rest of the world for so long, it might seem strange that a society that once knew how to make pottery bowls and containers would stop doing so. Numerous theories supposedly account for this: the unavailability of suitable clays or tempers on some islands, the loss of the requisite knowledge of forming and firing, the inconvenient fragility of pottery while travelling. The simplest explanation though is that the Polynesians' lifestyle had changed so that they no longer had any need for pottery; they had presumably developed cooking methods (like the earth oven) which — for them — were preferable to using cooking utensils, and had found better alternative liquid containers.

By 2500 years ago the basis of a distinctive Polynesian culture, its language and the physical type had been established in the western islands of Polynesia. Then, between 2000 and 1500 years ago, people began to spread to the east, to the previously uninhabited islands of the Marquesas, to distant Easter Island, and even to Hawaii in the north. Further changes in language and culture took place, differentiating them from those of the western islands of Tonga and Samoa.

So we come to Eastern Polynesia, that vast area of the Pacific Ocean lightly peppered with small islands (*Poly* = many; *nesos* = islands). Excluding New Zealand, the islands of Eastern Polynesia comprise mainly the groups of Hawaii, Society (or Tahiti), Marquesas, Tuamotus, Cooks and Easter, with a scattering of others around the Tropic of Capricorn — the Australs and Pitcairn being the best known.

Physically the people of Eastern Polynesia are much more homogeneous than, for example, the present-day Melanesians, and vastly more so than Europeans. This would suggest that they descended from a relatively small 'founding' group, and that there has been little contact with other groups that might have introduced different physical characteristics. In general, they are tall, well-built people with light brown skins and straight or wavy black hair. Studies of their skeletons have indicated a number of distinctive characteristics by which they may be identified.

As Banks noted, the people of Eastern Polynesia also share a common language. Many archaeologists tend to be wary of historical reconstructions made by linguists, particularly when it is realised how limited and poorly recorded the vocabularies from some islands are. Yet we are dependent on language studies to fill a number of major gaps that archaeology has not yet filled. For example, it is generally agreed that the variations spoken on all the islands in Eastern Polynesia were derived from one 'Proto-Eastern Polynesian' language, with Tongan and Samoan having split off earlier. This correlates with the archaeological evidence and provokes little argument.

For a people who were technologically dependent on stone rather than metal, the availability of suitable rocks had an important bearing on the type and shape of tools they could make, and indeed on the development of that technology. The islands of Eastern Polynesia are generally basaltic (volcanic) rock, although on some little or no basalt is actually present on the surface, the main 'rock' being a coral limestone which has formed upon basalt that was just below the surface of the ocean and which has subsequently been exposed. Where fine-grained basalt was procurable, however, the Eastern Polynesians perfected the design and manufacture of distinctive stone adze heads for wood working. A special innovation here was the provision of a shaped 'tang' or grip on some

The main direction of the settlement of Polynesia was from the west and then extended to the north and south, often in the face of opposing winds and ocean currents.

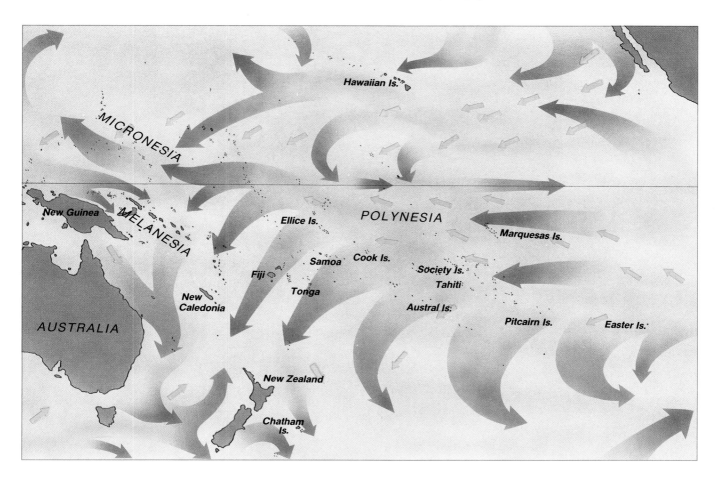

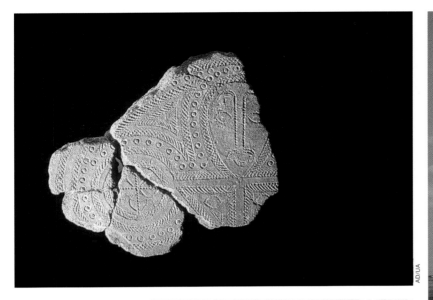

AD/UA

Lapita pottery (above) has provided some of the most important archaeological evidence for tracing the origin of the Polynesians.

John Coster

Examination of undisturbed stratigraphy (right), which may represent hundreds of years of human occupation, has enabled archaeologists to establish a chronology relating to Polynesian origins.

Sites on which Lapita pottery has been found, such as this one at Vava'u, Tonga (below), were often coastal villages where both fish and shellfish were important items of food.

Janet Davidson

forms to facilitate hafting them to their wooden handles. This feature has proved to be of immense value, along with the general shapes of the artifacts, to prehistorians in tracing the origins and connections of the Polynesians.

Besides having a restricted range of rocks, other land resources on most of these eastern islands were also fairly limited. The Polynesians brought most of their important food plants with them from the west. These included the coconut, banana, breadfruit, taro and yam. The kumara or sweet potato was also introduced into Eastern Polynesia, though this time from the east, from South America, at least 1000 years ago (there is no evidence that kumaras ever got into Western Polynesia prior to European contact). Horti-culture became crucial to their economy. The usual system of cultivation, still practised in some islands today, was to clear a plot of land, largely by burning, and to plant cuttings or tubers in holes made in the ground with a stick. After a few years cropping, the ground would be left idle to revert to natural bush.

As well as plants, the Polynesians introduced the dog, pig, hen and rat as food animals all deriving from the west. The first three were undoubtedly domesticated, but we know little about the status of the rat. It was certainly taken deliberately to the various islands and its bones in midden deposits testify to its importance as a food item, but whether it was domesticated or allowed to run wild is unknown.

They also made full use of the available coastal resources, the ocean and its fish. New types of fish hooks were developed — trolling

A coral atoll in the Fiji Group (centre). Many of the Pacific islands are low coral atolls with only limited resources, and the economic and cultural development of the settlers was often dependent on the importation of plants, animals and even stone.

The coconut (above) was one of the most important plants of tropical Polynesia, providing food, drink and material for cordage, basketry and shelter.

Basalt adze heads from the Society islands (left) show similarities in shape and method of manufacture to those from early New Zealand sites. Such similarities became less evident as the early Maoris discovered and experimented with the new rock types they found in New Zealand, which allowed the development of new manufacturing techniques.

hooks, mostly from pearl shell to act as sparkling lures as they were pulled through the water, and two-piece bait hooks, larger and stronger than could be made in one piece with the materials available. Although the shanks of these hooks were often made of wood and are thus rarely found on archaeological sites, the more durable shell lures and the bone and shell points provide valuable clues to interpreting the past histories of island Polynesia. One-piece hooks were made of stone on Pitcairn and on Easter Island.

With most of the islands of Eastern Polynesia in the tropics, there may not have been much need of clothing for warmth, but a form of 'cloth' was made from the bark of the paper mulberry tree, largely for decorative or ceremonial purposes, and although the bark cloth (usually called *tapa*) does not generally survive in archaeological contexts, the hard wood beaters used to make it are sometimes found in caves and other places where preservation conditions have been suitable.

Such evidence as the bark cloth also suggests that the activities of the Eastern Polynesians were by no means restricted to subsistence endeavours; although ornamented pottery was no longer made, many of their artifacts show a beauty of design not related to purely functional requirements. They also wore distinctive personal ornaments, and grooved 'reels' (cylinders of bone, shell, or stone) and tooth-shaped units (usually of bone), both of which were drilled and strung as necklaces, are particularly significant when trying to trace

origins by way of the distribution of artifact types. These two forms illustrate the problems of unravelling Polynesian prehistory. For example, the island of Niue is considered to belong to Western Polynesia yet both a tooth-shaped unit and an unfinished reel, which we might expect from Eastern Polynesia, have been found there in archaeological sites.

The distinctive race of people, the Polynesians, developed their physical characteristics, their language and their culture in the Pacific Ocean. They were a mobile people, successfully travelling across greater distances of ocean than anyone, anywhere in the world, had done before them. By 1000 years ago they had settled most of the vast Polynesian triangle, from Tonga in the west to Easter Island in the east, and as far as Hawaii in the north. About this time, too, they reached their southernmost point of settlement, New Zealand, thus completing the triangle. Although ethnologically New Zealand was to become Polynesian, geologically and geographically it differed greatly from the islands to the north — a fact which was to greatly influence the development of the Polynesian people who were to become the Maoris.

Islands of Origin

'From the similarity of customs, the still greater of Traditions and the almost identical sameness of Language between these people and those of the Islands in the South Sea, there remains little doubt that they came originally from the same source: but where that Source is future experience may teach us . . .'

JOSEPH BANKS, 1770

POTENTIALLY there are many sources of information as to which Eastern Polynesian island (or islands) the original settlers of New Zealand came from. These would include close similarities in language, physical appearance, blood groups, material culture or traditions, and that the plants and animals they brought with them occurred on the source island at the time this country was settled.

Unfortunately, none of these — or any other lines of research — indicate with any degree of certainty where the Maoris' homeland was. The problems lie in a general homogeneity of all the Eastern Polynesians and their culture, their propensity for taking plants and animals with them wherever they travelled, and in the ensuing changes that have taken place, especially since European contact.

New Zealand prehistorians today generally accept that the Marquesas or Society Islands are the most likely homeland of the Maoris, but few would be dogmatic in their choice of either. And there is considerable divergence of opinion as to whether the country was settled by a single group of people only, if there was a second immigration (possibly from a different island), or even if several groups arrived over a period of some centuries.

James Cook and his contemporaries noted close similarities between the speech of the New Zealand 'Indians' and those of the 'South Sea' islands, to the extent that Tupaia, a Tahitian whom Cook had aboard in 1770, could converse with the Maoris 'tolerably well'. Although modern linguistic studies are by no means in complete agreement with each other, they tend to group the Maori language with Tahitian (the Society Islands), Rarotongan (Cook Islands) and

Tuamotuan. Some of these studies, however, are of limited reliability, being based on data collected long after European contact, and, more to the point, after undoubted influence by Polynesian-speaking missionaries from other areas. Another problem is that dialectual variation within New Zealand was such that the speech of southern New Zealand, for example, was probably closer in some respects to that of Atiu in the Cook Islands than it was to that spoken in the North Island — a fact ignored by early missionaries in New Zealand when recording the Maori language, which they standardised according to that used in the north.

Because it is possible to obtain genuinely prehistoric data, physical characteristics based on bone measurements should be more reliable than language as a source of information on Maori origins. Sadly, studies of different characteristics give different results. One study suggests that the New Zealand Maoris have their closest relationship with the people of the Marquesas, Hawaii, Easter Island and the Chathams; another suggests that Hawaiians and Easter Islanders have a more distant relationship, which is not unexpected, but surprisingly brings in Tonga and Samoa from *Western* Polynesia! The similarities in bone structure and bodily form of people throughout Polynesia are so strong, and the total amount of research material readily available to physical anthropologists so limited, that the apparent differences noted have little statistical significance. And, like language, there is a considerable range within New Zealand itself.

To many archaeologists the evidence of artifact types is more acceptable. Although it is possible for communities of different places to develop identical tools independently, the

Evidence that the Polynesians made ocean-going voyages can be seen from this drawing of a Polynesian canoe which was discovered out of sight of land by Schouten and Le Maire in 1616. (From Burney, 1806)

likelihood of this is not great, especially if the environments — and hence the uses for the tools — the conditions, and even the raw materials are different. The argument against independent invention of identical ornaments is even stronger since there would appear to be even fewer common factors that could influence the shape and design of an object that did not have a principally utilitarian purpose. (In fact, there was also a considerable degree of aesthetic appreciation applied to the final shape — and finish — of many tools and implements.)

Parallel or antecedent examples of most Maori artifacts can be found in other Polynesian islands. Adze heads, one-piece and two-piece fish hooks, trolling hooks and a number of other artifact types share a common Eastern Polynesian similarity. If a particular design of artifact occurred only in New Zealand and one other Pacific island, that island could well be the place from which New Zealand's Polynesian

settlers came. Because artifacts were not mass produced, however, no two are exactly alike — even those made by the same craftsman will have slight variations. We are left with a somewhat subjective assessment of similarity unless we can find some very distinctive feature, a *type* of artifact, rather than simply a variation of design.

One type of tanged, quadrangular-sectioned adze head found in early New Zealand contexts has a pair of rounded knobs on the poll. These are probably ornamental because they occur mostly on finely finished tools, though they could also have some function in binding the stone head to its wooden haft. Apart from New Zealand, they have been found only in the Society, Cooks, Australs, Pitcairn and the Chathams. As it is extremely unlikely that such a feature would be invented independently in two different places about the same time, the argument can be made that settlers from one of these islands came to New Zealand. Small tooth-

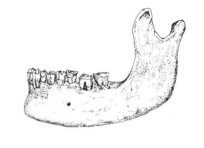
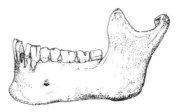

The lower edge of the Polynesian jawbone (top) is typically rounded, with the result that it will 'rock' when placed on a flat surface — hence the term 'rocker jaw'. The lower edge of the European jawbone (bottom) is flat or even a convex.

A word list from Hawkesworth (far left), 1773. Early European explorers noted close similarities in the languages spoken on different island groups.

A 37-metre long wall (below left) of large slabs of coral limestone mark the site of Vairakaia on Atiu, one of the Cook Islands.

Part of a complex of eight prehistoric rectangular stone enclosures (below) made of coral limestone, on Atiu, Cook Islands. Although believed to have had some ceremonial significance, the purpose of these structures must await archaeological investigation.

Marquesan trolling hooks (right). When available, in Polynesia, use was made of pearl shell for the lure shanks of trolling fish-hooks.

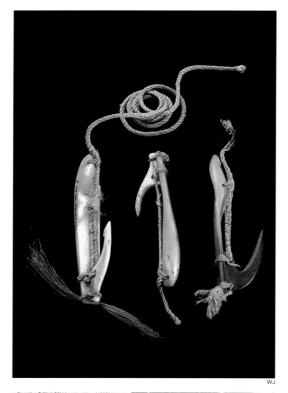

WJ

Excavations (right) on the island of Hivaoa, Marquesas.

Stone wall of a paepae (below) at Taiohae on the island of Nukuhiva, Marquesas. Although relatively common on many Polynesian islands, ceremonial stone structures of this type were not made in New Zealand.

AD/UA

shaped necklace units (*see page 48-49*) share a distribution with Niue, the Society and Marquesas Islands — reducing the apparent likely homeland to the Society group of islands. However, reel-shaped beads for necklaces have been found on early New Zealand sites in both the North and South Islands, and although they have been made of several different materials and vary in their size and proportions, they are distinctive in that they have grooves and ridges around their circumference. Beads with the same distinctive features have also been found on the Marquesas, thus equally strengthening the case for a Marquesan origin of the Maoris.

Harpoon heads are common to both the Marquesas and New Zealand. Most of these are not particularly distinctive but one harpoon head, of a design so far unique in New Zealand, was excavated from the 900-year-old Fyffe site in Kaikoura — and is very similar to one found in the slightly older Hane site in the Marquesas. Tattooing chisels from Hane are also similar to those found in New Zealand. It is evidence of this sort that makes it highly plausible that the Marquesas Islands were the homeland of New Zealand's first settlers.

A major flaw to this argument, however, is that such harpoon heads may well have been made on other islands but simply have not yet been found. The same, of course, applies to other distinctive artifacts. For the present, on the grounds of available archaeological evidence, we must opt for the Marquesas being the probable Pacific homeland of the Maoris, with the Society Islands as runner up. In fact, there is every

AD/UA

AD/UA

likelihood of further research turning up convincing evidence from closer island groups. The Tuamotus and southern Cooks are both geographical contenders, and it is certainly most unlikely that a voyaging canoe would have completely by-passed the many islands that lie between the Marquesas and New Zealand.

The plants and animals that were successfully introduced into New Zealand — the kumara, yam, taro, gourd, tropical cabbage tree, paper mulberry, the kuri and the kiore — do not provide any clues to where the people came from. Other important species of both may well have been brought but not survived either the journey or their introduction to the new land. It is easy to imagine that pigs and hens might have been sacrificed for the immediate requirements of food on a long journey.

Although it is theoretically possible for the Maori population of New Zealand, estimated as at least 100,000 by the end of the eighteenth century, to have descended from as few as six people 1000 years ago, there are several reasons for believing that it was more than this small number. A very small 'founding population' is less likely to have survived, the gene pool may have been too limited to produce the variety of physical characteristics that developed, and it would have been more difficult for few people to bring with them the varied skills and cultural traits that link New Zealand so closely with the rest of Eastern Polynesia. A few years ago a computer study indicated that a group of seven men and seven women (the latter aged 18 to 20 years) would have had an 85 per cent chance of

founding a permanent population. It seems probable that what must have been a major expedition of exploration and settlement would have had more members than this, and we could expect several times this number to have travelled on a large ocean-going canoe.

There remains the question of a single or multiple settlement. Recently several prehistorians have resurrected the idea that more than one group of people settled here in prehistoric times, although this raises the question of why pigs and hens — so important in Polynesian economy — were not imported on a subsequent voyage. One proposition is based on the marked cultural differences in southern New Zealand, suggesting that the South Island was settled by a different area from the North — but without going so far as to propose where such an area might be. This is somewhat reminiscent of earlier arguments for multiple settlement which maintained that certain North Island artifacts and art forms had non-Polynesian attributes, or that East Coast and Central North Island Maoris had some physical characteristics that separated them from the rest of New Zealand. Another proposition contends that a fishing lure of tropical pearl shell found on the 600-year-old Tairua site on the Coromandel must have been brought to New Zealand long after the time of first settlement. An obvious alternative explanation — assuming the identification of pearl shell is correct — is that the lure was regarded as an heirloom from the old country, and retained for several generations before being lost in a North Island shell midden.

A crop of taro (far left) growing over the remains of an earlier Niuean occupation dating back several centuries. Prehistoric horticulture in Polynesia was probably carried out in much the same manner.

Archaeological and linguistic evidence suggests that the two most likely islands of origin for the first settlers to New Zealand are the Marquesas and Society groups.

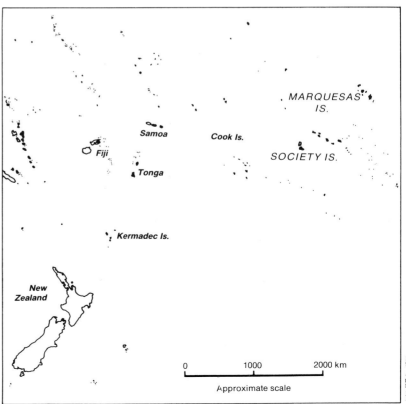

Julie O'Brien/CM

Navigation

SINCE the earliest European exploration of Oceania, there has been much speculation as to how it became settled. Many writers noted how difficult deliberate journeying from one group of islands to another must have been once the craft were out of sight of land. And although archaeology may not be able to tell us a great deal about prehistoric seafaring and navigation *per se*, we do have a considerable amount of factual information upon which theories may be based.

We know, for example, that the general spread of people was from the west to the east, and radiocarbon dates provide some indication of when each group of Polynesian islands was settled. We have detailed data on winds and currents, and must take into account that west to east movement is against the prevailing winds and currents (except at the equator). We know that the Polynesians must have had contact with South America to get kumaras. And we have eighteenth-century descriptions of their canoes and sailing abilities.

Although the Polynesians used (and still use) outrigger canoes for fishing and for travelling short distances around their islands, the principal long-distance vessel was the double canoe. Cook and his contemporaries described several of these in use or being built in the latter part of the eighteenth century. They had lengths of up to 33 metres (longer than Cook's *Endeavour*) and could carry over 200 people, although for long-distance voyaging the number was probably much less. The twin hulls, not necessarily of the same size, were held together by a platform which often had some form of shelter built on it. Typically they appear to have had a triangular or 'crab-claw'-shaped sail, sometimes two sails. During the nineteenth century Europeans were told that journeys of 20 days were well within the capabilities of the craft and its sailors.

In the earlier days of this century in New Zealand, when the traditionalists reigned supreme, all too little thought was given to the difficulties of navigating across great ocean distances without instruments. It was generally believed that Polynesian sailors could travel between island groups at will, although it was puzzling that they were apparently no longer making such journeys at the time of European contact. Then in 1956 Andrew Sharp stated quite baldly that the longest deliberate offshore voyages made by Polynesians had probably been no more than 300 miles (483 kilometres). He maintained that locating small islands in the middle of the Pacific Ocean would have been almost impossible and compared it to the journeys on the land-locked seas of the old world where voyagers could cross with the certainty of hitting land, and then make their way along the coastline.

When the furore resulting from Sharp's assertions died down, many people were left thinking that the Pacific had been settled largely as a result of 'accidental drift', which rather overstated his hypothesis. The lie to this was given by a computer-aided study by Levison, Ward and Webb which showed that it was most unlikely that many islands would have been settled at all had canoes simply drifted where

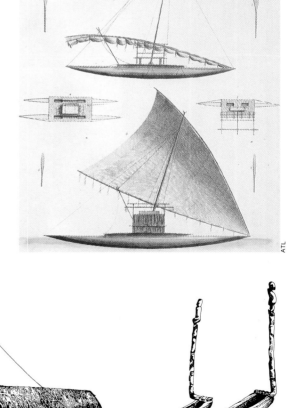

A Tongan canoe (right) from Dumont d'Urville's account of his 1826-29 voyage, *Voyage de la Corvette Astrolabe*. The type of canoe in which the original Polynesian settlers came to New Zealand may well have been similar to the one depicted here.

Much Pacific travel was undertaken in large double canoes similar to this one which was depicted by the artist Webber who accompanied Cook on his third voyage, 1776-1780. Such canoes were capable of carrying considerable numbers of people over long distances.

winds and currents took them. To get to New Zealand must have required a deliberate intention to sail in a southerly direction.

Oceanic yachtsman David Lewis maintained that the non-instrumental skills of Pacific sailors had been vastly under-rated, and although such skills may have been forgotten by modern Polynesians, there were people in Micronesia who could sail accurately over long distances. To put the matter to the test, anthropologist Ben Finney organised the construction of a 19-metre-long double canoe, which in 1976 was sailed from Hawaii to Tahiti guided by a Micronesian master navigator, Mau Piailug, using traditional non-instrumental methods. (At that time no Polynesian could be found who was familiar with the ancient navigational methods.) In 1980 Nainoa Thompson, a Hawaiian pupil of Mau, sailed the canoe from Hawaii to Tahiti and back without using instruments, charts or other modern devices. An even longer journey to New Zealand was made in 1987. These ventures did not prove what had been done in prehistoric times — all they showed was that it was possible to arrive at a chosen destination, given prior knowledge of position and the prevailing winds and currents, without the use of instruments.

In order to navigate successfully across the open ocean the Pacific sailor had to be able to determine the required direction and also keep track of the distance and direction actually travelled so that any necessary course corrections could be made. There is no great problem in setting a course: this can be done basically from the rising and setting positions of appropriate stars (requiring a sound knowledge of the whole of the night sky so that direction can still be found when the key stars are too far above the horizon or obscured), together with reference to the sun, the pattern of ocean swells and the prevailing wind when the stars are not visible. A canoe's position when travelling in a north-south direction can be judged from the height of known stars above the horizon; for east-west movement, however, reliance must be placed on 'dead reckoning'. In his 1980 voyage, Nainoa Thompson kept track of the vessel's position by continually estimating how much it deviated from an ideal course which took into account the winds and currents between Hawaii and Tahiti.

Another important aid to early Pacific navigation must have been the ability to recognise the proximity of land by such means as cloud formations, light being reflected on to clouds from shallow lagoons, changes in swell patterns, or the presence of birds.

Anthropologist Geoff Irwin — he is also a Pacific yachtsman — believes that the Polynesian sailors would not have recklessly ventured forth into an unknown ocean without hope of return, but that they would limit any journey of exploration to the point from which they could expect to be able to return to their home island. In other words, they would not deliberately sail beyond the 'point of no return'. If this were so, there is an advantage in sailing out against the prevailing winds and currents as these would be of considerable assistance on the homeward journey if no new landfall was made. This theory provides an explanation for the west to east settlement of Polynesia.

Most of the exploration and settlement of Eastern Polynesia took place 1-2000 years ago, and it has been widely assumed that long-distance voyaging then ceased. Suggested reasons for this have ranged from hypothesised changes in wind and current patterns to the possibility that once all major island groups were settled, expeditions returned with the news of no more uninhabited land, thus rendering any further exploration pointless. There is, however, no supporting evidence for such notions.

The experimental double canoe Hokule'a (left), undergoing sea trials in 1975. Although built of modern materials, it conforms to prehistoric design. The Hokule'a has since been successfully sailed on several long-distance voyages in the Pacific without the use of navigational instruments.

New Zealand (below) from 150 kilometres out to sea. The curvature of the earth prevented canoe voyagers from seeing distant land even in clear conditions, but distinctive clouds positioned above islands often indicated their presence long before the land itself could be seen.

Polynesian Voyaging Society

A New Land

*T*O the first Polynesians to arrive in New Zealand 1000 or more years ago, this country must have seemed like a completely different world. It was a world far bigger than any island they had known before, stretching over 13 degrees of latitude; it was 25 times larger that Hawai'i, the largest of the Eastern Polynesian islands to the north. It was 160 times larger than the combined Society Islands and 200 times larger than the Marquesas, the most likely places of origin for the Maoris.

As well, the structure of the new land was completely different. Although New Zealand comprises several islands, these are actually pieces of a large continent emerging from the sea. Unlike other Eastern Polynesian islands, they are geologically complex, composed of a whole range of sedimentary, igneous and metamorphic rocks, with numerous high mountains and volcanoes with deep lakes and large, swift rivers.

The climate, too, was unlike any they had known before, the temperatures ranging from sub-tropical in the northernmost areas to distinctly sub-Antarctic 1600 kilometres away in the south. Today the mean annual temperature at sea level ranges from 15°C to 9°C, north to south, and although there has been much speculation that it may have been warmer when people first arrived, any increase is likely to have been small — probably no more than one degree. The amount of rainfall may also have been slightly different from that experienced today, but the wide range would have been comparable — currently mean annual rainfall varies from 300 millimetres in Central Otago to over 8000 millimetres in the Southern Alps. This was a land that did not readily lend itself to the horticultural practices the settlers had developed in their tropical homelands — not only was it colder, but seasonal changes were much greater. Some imported tropical plant species, even if they survived the long ocean journey, would either die during the winter months or be restricted to growing in warmer parts of the country.

Eighty per cent of the land was covered with dense evergreen forest rising from the coast, inland and upwards to the alpine timber limits. This would supply almost limitless timber for a variety of purposes — particularly the 'softwood' conifers, such as totara, that resisted weathering and rotting in the ground, and were to be later used for carving, canoes and house structures. There was kaikomako — used for firemaking; houhere or lacebark, from which they would try to make barkcloth; tough kanuka for the shafts of digging sticks, and numerous others. Yet it would take generations of experiment and trial and error to discover all the attributes of the wealth of timber in this new land.

Much of the animal life, too, was new and different. While the coastal waters abounded in fish, shellfish and marine mammals, and on shore there were seals and seabirds, the land fauna was more unusual. Of the larger animals, the few amphibians, reptiles and mammals were to be of little significance. The most important denizens

of the forest were birds. Many of these had evolved from species which were isolated in New Zealand when it broke from the original continental mass of Gondwana and became an island — more than 80 million years before. In an environment free from mammalian predators, some had become completely flightless, many could fly only heavily and for short distances. Such features would make them vulnerable to any incoming, large predator.

This was the strange country to which the first Polynesians came. On plants and animals that resembled familiar species they had left behind they would bestow the same names, such as *weka* for the woodhen. Some were more imaginative: the huge moa was given the name of the Polynesian domestic fowl. Many place names were also imported, some of which had already been applied to geographic features on more than one Pacific island.

The actual landfall site is unlikely to ever be identified. Their initial settlement would have been small and probably of a very temporary nature, occupied only long enough for the travellers to get their bearings, recoup their strength, and prepare to explore their new country, although they may have planted the tubers and cuttings they brought with them. It is likely that they landed somewhere in the north. Apart from this being the nearest part of the country to their homeland islands, the northern climate would have been more conducive to the successful initial survival of kumara. And, as well, the presence of artifacts of Mayor Island obsidian on very early sites throughout New Zealand suggests that the northern area was known from an early date.

Over the next eight or ten centuries these people would thrive, irrevocably altering the face of the new land. But in the beginning we may picture them, a small party struggling ashore. Did they even have the strength to securely beach their canoe? We cannot say; we only know with certainty that they arrived — and survived.

Upper Rakaia River. The geography of the new land confronting the first Polynesian settlers would have been unlike anything they had experienced before.

Andris Apse Ltd

35

Early Settlement and Shelter

A watercolour (right) by T. S. Cousins of Haast at the Weka Pass rock art shelter, North Canterbury, 1876. Many of the early shelters were simply rock overhangs that offered little protection against the weather.

Where they were available, natural rock formations (below right) often afforded convenient shelter to the early Maoris. In inland Canterbury and North Otago many hundreds of shelters, such as this one in Duntroon, contain archaeological evidence of prehistoric occupation.

Excavations at the Ototara Glen rock shelter site (below), North Otago, showed that most of the occupational activity actually took place immediately outside the limestone overhang; this possibly indicates that the most sheltered area was kept clear for sleeping quarters.

*O*NCE the immediate — and possibly urgent — needs of finding food and water had been met, the next important consideration for the first arrivals must have been shelter. Some sort of weather-proof dwelling place would have been essential. In some of the more sheltered parts of the northern North Island, it may well have been possible to live in the open all the year round, but it is unlikely that people whose ancestors had for many generations lived on tropical islands could easily become immune to the southern winters.

Doubtless the very first shelter was that afforded by natural rock overhangs and caves, and these continued to be used to some extent throughout the whole of the prehistoric era.

Rock shelters — they are generally too shallow to be called caves — were used wherever convenient throughout the country, mainly to provide temporary accommodation on hunting and fishing trips and on cross-country journeys. The best known are the inland South Island limestone shelters in which the occupants drew on the light-coloured walls. Although the drawings make it obvious that the rock formations have been used in the past, there are probably at least as many shelters with no drawings — the rock surface may have been unsuitable, the artwork may have since disappeared, or simply because no drawings were ever made in them. Excavation of shelter floors, however, will often reveal food remains, artifacts or charcoal and burnt, broken stones from domestic fires. Usually, the shelters had only temporary, sometimes intermittent, occupation — particularly if they were small or shallow. Some shelters did not have any overhang at all but simply comprised a rock face against which people camped. Obviously, the distribution of rock shelter sites throughout the country is dependent on the distribution of suitably weathered outcropping rock.

In 1962–63 the North Otago Scientific and Historical Society investigated a fairly typical limestone rock shelter at Ototara Glen. The shelter itself was about eight metres wide and had up to two metres overhang; there were no drawings or other obvious indications that it had been occupied. Beneath the surface of the ground, mostly outside the area covered by the overhang, the remains of a cooking fire, midden bones, shells and artifacts indicated that a small party of people had camped there some 550 years ago. They had fed on fish and birds, including the extinct moa, goose and swan. And although they were primarily engaged in fowling, they had brought fish, seal, shellfish and echinoderms from the coast some two kilometres away. Archaeologists were even able to tell that they had dropped the shells of the catseye, *Turbo smaragda*, in one place and the operculum (the actual 'eye') from them in another.

Interestingly, Ototara Glen was used as a camp site by Walter Mantell and his survey party in 1848, and subsequently by others engaged in early farming activities, and remains of their occupation were found in the top few centimetres of soil.

Although the Maoris generally did not favour deep dark caves, Moa-bone Point Cave

near Christchurch was a remarkable exception. The cave itself comprises three main chambers: the first and largest of over 600 square metres was poorly lit from a restricted entrance (the opening has since been considerably enlarged by the construction of the Redcliffs main road), the two inner chambers being quite dark. Yet prehistoric occupational debris occurred from a depth of two metres near the entrance to about 30 centimetres at the far end. Its main period of occupation was about 600 years ago, and it appears to have been used at about the same time as a comparatively large settlement in the adjacent Redcliffs sand dunes. People clearly used the cave for a variety of activities, including eating and the disposal of food remains, and for some manufacturing industry; hanks of human hair had been placed in crevices, and a folded burial was dug up from the main chamber last century. Interestingly, remains of posts indicate that a structure had been built inside the cave, and one interpretation of this is that it provided a cover over a canoe to prevent fragments of rock from the cave roof falling into it (though why a canoe should be more vulnerable than people to damage from rocks remains a mystery). The cave thus appears to have been used for several reasons, but the main one was undoubtedly in providing shelter for the occupants of the Redcliffs settlement when they required it.

A North Island example of an early cave shelter is the Whakamoenga Cave on the shore of Lake Taupo. This cave has a floor area of about 180 square metres and had four main periods of occupation, the latest dating to early European times. It was first occupied 5-600 years ago by people who hunted moas. Different parts of the cave were used for different purposes. Near the entrance was a sort of vestibule, there was a cooking area to one side, and a working area in one part where the floor was rocky. It

was not possible to recognise any discrete sleeping area from material in the occupational deposit, but there were sheltered and rock-free areas towards the back of the cave that could have been used for sleeping.

Although there are both good archaeological records and eye-witness descriptions of houses at the end of the prehistoric era, we have very little information about the dwellings constructed during the first few centuries of occupation. What evidence there is is sparse and largely unsatisfactory. Houses then were constructed almost entirely of perishable materials, mostly timber and other plant products; the small amount of stone used — such as for fireplaces — does not provide much information on the buildings themselves, while modifications to the ground surface — hollowed-out floors and raised earthen walls — are subject to infilling and erosion respectively. Finally, most of the house structure was above ground level, adding to its vulnerability through rotting, burning, weathering and ageing.

Nevertheless, a number of early investigators reported evidence of houses or huts on moa-hunter sites. Julius Haast noted that there had been a rectangular hut, 4.6 metres long by 2.1 metres wide, with an opening facing north, adjacent to the moa-hunter site at the mouth of the Rakaia, and David Teviotdale said there were at least 36 huts defined by stone fireplaces at the mouth of the Shag River, another important moa-hunter site. At Waitaki, Teviotdale thought there were both circular and rectangular huts adjacent to the moa-bone middens, though his interpretation of the evidence has since been questioned. Dwellings were of little interest to earlier investigators (except possibly as indicators as to where portable artifacts might be found) and as a rule no record was kept of the remains of structures, even when they were noticed.

Wairau Bar excavations (below left). Although extensive excavations were carried out at Wairau Bar in the 1940s and early 1950s, these yielded only limited information on the moa hunters. Using better techniques which included digging in 'squares' subsequent excavations were aimed at learning more about the site and its occupants of over 600 years ago.

Part of an array of post holes (below) which showed up in 1959 excavations at the Wairau Bar moa-hunter site; some of the posts appear to have formed a building as outlined. However, there has been very little archaeological study made of structures relating to this early period of prehistoric occupation.

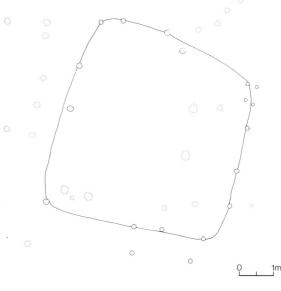

0   1m

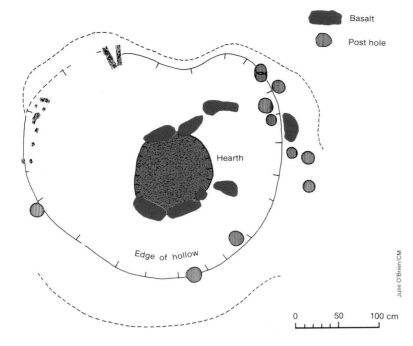

Basalt

Post hole

Hearth

Edge of hollow

0   50   100 cm

Julie O'Brien/CM

Towards the end of 1987 archaeological excavations were undertaken at an early sand dune site at Tumbledown Bay on Banks Peninsula, with the object of recovering data on the prehistoric occupation before it was destroyed by wind erosion and the various activities of visitors to the Bay. Evidence was obtained of the site having been occupied on a number of occasions over a period of time, the earliest being associated with moa hunting. One of the most important discoveries in the lower levels was evidence of a roughly circular dwelling, the floor of which comprised a shallow saucer-like pit similar to those found on the much later Peketa Pa at Kaikoura (*see page 73*). Post holes and scattered charcoal around the edge were probably the remnants of a shelter that had been built over the hollow, which contained an ash-filled fireplace marked with basalt stones.

In the Marlborough Sounds there are pits that although not directly connected with moa hunting are thought by some investigators to be the remains of early house sites. Some North Island archaeologists, on the other hand, claim that they are kumara storage pits, although this is hard to sustain considering the size of the pits, their distribution and the absence of any nearby garden areas. They are rectangular in shape, up to 45 square metres in size, and occur mostly towards the end of spurs and ridges. Their early age is suggested by the fairly large trees in the bottoms of some pits. While the only ones to have been investigated archaeologically have been no more than about 400 years old, this does not mean to say that others are not much older.

Modern archaeologists have been largely frustrated in their efforts to learn more about early housing in New Zealand. At Foxton, north of Wellington, a hearth and associated post holes indicated a rudimentary shelter; at Tai Rua in North Otago small fireplaces and post holes have been interpreted as indications of dwellings. This sort of evidence would suggest that the early people did not build substantial houses, and this may be because their lifestyle was of a more itinerant nature than that of their descendants of, say, two centuries ago. Yet this is not a very satisfactory explanation. The range of tools used by the early people include several types of adze heads, chisels and drill points, indicating that they were experienced wood-workers, and in at least two early sites — Pounawea in South Otago and Hohopounamu in North Canterbury — there were rows of post holes, which if correctly

Mutton-birder's huts, which are probably very similar to the temporary shelters built in prehistoric times, were still being constructed in southern New Zealand early this century.

A. Phillips Coll./CM

interpreted as fencelines suggest a degree of permanency which might warrant equally permanent houses.

Although much of the work at Wairau Bar was aimed at recovering portable artifacts, excavations in the late 1950s and early 60s revealed an array of filled-in post holes in the sub-surface deposits. There was no obvious pattern to them but they clearly represented the remains of a number of structures. Recently, Atholl Anderson has made the tentative suggestion that one group relates to a 4.5 metre-square building. And at Tumbledown Bay on Banks Peninsula, Brian Allingham has excavated what appears to have been a sub-circular house, roughly three metres in diameter, with a central fireplace.

A substantial and relatively well-preserved house site excavated at Moikau in the south of the North Island is widely believed to be of an early age. It had been identified on the surface by a stone-lined hearth in a rectangular depression. The walls were delineated by squared totara post butts forming a rectangle 6.7 metres long by nearly 4.5 wide inside the depression. As well, it had an internal division of some sort and a door facing roughly south-west. The archaeologists working on the site recognised that the general plan of this house differed little from that of those used in the nineteenth century. Indeed, it may well be that it is far more recent than the 770 years charcoal radiocarbon dating suggests (being a porous substance, charcoal tends to absorb organic material from the surrounding soil, and this can affect the date).

Because we know so little about the actual dwellings, we tend to think of the places where people lived as camp sites or encampments, as if they were temporary, rather than permanent, in nature. Nevertheless, some useful information has been obtained on the organisation and layout of some of the early settlements. For example, most of the large early settlements were at the mouths of rivers (especially in the South Island) where there was access to the interior and freshwater and coastal foods were at hand. Although there are some notable exceptions — such as Wairau Bar — the majority were not occupied for any great length of time; rather, it would seem, the people came into an area, exploited the readily available resources such as moas, and then shifted on to another area. While the total population was relatively small such a resource strategy may have been viable.

One such site near the mouth of the Kaupokonui River in Taranaki was exposed by wind erosion in 1962. It was identified as being of moa-hunter age although there was evidence of more recent occupation nearby. The site has been radiocarbon dated to about 600 years before present, and although it was primarily a butchery site where a large number of moas — one estimate is of up to 400 — were eaten in a relatively short time, the inhabitants clearly observed different areas for different activities. Excavations carried out by Alistair Buist and Richard Cassels concentrated on the moa-hunter beach midden (*see pages 52-53*). The early occupants had left an abundance of moa bone, together with the remains of many other species

Rectangular pits, up to 11.5 metres long and sometimes cut into rock, are a common feature of the archaeological landscape in the Marlborough Sounds (left). Most were interpreted by early investigators as 'pit houses', and recent research indicates that they were more likely to have been used for habitation than for storage. Many are nowadays covered with bracken or scrub.

Depressions on a Kaikoura hillside (below), indicating the presence of largely filled-in pits, provide a tenuous reminder of past occupation. Their visibility varies with the length and colour of the grass.

of birds, and some dogs, rats, seals, fish and shellfish, and a variety of artifacts and other evidence from which it was possible to learn something of the organisation of their village or camp. A cooking area was easily distinguished by the quantity of charcoal and burnt stones; an oven depression that was partially uncovered was about three metres in diameter and 15 centimetres deep. Of special interest were three butchery areas. There was a primary butchery area where moa carcasses were cut up, and where there were relatively few stone tools. Nearby was a secondary processing area where there were mostly leg bones of moas and bones of sea mammals, and where there were more tools. And there was a tertiary processing area where the bones were either naturally small (there were over 50 species of birds represented on the site) or were broken pieces of larger bones. Here were large quantities of stone material, mostly obsidian and chert, but also flakes from adze head manufacture. There was also a fish-processing area and, after the main period of moa butchery, an area where dogs were tethered — attested to by their numerous droppings.

The North Otago site at Tai Rua (not to be confused with Tairua on the Coromandel) was also divided into activity areas. It was discovered in the late 1950s when farm ploughing turned up an area of midden, oven remains and artifacts at the northern end of a coastal flat immediately behind a sandy beach. Initial salvage work to recover material from the disturbed ground soon indicated that it was a moa-hunter site and that there was undisturbed occupational material beneath the plough depth. Over most of the site there was only one occupational deposit, although it was divided into three different layers in some places, and its composition varied in different areas. Since the time of occupation it

had been covered with wind-blown sand in the top of which a stable soil had developed.

At the back of the site furthest from the beach was a butchering area with large numbers of moa bones, and there was a cooking area between here and a small watercourse or swamp. Although wastage of moa carcasses was not as great as at Kaupokonui, whole necks had certainly been cast aside. A broken harpoon point was also found here — giving weight to the possibility that harpoons were used to catch moas — as well as a quantity of moa egg-shell, possibly from formed but unlaid eggs.

Closer to the beach was an area containing numerous post holes and small fireplace hollows which indicated a living area. Because there were no discernible alignments in these post holes, the huts or shelters must have been subcircular or irregular in shape.

Between the living and the butchering and cooking areas was a large accumulation of rubbish — bones, shells, burnt stones, charcoal and artifacts. Lesser quantities of this midden material were also scattered over most of the site. By analysing the midden it was possible to tell that moas and shellfish had been the most important foods, followed closely by fish and small birds — of the latter, four were extinct

Strata in the Tai Rua site, North Otago (right). The bottom layers were produced by various activities of moa-hunter occupation 500 years ago, while the upper layers reflect present-day farming processes.

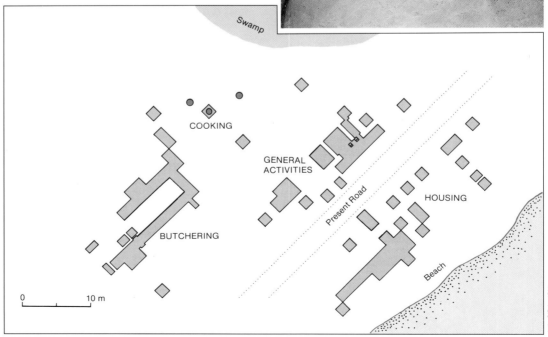

Some 500 years ago a small group of people lived on the coastal North Otago site now called Tai Rua. Various activities such as butchering moa carcasses, cooking food, making fish-hooks, sheltering, and the dumping of refuse were for the most part carried out in separate areas of the site. At intermittent times during the late 1950s and the 1960s a series of excavations, indicated by squares on the plan, provided information about the inhabitants and the layout of their settlement. Today the site is bisected by a modern roadway.

Swamp

COOKING

GENERAL ACTIVITIES

Present Road

HOUSING

BUTCHERING

Beach

0   10 m

Julie O'Brien/CM

species, and the remainder mostly from marine or freshwater habitats. Some dogs and seals were also eaten. A total of 1624 artifacts was found, over 55 per cent of them being cutting and chopping implements or waste flakes produced during their manufacture. There were 11 sinkers and 43 drill points and over 300 unfinished, broken or complete fish hooks. These artifacts indicated that an important aspect of the occupants' lives was manufacturing fish hooks of a variety of different shapes and sizes from moa bone. A series of radiocarbon dates gave an age of about 500 years before present.

The distribution of these early sites is interesting: there are more known early sites in the South Island than in the North. There were doubtless two main resources that attracted the early Polynesian settlers to the colder parts of the country. One would undoubtedly be the greater range of stone materials, much of the North Island being covered in relatively soft or otherwise unsuitable rocks for a stone-age technology. The other important resource that flourished in the South would have been the moas. They were present in the North Island but not in such great numbers — much of the North Island forest had been devastated by volcanic eruptions. The only real disadvantage in the South would have been the colder climate, which made kumara cultivation more difficult — and, indeed, impossible in the southern half of the island. But kumaras were not particularly important in the early days when there was such an abundance of natural food available.

In the Moikau Valley, Palliser Bay, a stone-lined hearth in the centre of a rectangular depression was identified as the remains of a prehistoric house. Excavations in 1971-72 revealed post butts and timber demarking the walls of a one-roomed building with a porch facing the south-west. This is very similar in design to houses that were being used into the historic period.

Garden wall

Porch

Fireplace

0 1 2 m

More than 600 years may separate the Moikau house and this nineteenth-century dwelling below, also found in the Wairarapa. During that time basic house design does not seem to have changed significantly.

Binsted's Studio

Early Stone Tool Technology

*T*HE technology of the pre-European Polynesians in New Zealand was based on their ability to shape stone of selected varieties into tools, weapons and ornaments. In the Pacific Islands the range of available stone materials had been limited — coral limestone and some volcanic rock, mainly basalt. Despite this they had developed considerable skill in shaping stone materials and designing and using tools made from them.

The principal technique that was used to shape stone is known as 'flaking'. Bascially, this involved striking flakes of stone from the parent material, using a hammer stone; the flake sizes could vary from very large pieces, such as would be struck off when quarrying, to tiny fragments chipped off to sharpen a cutting edge or to produce the exact shape of an artifact. Some materials were more suitable for flaking than others — usually the finer and more evenly grained the material was, the easier it was to flake in a controlled manner — but other qualities also had to be taken into account. Although obsidian could be flaked to produce a very sharp edge, the material was too brittle for adze heads.

To the first Polynesian settlers the land with its wide range of continental rock types must have seemed like a treasure-house of precious stones. From the range of different kinds of worked rocks that occur in even the earliest known archaeological sites, we know that the new arrivals must have explored the country to find suitable stone materials. And these were found in abundance: volcanic glass (obsidian) from Mayor Island and Taupo, argillite (indurated mudstone) from Nelson, greywacke from Canterbury, porcellanite and orthoquartzite from Otago, chert from the east coast limestones, and a wide variety of igneous rocks — basalts, andesites and tuffs — from all over the country.

Some of the rocks they located were a complete novelty and many trials and errors must have occurred during an initial search for stone suitable for flaking. Evidence of such experimentation is found on some early sites — for example at Clarence Mouth and at Kaikoura — where readily obtained local materials such as mudstones and silicious limestones were tried although neither of these proved particularly successful for tool-making.

The metamorphic rock greenstone (nephrite or pounamu) was also tried in this early period, although unsuccessfully. At first the efforts of these skilled Polynesian craftsmen produced only crude artifacts: the fibrous nephrite, with its tenacious internal structure, did not fracture cleanly when struck.

Some rocks suitable for tool-making could be found in conveniently sized pieces in river beds or on beaches. At Wakanui, Rakaia and Kaitorete Spit thousands of simple but effective knives were made by knocking flakes off locally obtained greywacke beach cobbles. Such knives were mostly oval in shape, from five to 15 centimetres long, and were used for a variety of purposes including butchering moa carcasses. For better quality cutting implements it was often necessary to travel some distance to the source of suitable stone, which may have required quarrying from an outcrop. The material most widely distributed in archaeological sites is obsidian, a black volcanic glass which occurs naturally only in a few places in the North Island, and which can be broken to produce a very fine cutting edge. At first the most popular source of it was Mayor Island in the Bay of Plenty, and flakes from here are found throughout New Zealand. One very large piece, weighing 48 kilograms, was found in the 750-year-old moa-hunter site at the mouth of the Hurunui River, over 1000 kilometres from its Mayor Island source. Fine-grained basalts and argillites were also highly sought after for the manufacture of adze heads. Stone from the Tahanga basalt quarry on the western side of the Coromandel Peninsula was taken and used on sites from Tauranga to Kaipara; argillite from Nelson has been found on sites all over New Zealand.

The flake knife was the most widespread tool used during the whole of the prehistoric period and was particularly important during the early moa-hunting era. In its most simple form it consisted of a single flake struck from a cobble or a prepared 'core' — the natural sharp edge being used for cutting. The form and size of these knives varied according to the material used and the area of the country in which they were manufactured, as well as the use for which they

Sources of the main kinds of stone used for tool manufacture during the early period of prehistory. This map also shows the main sources of nephrite, or greenstone, which did not become popular until a later period.

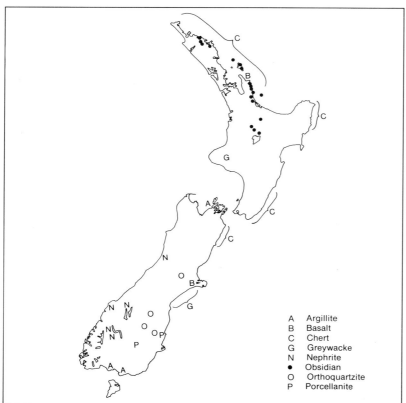

A	Argillite
B	Basalt
C	Chert
G	Greywacke
N	Nephrite
●	Obsidian
O	Orthoquartzite
P	Porcellanite

Julie O'Brien/CM

were intended. Large and beautiful examples of such knives, often called blades, are found on early archaeological sites in southern New Zealand, where their primary use was undoubtedly the butchering of 'big game'. The manufacture of these large knives declined after the extinction of moas and the reduction of the seal population.

Other really important tools, which were shaped almost entirely by flaking during the early period, were adze heads and chisels. Large flakes were first struck from a suitable piece of stone (usually argillite or basalt) to form the general shape of the adze head — often called a 'blank', 'rough-out' or 'preform'. These were sometimes left in this basic form except for the grinding of the cutting edge. Throughout the Marlborough Sounds, not far from the main sources of argillite, huge quantities of waste flakes were produced by people making tools by flaking. Some adze heads had the surface further reduced by 'hammer dressing', and a proportion were then polished all over. Some were roughened or reduced to a 'tang' at the poll end to facilitate binding to a wooden handle, others were simply tapered.

The wide range of adze heads and chisels found on sites suggests that the Polynesian settlers were skilled and comprehensive woodworkers. Several ethnologists have set up 'typologies' by which they have classified adze heads and the one in most common use was devised by Roger Duff. It comprises over 20 different varieties, although there is no evidence that the craftsmen who used them recognised this many or that they were used for different purposes. Some early adze heads that have been found are so large and heavy that they may have been only used for ceremonial purposes.

Drill points, principally of flint, but sometimes of other suitable materials such as argillite, were also manufactured by flaking. The principal requirement was that the rock was not too brittle for use. Mounted on a wooden spindle, the drill point was used with a rotary motion (usually by way of cords twisted around the weighted spindle) to bore holes in bone, shell, wood and stone.

Although flaking was to remain a basic element of stone tool technology throughout the whole era of human prehistory in New Zealand, it attained its highest standard during the early period when craftsmen made greatest use of the whole range of stone resources available.

Waste flakes of basalt (far left) produced during the manufacture of adze heads on Browns Island, Auckland, some centuries ago. Quantities of flakes like these are the most commonly found evidence of stone tool manufacture.

An assemblage of early adze heads (below left) found in the partly drained bed of Lake Ellesmere. Many of these clearly show flake scars from the manufacturing process. It has been suggested that they may have been lost when a canoe overturned on the lake.

Flaking techniques were used (left) to make a variety of early stone tools, using both locally obtained materials and others brought in from distant sources. This selection is from the 550-year-old Rakaia moa-hunter site and includes rock from as far away as Mayor Island — a distance of over 1000 kilometres.

A Canterbury Museum reconstruction (below) of moa hunter Maoris quarrying argillite rock for the manufacture of adze heads. This diorama was made by Leo Cappel from archaeological data supplied by Roger Duff.

Early Wood Carving

THAT the Maori people have been carving wood since the earliest period of their occupation of New Zealand is evident from the whole range of stone wood-working tools found on early sites. Unfortunately, few examples of early wood carving are known because the wooden objects themselves are not often preserved. Those that have survived are of a style quite different from those of the later era and in many ways resemble the early rock drawings and ornaments.

The outstanding feature of most of the very early wood carvings is the generally angular or rectilinear style of much of the decorative element. There is little evidence of the spirals and curvilinear styles so characteristic of later Maori art (*see pages 82-85*) and which feature so prominently in major museum displays and publications about Maori culture. In this, it is not surprising that many of the early New Zealand carvings bear a closer resemblance to some Pacific Island art motifs.

Most known examples of this early wood carving have been located in swamps or caves. In swamps a lack of oxygen excludes the bacteria which cause decay, while caves may provide dry conditions which inhibit the rotting of wooden items. Many of the wooden artifacts found in swamps were possibly placed there deliberately; the Maori people were certainly aware of the preservative qualities of swamps and may have used them to conceal precious pieces. Immersing the wood in mud could also have made it more easily worked during further carving.

A number of fascinating early carvings have been recovered from swamps throughout the country, most notably at Kaitaia, Kauri Point and Waitore in the north, and Temuka and Jacksons Bay in the south. And it is not only in the ornamental detail of the carving style that they differ from more familiar later pieces. Some are so different in their overall form that there is no certainty as to how they were actually utilised by the people who carved them. The 'Kaitaia lintel' is a good example. This well-known carving, currently displayed in a special case in Auckland Museum, caused considerable controversy when it was found in a swamp at Kaitaia (near Awanui) in 1921 to the extent that some reliable Maori 'authorities' denied that it

was of Maori origin. Nevertheless, it became popularly known as a lintel (a horizontal timber over a doorway) although an examination of it suggests that such a function is most unlikely. To this day its purpose is unknown.

Caves throughout New Zealand have also yielded a variety of early wooden pieces, including many smaller items that have seldom been preserved elsewhere. Probably the best known of the early sites are Moa-bone Point Cave and Moncks Cave — both located in the volcanic rock of Banks Peninsula and both extensively excavated last century.

Moa-bone Point Cave has been discussed in the introduction. This large cave contained floor deposits which in some places were up to two metres deep, and ranged in age from a lowest early moa-hunter level, through later Maori and into the European period. It was an ideal environment for preserving organic material and a number of wooden artifacts were found both by Julius Haast in the 1870s and by archaeologists this century. A unique head comb recovered by Haast has the notched ornamentation typical of the archaic period, while a small wooden head found in 1957 has simple angular lines and flat planar surfaces. (A wooden figure recovered from a cave on Otago Peninsula shows the same simplicity and undoubtedly dates to the same early period — its

One of the unique wood carvings (right) recovered from Moncks Cave was this small head, which was designed to be attached to a handle or shaft. This is another of the carvings which H. D. Skinner described as having 'crocodilian' features.

One of the best known examples (below) of early wood carving was found at Kaitaia in the 1920s. Today it is on display in the Auckland Museum. The central figure has a very 'Polynesian' appearance, while the chevron shapes occur in other early Maori art forms such as pendants and drawings.

Andrée Brett/AIM

style being much more in character with the art of Polynesian Islands like the Marquesas.)

Probably the most important of all cave discoveries was made in 1889 when workmen obtaining material for road construction uncovered the entrance to a cave at the base of a cliff on the property of a Mr Monck at Sumner, Christchurch. The cave, consisting of three chambers, appeared to have been sealed off for centuries by a rock fall and was to prove a precious time capsule for wooden relics of the early period. Regrettably, the contents of the cave (which included a range of artifacts and food remains, as well as things such as the occupants' hair clippings) were much disturbed, and material had been removed before it could be examined officially. There seems to have been a great deal of 'unofficial' digging with stories of treasure-hunting excavations carried out at night by the light of lanterns with a sacking screen over the cave mouth.

This indiscriminate digging destroyed the stratigraphy of the floor deposits of Moncks Cave. However, there still remain five extremely important pieces of early wood carving that were recovered at the time: an outrigger, a painted canoe paddle, a canoe bailer of unique design, a small carved wooden head and a three-dimensional carving of a Polynesian dog or kuri.

While it is clear that wood carving was important to the Polynesian people at all periods in New Zealand, most of the early pieces recovered throughout the country have been relatively small, even portable, items. This undoubtedly reflects in part the environment of preservation; larger, less portable items are not so likely to have been placed in swamps or caves. But the size of these pieces may also reflect something of the lifestyle of the earlier people. In a less-settled, more mobile existence, based on a hunter-gatherer economy with few permanent buildings, large ornate carvings would be inconvenient and difficult to move. Treasures that were small, on the other hand, could be carried and make familiar every new resting place.

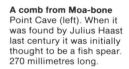

The head of a god symbol (far left) recovered in a swamp at Katikati. The multiple-lidded eye and head shape are found in similar carvings of the Cook Islands.

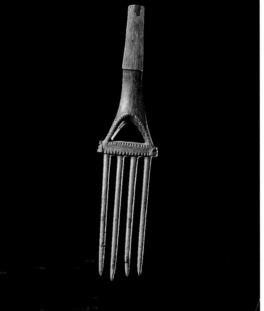

A comb from Moa-bone Point Cave (left). When it was found by Julius Haast last century it was initially thought to be a fish spear. 270 millimetres long.

The so-called 'god-stick' (below left) head from Moa-bone Point Cave displays the distinctive angularity of much early Maori wood carving, and is more reminiscent of the art styles of some of the Pacific islands than of the classic New Zealand Maoris.

There is still no certainty as to the original purpose of this unique crescent carving (below) recovered from a swamp near Temuka, South Canterbury. It measures 940 millimetres across the tips of the crescent which may have been intended to sit on a post rather than form part of a building, and possibly had some ceremonial significance.

Rock Art

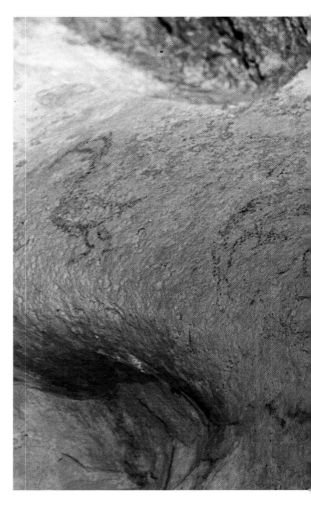

*O*F all the archaeological remains relating to the prehistoric Maori, rock art has perhaps had the most interesting and controversial history of research. This is largely because of the marked dissimilarity of most rock drawings to the more familiar Maori art forms — a problem that was compounded by the apparent lack of knowledge of the drawings by the eighteenth- and nineteenth-century Maoris.

Many investigators last century considered that the rock drawings were the work of either a much earlier race than the Maoris, or even of non-Polynesian visitors to New Zealand (*see page 11*). Although it has been recognised for most of this century that they are undoubtedly the work of Polynesian New Zealanders, they were usually considered to be of 'pre-Fleet' age, or even the work of an early Maori 'lost tribe'. Even quite recently Maori rock drawings have been 'interpreted' as Polynesian writing, as referring to celestial locations, and as showing influence by extra-terrestrial beings.

A common twentieth-century tendency until the 1960s was to study the drawings primarily as an art form, without making any real attempts to place them in the overall context of prehistory. During the last 20 years, however, a serious archaeological study has been made of rock art, and the results of excavating a number of shelter floor deposits, together with radiocarbon dating, have established its place as an important component of early Maori culture.

Like people everywhere, the early Maoris liked to draw. As a canvas they used the smooth, light-coloured surfaces of the walls and roofs of rock overhangs — usually of limestone — in which they sheltered during hunting trips into the forest. Their drawing materials were principally charcoal and red ochre, almost always used dry rather than as a paint. More rarely, they carved designs in the soft rock surface or scratched it with another rock to produce a whitish mark.

Several hundred rock art sites have been discovered in New Zealand, mostly in the South Island, with the greatest concentration of sites being in North Otago, and North and South Canterbury. Besides containing drawings, many shelters have earth floors, within which are preserved other relics of past human occupation.

Almost all South Island prehistoric rock drawings have a strong 'family likeness'; they are mostly of individual subjects with virtually no attempt at composition. The most common and easily recognised subject is the human form. This is stylised and typically presented as a frontal silhouette with flexed arms and legs — facial features are never shown. Other recognisable animals — dogs, birds and fish — are usually drawn in profile, and most often face the viewer's right. There are, however, notable and spectacular exceptions. At a locality called Earthquakes in North Otago one drawing depicts a man sitting in profile, knees upraised, and an arm with a large three-fingered hand stretched before him, looking over the valley. And at

One of the few compositions in Maori rock art, this group at Ngapara, North Otago, comprises variations of the human form. Because of the way the figures appear to 'dance' across the rock face, its European discoverers in the 1960s named it the 'Ngapara Twist'.

Craigmore, in South Canterbury, an ancient bird, wings outspread and beak hooked, hovers on the roof of a cave-like shelter — surely a representation of the giant extinct eagle, preserved for centuries in charcoal outline. But also at Craigmore, conventionally shown in profile, are a group of moas — perhaps the only definite drawings from life of these great creatures and close by a 'big dog' or kuri stands patiently facing the right. Men with clubs, men in a mokihi, stick figures or 'in the round' — hollow-bodied or infilled — birds and birdmen, fish and whales, red, black, or incised, such drawings are found from Southland to Marlborough.

Not all South Island drawings, however, are recognisable as belonging to the everyday world. Some appear as mythical creatures — or perhaps they are so stylised as to be unrecognisable by today's investigators. Others are quite clearly designs — chevrons or triangles, concentric circles or, more rarely, spirals. Some have features markedly similar to those of archaic wood carvings and some of the personal ornaments of the early period.

Among the best known of the more abstract artwork is the black design commonly known as the 'Opihi taniwha', which some years ago featured on a postage stamp. The popularity of this five-metre-long composition seems to derive

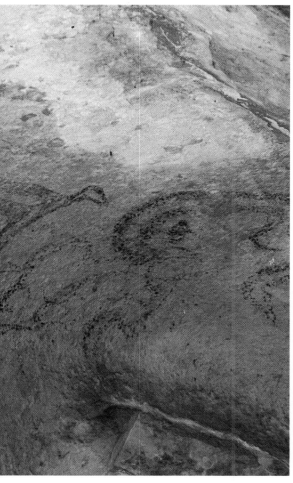

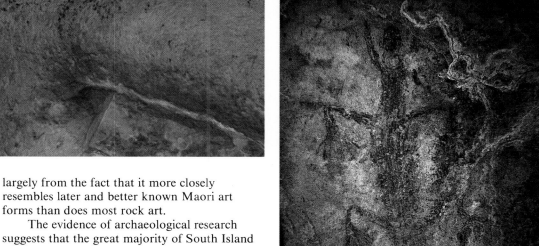

largely from the fact that it more closely resembles later and better known Maori art forms than does most rock art.

The evidence of archaeological research suggests that the great majority of South Island rock drawings were executed in the first 500 years of occupation during the hunter-gatherer period. Parties of early moa-hunter Maoris, including family groups, travelled inland from their coastal villages to hunt for birds and rats, taking with them tools and some food, including shellfish. They used the rock overhangs in the hunting area as shelter on these trips and during their stay they drew on the walls and ceilings, using charcoal and sometimes red ochre which they brought with them. They also left on the shelter floors food remains, such as shells and bones, the stones and charcoal of their cooking fires, and some of their tools and other possessions.

After the destruction of the forest (*see page 53*) these inland areas were largely deserted until with the advent of European explorers some of their accompanying Maori guides once again drew on shelter walls, this time depicting subjects like sailing ships and horses.

Far fewer rock art sites are known from the North Island and these are quite different from those of the South. Most are engraved, and where pigments such as ochre and charcoal have been used they are often applied as a paint rather than used as a dry 'crayon'. Nor do individual sites exhibit the same cultural similarity, one to the other, as they do in the South. They also seem to have been executed at a much later date so that the marked regional variations probably reflect a more settled agricultural lifestyle with more clearly defined tribal differences.

The favourite subject of North Island rock art is the dug-out canoe — a subject not depicted in the South. Human beings are sometimes given facial features or are even simplified to these features alone. Some recent work in Taranaki has revealed a previously unknown series of rock carvings or petroglyphs, mostly consisting of spirals, rendered in volcanic rock. They form a discrete group in a relatively small area.

Part of a series of rock carvings (above) depicting canoes, Kaingaroa Forest. This example is decorated with spirals, which supports the idea that North Island rock art is later than that of the South. The Maori use of spirals for decoration is believed to have developed in New Zealand; older South Island drawings and carvings generally show concentric circles.

A charcoal drawing (centre) on the ceiling of a North Otago limestone rock shelter. The principal figures are usually interpreted as dogs, despite the absence of tails. An alternative identification would be that they are seals, but the prominent penis makes the former more likely.

This stylised human figure (left), executed in red ochre, shows an unusual disposition of limbs with elongated extremities. Bilateral extensions to the head as occur here were used by the author Eric von Daniken to suggest extra-terrestrial contact with New Zealand.

Personal Ornaments of the Early Period

PERSONAL ornaments, particulary neck pendants, were evidently popular during the entire prehistoric period. The best known of these is the *hei tiki* (*hei* meaning worn around the neck and *tiki* meaning a human form), and because of the great interest shown in the *hei tiki* by Europeans, it has largely overshadowed the wide variety of ornaments worn, especially those of the early period.

Most early types of personal ornament are known principally from being found on archaeological sites, and are of types which had ceased to be made or worn by the time Europeans arrived. During the nineteenth century ethnologists thought that the native inhabitants of New Zealand had never worn necklaces of perforated beads, and even well into this century some necklace units were thought to be weights for drills; it was not until they were found in position around necks of human skeletons at Wairau Bar that their real purpose was recognised.

Many early pendants are unique or known from only a few examples; some clearly reflect the still-prevailing cultural influences of the Pacific Islands. Some pieces are frequently referred to as 'amulets', a term that means a charm worn to guard against evil. Unfortunately, archaeology simply cannot tell us enough of their original purpose to allow any firm conclusion to be drawn as to their significance.

Stone, bone, ivory and shell were all utilised in their manufacture. (Notably, virtually no use was made of nephrite — greenstone or pounamu — which was so popular at the time of European contact because at this early period the Maori people had not yet learnt how to work it effectively.) Most known ornaments appear to have been designed to be worn around the neck — either a series of units threaded together to form a necklace, or single, larger pieces, perforated for suspension as pendants. Sometimes the two were combined and an individual breast ornament was worn as the centrepiece of a necklace.

The most simple and basic necklaces comprised natural teeth or shells, perforated and strung together. Some of the best examples of these were found on the moa-hunter site at Wairau Bar in Marlborough and included strings of porpoise teeth — there were 412 teeth in one necklace, 386 in another — shark teeth (38 units), and 14 drilled left valves of a small bivalve shellfish, *Myadora*, which would have been worn with the inner pearly surface facing outwards.

Necklace units were also artifically shaped from a variety of materials. Large and small 'reel'-shaped beads seem to have been popular with the moa hunters. The larger forms were most often made from pieces of the central shaft of moa leg bones, but they were also occasionally made of relatively soft stone such as serpentine or of whale tooth ivory. Small reels were made of ivory from seal teeth, bird and mammal bone, or even cut from the fossilised shells of the mollusc, *Dentalium*.

Necklace units shaped like teeth were also cut from whale ivory, moa bone and, more

This rare partly-divided stone sphere (right) is generally considered to have been a pendant. Because of its similarity to similar objects from the Cook Islands, some researchers believe it to represent human testicles.

Shells and teeth (below right) were two of the natural items most commonly used by the early Maoris to fashion into necklaces. The shells pictured here (at top) are the left valves of *Myadora*, while the teeth are from porpoises (centre) and sharks. All of these were recovered from the Wairau Bar site.

A unique stone pectoral pendant from Okains Bay, Banks Peninsula (below). It is 178 millimetres wide with two fish carved in low relief.

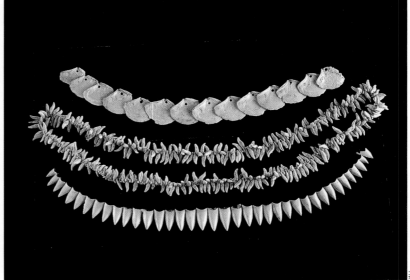

rarely, human bone or shell, as many as 23 of these forming a single necklace. From his work at Wairau Bar, Roger Duff thought it probable that these 'teeth' were also worn as bracelets.

Teeth seem to have been important for either decorative or ritual wear in the early period. Certainly 'tooth' pendants were a feature of the culture of a number of the Pacific Islands; even today the sperm whale tooth *tabua* has special value and is used for ceremonial purposes in Fiji. In early New Zealand full-sized (or even larger) replicas of sperm whale teeth were sometimes carved from stone and worn as the centrepiece of a necklace. This may have been a development brought about by demand exceeding the availability of the 'real thing'. However, there is one genuine sperm whale tooth pendant, ornamented with decorative notching in an early style, which is reputed to have been one of three brought to New Zealand from 'Hawaiki', the homeland, and kept for generations as an heirloom by a Kaikoura family. It was said to be a 'tohi' and in times of war it was invoked and if it stood on its tail it was a good omen.

A very rare type of stone pendant is the 'pectoral' (breast ornament). This is almost certainly a rendering in stone of the large pearl shell pectorals known from the more northerly Pacific. An outstanding example is one of black stone from Okains Bay on which two fish forms have been carved in low relief; it has been seriously suggested that the fish are a traditional rendering of the bonito or albicore.

Two other groups of pendants deserve mention. The first is the 'twin-lobed' (sometimes called 'divided sphere') pendants of which seven examples, all slightly different — plus three broken parts — are known from sites ranging from the northern South Island to Auckland. They were formed by nearly dividing a single piece of rounded rock with a deep cleft. Similar forms occur in the Cook and Austral Islands and it is assumed that they represent stylised human testicles. These pendants are not drilled or perforated for suspension, and must have been lashed to a suspension cord when worn.

The other important group is of whale ivory and belongs to a class usually referred to as 'chevroned pendants'. They fall into two sub-groups, the single or symmetrical, and the paired or asymmetrical forms. All differ slightly — particularly the single pendants — but have a marked resemblance in the angularity of their decoration to the two other early art forms of wood carving and rock drawings.

Very little is known about these early personal ornaments. Many have unique features — such as the fish on the Okains Bay pectoral — which may have had some special significance to the maker or wearer. Others are unique in their overall design; one found at Flaxbourne is shaped like a capital 'E' in polished black stone. And although the objects found in archaeological contexts have outlasted any memories of them, it is clear from the number interred with burials or secreted in 'safe' places that they were highly important — yet what significance they held, we cannot say.

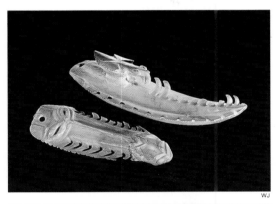

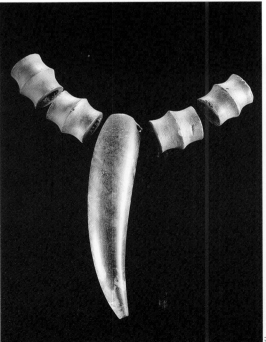

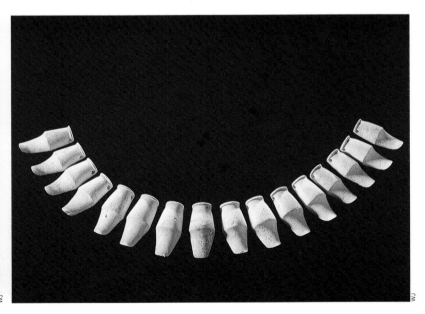

The most intricately carved personal ornaments (left) were made from the teeth of whales or elephant seals. They comprise a class referred to as chevroned pendants from the chevron shapes incorporated in the design. Like most of the early ornaments, they had ceased to be made or worn by the time of European contact.

A stone replica of a sperm whale tooth (below left), 225 millimetres long, and reel-shaped beads cut from moa bone, were worn on a cord around the neck by moa-hunter Maoris. These specimens are from Fortrose and Wairau Bar respectively.

Necklace units fashioned from moa bone (below) in the shape of the stylised teeth of a small whale. Each is drilled for threading on a cord. Units similar to these Wairau Bar specimens have been found on the Society Islands, Marquesas and Niue.

Man, Moa and Forest: Prehistoric Overkill

*U*NTIL the coming of man about 1000 years ago, New Zealand had been isolated for some 80 million years during which time a variety of highly specialised birds had evolved to inhabit the heavily forested land. The most spectacular of these were the moas or Dinornithiformes of which a dozen different species lived in the forest and, in particular, its margins. All were large — the smallest was a metre in height, while the largest with head erect stood up to three metres. The moas were ratites and like all other birds of this group, such as ostriches and emus, they were flightless although descended from an original flighted ancestor. In New Zealand they had lost all trace of wings, developing instead immensely strong, heavy legs adapted to a ground-dwelling existence. In some of the medium-sized species leg thickness and associated body weight had developed to cumbersome extremes. The range of sizes and different shapes of their beaks indicates that they filled a variety of niches, to some extent taking the place filled by browsing animals in some countries.

Moas were not the only flightless species in New Zealand. There was *Aptornis*, which was like a giant rail or woodhen as large as the smaller moas, and the kiwi, *Apteryx*, the moa's closest relative. There were, as well, other unusual and specialised species which, if they could still fly, could do so only in a very limited fashion. A small duck, *Euryanas*, had remarkably heavy legs and considerably reduced wings; kakapo, the large ground parrot, could do little more than glide after having climbed to achieve some height. Birds like the kokako and the huia spent much of their time on the ground — their flight was not as limited as that of the kakapo but was largely confined to short gliding bursts from tree to tree.

All these birds — and others as well — were extraordinarily vulnerable to any form of predation. Not only were they slow moving,

many of them ground-bound, but with no predatory mammals in the country they had not developed any effective defenses. A number had also evolved a very low reproduction rate, which until then had been all that was necessary — investigations of moa nests in Hawke's Bay and in Canterbury suggest that only one egg (or at most two) was laid. Although species such as the hawk and falcon undoubtedly preyed on New Zealand's smaller birds, the only creature which could possible have posed a threat to giants like the moas and the rail-like *Aptornis* was the New Zealand eagle *Harpagornis* with its three-metre wing span. And although it has recently been suggested that *Harpagornis* might have been capable of attacking and even killing a moa, all the evidence indicates that this eagle was basically a carrion eater, living off the carcasses of the larger birds.

The impact of the incoming Polynesians on a fauna such as this was devastating and evidence of that impact is found in middens all over the country. By the time the Europeans arrived 200 years ago many species were extinct.

Once early researchers had established that these birds had actually been alive at the time the first Polynesians arrived in the country, questions were asked as to how such widespread and sudden extinctions occurred. Investigators last century had few problems in accepting that the early Maoris had killed large quantities of moas — the abundant remains on sites, particularly on the east coast of the South Island, provided adequate testimony. The work and observations of researchers such as Mantell and Haast has already been noted but they were not the only people last century to record the results of moa hunting clearly visible on archaeological sites. As early as 1851 Charles Torlesse had noted in the sand dunes at Redcliffs, Christchurch, the abundant remains of moas which were 'apparently the refuse of former native feasts'. At Puketoi, Otago, Murison in 1865 found numerous ovens containing great quantities of

Vast quantities of moa bones were found by European farmers when they first ploughed the ground at some of the large moa-hunter sites. This early photograph shows one of many heaps of bones at the Waitaki Mouth site, North Otago.

David Larnach

moa bones, together with amounts of moa eggshell which indicated that 'a vast number of eggs must have been consumed as food'. Haast's findings at Shag River were later supported by Augustus Hamilton who reported finding on this same site between 50 and 60 moa necks, mostly with skulls attached, thrown aside as useless. Still from Shag River, late in the nineteenth century, several wagonloads of bones were gathered up and sent to the Dunedin bone mills to make bone flour. (Even as recently as the 1950s quantities of moa bones could still be found among the sand dunes on site.) And there were many other sites which produced ample evidence of large-scale, often wasteful moa hunting.

In the 1960s Paul Martin of the University of Arizona introduced the term 'prehistoric overkill' to summarise the widespread and sudden extinction of large, vertebrate animal species throughout the world, coincident with the arrival of man into any area for the first time. Despite the universal recognition of this phenomenon by scientists there has been an equally widespread reluctance to accept that man was ultimately responsible for the demise of so many species, and this has been particularly true in New Zealand.

In 1962 Kenneth Cumberland in a review of the relationship between moas and man discussed at length the available evidence, and particularly man's use of fire in the early period. He had no doubts as to what had occurred, describing '. . . countless fire-blackened hangi [or umu, 'oven'] stones, charred bones, greasy layers of ash. . . . The ghostly remnants of the forest and the bones of the destroyed avifauna littered the ground for centuries.' Yet despite this, he still believed that this was 'one of the few known cases in which aboriginal man harried a wide range of animals to extinction'.

Also in 1962 British archaeologist Jack Golson, working in New Zealand, observed in a review of the previous decade's archaeological findings in New Zealand, that the one definite

The giant eagle Harpagornis (left below) died out about the same time as the moas when its main source of food, moa carrion, was no longer available. Harpagornis was probably the largest eagle that ever lived.

New Zealand forest cover (below) at the time of Polynesian settlement (left) and European settlement (right).

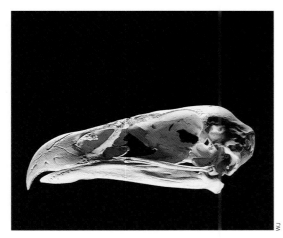

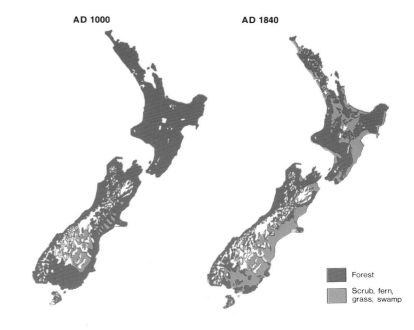

AD 1000   AD 1840

Forest

Scrub, fern, grass, swamp

Julie O'Brien/CM   Sources: Atholl Anderson and Matt McGlone

A full-sized reconstruction (far left) from Canterbury Museum of Euryapteryx, the moa most commonly hunted in the South Island.

These burnt totara trunks (left) from Banks Peninsula bear mute testimony to the former presence of forests. Radiocarbon dating indicates that there was widespread burning 500 to 800 years ago.

51

result that had emerged was that 'man, as the moa's first mammalian predator, was the prime instrument in its extinction'. Nevertheless, it was still popularly maintained that the main causes of moa extinction were probably genetic weakness or climatic change — despite the fact that moas had successfully survived 70 million years of much more dramatic climate variation than had occurred in the last 1000.

One of the problems was that twentieth-century investigators had not at that time repeated the early discoveries of such large quantities of moa bone on sites, and were reluctant to accept evidence of workers almost a century earlier. Since then, however, those early observations have been supported by further research. At a moa butchering site at Tai Rua in North Otago, excavations in the 1960s revealed complete moa necks in position of articulation — some with heads attached, discarded whole, as had previously been reported from Shag River by Haast and Hamilton. Similar wastage was found at Hampden. During a re-investigation in 1972 of the Rakaia site, first examined by Haast

in 1872, an undisturbed oven was located which confirmed Haast's earlier descriptions of hollows containing numerous burnt stones, broken moa bones and flake butchering knives. An earth oven hollow at Wakanui a little further south was also found in 1972 to contain tightly packed moa bones and a number of similar ovens were located nearby. And in 1988 Atholl Anderson found that bone-rich deposits still existed at the Shag River site.

Perhaps the most spectacular archaeological findings on moa hunting of recent years were those made at Kaupokonui in Taranaki, which rivalled those on the great South Island sites. The general plan of this early village site has been described in the section on early settlement, but it was its moa-hunter middens which excited the greatest interest. These were conspicuous for the number of moas which had been slaughtered over a very short period and even more for the wastage of flesh and bone. (Moa bone was an important material for the manufacture of items such as fish hooks, harpoon points and ornaments.) The investigators could not reconcile

Excavation of a moa-hunter site at the mouth of the Kaupokonui River, Taranaki, in the 1960s and 1970s showed that different parts of the site had been used for different activities. In particular, Richard Cassels in 1974 identified specific zones where the butchering of carcasses had been divided into three processes. The investigators were amazed at the amount of wastage of large portions of moa carcasses at this site.

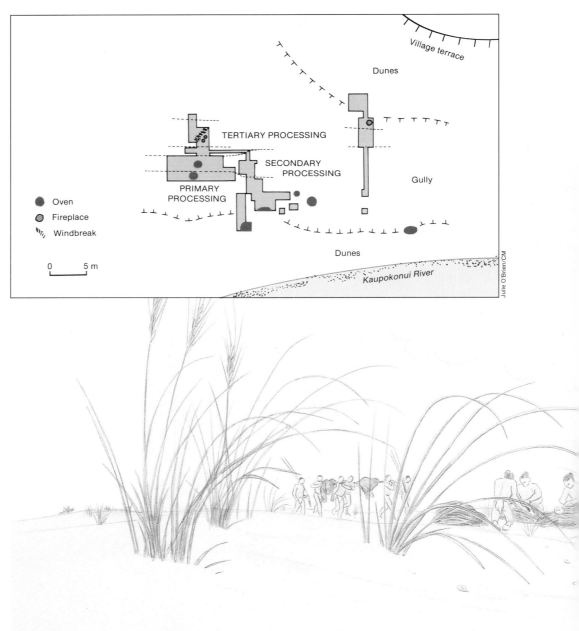

the wastage with a prehistoric economy dependent on moas as food and suggested that the site represented the result of a major hunting expedition launched from elsewhere in the region. Whatever the reasons for the killing of so many birds at one time — clearly far more than could be adequately utilised — Kaupokonui provides strong supporting evidence for the reported findings of similar sites last century.

No species, much less highly specialised ones such as moas, could continue to withstand the sort of hunting pressure indicated by sites such as this. And there is also equally strong evidence from sites all over the country that other species besides the moas were also directly, or indirectly, victims of early Polynesian predation. The giant 'rail', the goose, a large swan and a duck were all hunted and eaten. All, along with the moas, became extinct about 4-500 years ago. The giant eagle, too, became a victim because with the disappearance of the larger, flightless species it lost its food supply. Eventually it also ceased to exist.

Recently, along with the acceptance that people were responsible for moa extinction, it has also been recognised that much of the forest was burnt off during the prehistoric period, and that this resulted from human activity. It is really only in the last 25 years that scientists have determined that forest or scrub originally covered most of New Zealand, from shore to treeline, and that this was what confronted the first humans who arrived here. (Prior to this it had been thought that the moas had been grass eaters, dwelling mainly on the supposedly tussock-covered plains, in clearings and on river flats. Analyses of preserved gizzard contents have now shown that they ate twigs, leaves and seeds of trees, shrubs, vines and herbs.)

Even when it was accepted that the land was forested, and that its terrestrial bird species were forest dwellers, there was still considerable argument as to how the forest disappeared. For example, it was popularly assumed that the burn-off resulted from natural phenomena — such as lightning strike — with an associated climatic change to account for the lack of regeneration. However, in the 1960s radiocarbon dating placed major forest burn-off firmly in the era of Polynesian settlement. Although there had been earlier natural fires before the arrival of man, it is now widely accepted that for one reason or other, these early people burnt off almost half of the original forest in a series of fires, mostly 500 to 800 years ago, and in so doing destroyed the greater part of the habitat and food supply of the moas and other species. It may be that the fires were entirely accidental, perhaps ignited by wind-borne sparks from a camp fire; alternatively, they may have been caused by deliberate forest clearing that got out of hand.

Today, faced with overwhelming and largely irrefutable evidence, it is acknowledged that during the first 500 or so years of man's occupation of New Zealand, there were widespread changes to the environment that included the extinction of a number of bird species — notably the moas — and that this resulted not only from direct predation, but also from the destruction of habitat as a result of forest burn-off. These environmental changes in turn necessitated major adjustments to the people's economy and accelerated alterations to their culture.

An artist's impression of butchering and cooking activities following a moa hunt. This is based broadly on archaeological evidence that was obtained from the Kaupokonui site, Taranaki, by Richard Cassels. Different zones can be distinguished where specific activities were performed.

Geoffrey Cox/BM

Kuri and Kiore

BEFORE the arrival of man to New Zealand, the only native land mammals were two species of bats, *Mystacina tuberculata* and *Chalinolobus tuberculatus*. The only other mammals were the seals and other marine mammals, which spent part of their time on shore. The Polynesians, upon their arrival, brought with them two other species: Polynesian dogs (*Canis familiaris*) called 'kuri', and Polynesian rats (*Rattus exulans*) called 'kiore'.

Evidence abounds of their past presence. Although the Maoris had no written language, they left a visual record of the kuri: black charcoal drawings found on rock overhangs in the South Island. They depict an animal with a characteristically long body, heavy forequarters and short legs. The face is pointed and the ears pricked. Similar features are displayed by a unique wooden carving found in Moncks Cave near Christchurch. Only the pricked ears are missing, replaced by a sort of top-knot.

The bones and teeth of kuri are not uncommon in middens throughout New Zealand; the dog was kept as much for food as for companionship. Such remains indicate a moderately sized animal similar to the Maori depictions of it. Ornaments and fish-hook points were also fashioned from the teeth and bones, particularly the relatively hard lower jaw.

The kuri also provided skins for clothing. Dog-skin cloaks were valued and many have survived in family ownership or in museums, while dog hair was also used to decorate objects. The kuri's coat appears to have been of variable length. The main body hair seems to have been about two to three centimetres long, with feathering or fringing of longer hairs in places — probably on the tail and legs.

When Europeans arrived the kuri was relatively abundant and, although detailed written descriptions are rare, the kuri (often referred to as the 'Maori dog') is mentioned in a number of early European accounts of New Zealand, and appears in some early paintings and sketches. One of the best descriptions is that of Crozet, who visited New Zealand in 1772:

> *They have absolutely no other domestic animal than the dog. The dogs are a sort of domesticated fox, quite black or white; very low on the legs, straight ear, thick tail, long body, full jaws but more pointed than that of the fox and uttering the same cry; they do not bark like our dogs.*

Cook described the dogs in a similar way, as did several of the men who accompanied him. All the early descriptions tally well and are supported by sketches, so that we have a reasonably good idea of the dog's general appearance. What is not so clear is its diet and general behaviour and temperament.

Early reports suggest that the Maoris fed their dogs on vegetable foods and fish; this is supported by the extreme rarity of chew marks on larger midden bones and the presence of small fish bones in their faeces. However, their skulls and teeth indicate that they would have had a strong bite, and the good condition of most kuri teeth is surprising if indeed they were fed principally on soft foods. It seems likely that their diet was not as restricted as it may appear.

Early Europeans described the New Zealand Polynesian dogs as sulky and treacherous. Polack, writing in 1831, noted that they were 'morose and unamiable to strangers', yet there is no indication that they were this way inclined with their Maori owners. But it is their possible role as hunters which has provoked most disagreement. None of the early European reports suggest that the kuri was used for hunting. There are later descriptions of Maoris using dogs to hunt ground birds but these reports were made at least 50 years after the arrival of Europeans when European dogs had already interbred with the kuri. It was probably these cross-bred animals which were used by the Maoris for hunting once they had seen the Europeans working their own dogs in this way.

After the arrival of European dogs and the consequent cross breeding, many of the resulting progeny ran wild in packs, threatening the livestock of the early European settlers. As a result they were shot in considerable numbers. The last dogs identifiable as being at least part kuri were destroyed in the 1850s and the breed then became extinct in New Zealand.

Kiore, the 'Polynesian rat' (*Rattus exulans*), was the other terrestrial mammal introduced with the dog. It has been suggested that it might have arrived as a 'stowaway' on the canoes that brought the Polynesian immigrants to New Zealand, but in view of its value as a food item it is more probable that it was deliberately introduced. However, unlike the kuri, the kiore was not domesticated, and lived wild in the forests.

The kiore is a small rat, widespread in the Pacific, and the first Europeans to describe it in New Zealand placed it in the same genus as the mouse (*Mus*). It is almost exclusively a vegetarian, although its distinctive tooth marks are occasionally found on bird bones in archaeological sites.

Kiore remains are common in Maori middens of all periods. Most often found are the jaws with their ivory-hard, rodent teeth. These are the most durable and distinctive parts of a rat skeleton, which may partly account for why they are so frequently recovered. However, the best interpretation of this midden evidence is that kiore was often cooked and consumed whole, only these indigestible portions being discarded.

James Hay observed the consumption of European rats in Canterbury in the 1860s:

> *When shifting the* [wheat] *stack . . . the Maoris came over . . . to assist in killing the rats. From fifty to seventy were collected . . . When one was wanted for cooking he*

A Maori dog or kuri redrawn from a sketch made on Cook's first voyage to New Zealand, probably by the artist Sydney Parkinson. The black and white spotted colouring is as described in several early records.

Vivian Ward

54

was covered with soft clay and put into the fire. When cooked he was raked out of the fire, and when cool enough to handle was knocked on a stone or hit with a stick to crack the baked cake encasing him. When opened out the hair and scarf skin adhered to the inner surface of the clay, and the flesh looked white like chicken. A dexterous twist with the thumb nail scooped out the entrails in a round ball. All was eaten save a few of the large bones and the tail.

The abundance of kiore remains on sites indicates that it was a popular part of the Maori diet. Even an early European explorer writes enthusiastically of his Maori guides cooking 'a meal of delicious little rats for dinner which, to my taste, are quite equal to the frogs in France'.

Although the early European visitors to New Zealand made little reference to the 'Maori rat', it is apparent the kiore was present in considerable numbers. There are well-recorded 'plagues' of kiore occurring in the Marlborough-Nelson area in the mid nineteenth century, and George Forster reported a similar over-abundance of the native rat during Cook's second visit to New Zealand in 1773.

The kiore was not able to compete with European rats once these became established. The ship or black rat (*Rattus rattus*) arrived in New Zealand on the first European sailing ships — probably some came ashore from Cook's vessels — and was closely followed by the brown or Norway rat (*Rattus norvegicus*). Both species spread quickly throughout the country. Predators, such as feral cats and mustelids (weasels and stoats), introduced by Europeans, must also have played a part in the reduction of the kiore population until today when its distribution is limited to some offshore islands and a few isolated areas of Fiordland and Stewart Island.

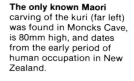

The only known Maori carving of the kuri (far left) was found in Moncks Cave, is 80mm high, and dates from the early period of human occupation in New Zealand.

Rat jaws excavated from Timpendean rock shelter in North Canterbury (below left). The shelter occupants had hunted the kiore in the surrounding area which was forested at that time, about 500 years ago.

Commonly referred to as 'Big Dog' (left) this charcoal drawing can be seen in a limestone rock shelter in South Canterbury.

This kuri skull (below) was excavated from Moa-bone Point Cave at Sumner, Christchurch. Its exact age is unknown. The teeth and well developed 'saggital crest' — the ridge on the top of the head to which the jaw muscles were attached — indicate that this dog would have had quite a strong bite despite the relative absence of dog-chewed bones on archaeological sites.

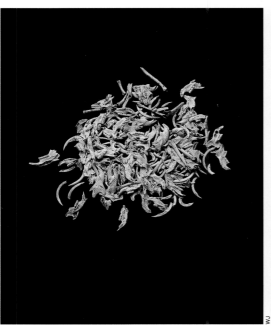

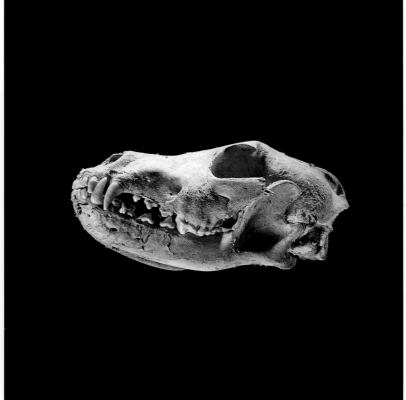

55

*H*ORTICULTURE has always been important to the Polynesians in their tropical homelands and when they came to New Zealand they brought with them a number of plants. Although there may have been some species which perished in the cooler New Zealand climate, those that we know survived were the kumara (*Ipomoea batatus*), gourd (*Laenaria siceraria*), yam (*Dioscorea* spp.), taro (*Colocasia esculanta*), tropical cabbage tree (*Cordyline terminalis*) and paper mulberry (*Broussonetia papyrifera*).

Most of these could never be grown anywhere in New Zealand except in the warmer climate of favoured areas of the North Island. However, techniques were developed by which kumaras could be over-wintered in colder regions as far south as Taumutu (a little south of Banks Peninsula), and this introduced plant was to play an important part in the economy and the lives of the Maori people.

Because of the dearth of organic remains which could be used for radiocarbon dating we do not know for sure how important the cultivation of introduced plants was during the first few centuries of occupation. It appears to have been well established by about 600 years ago; one site with an apparently associated garden area on the south bank of the mouth of the Clarence River in Marlborough has been dated as 750 years old and even earlier indications have been found in the North Island. Certainly some horticulture must have been practised from about 1000 years ago and continued throughout the whole prehistoric period. It is likely that kumara cultivation was not particularly important while the population was small and natural food resources were plentiful. Initially it may have been carried out only in the warmer areas of the North Island

where the winter temperatures were not harmful to the delicate tubers.

Although earlier workers correctly identified some archaeological features — notably low stone 'walls', storage pits and modified soils — as indicating prehistoric gardening, it was not until the last 20 years when a great deal of deliberate site recording has been undertaken throughout the country that it has been realised just how widely spread these are distributed. Most easily recognised of these features are the low 'walls' or long narrow piles of stones that probably marked the boundaries between individual garden plots. They are typically found on gently sloping sunny ground near the coast, and often form parallel lines five to 60 metres apart, running down the slope. The angle of the slope may be up to about 20° with around 7° being fairly common. Mostly the walls have been formed of stones cleared from the areas between the rows, and vary from less than a metre to several metres in width, depending on their distance apart and the quantity of stones to be cleared. Besides marking boundaries, they also provided a place to put the cleared stones.

At Wiri, south of Auckland, and at Palliser Bay in the Wairarapa, both very large horticultural areas of the North Island, these walls were composed almost entirely of stones. Both areas have been fairly intensively investigated in recent years and the researchers concluded that stone walls were principally built to establish boundaries and to clear stones from those areas used for cultivation.

The importance of constructing walls, even when stones were not available, was demonstrated by the results of work at Clarence in southern Marlborough. On this coastal site there was an area of over 15 hectares of garden plots divided by parallel walls. Investigations in

Mokena Pahoe of Waipiro Bay poses beside a type of food storage pit that became common in the nineteenth century.

Auckland Weekly News

1977 showed that the materials from which the walls were constructed differed according to what was most readily available in the immediate vicinity. Where large stones were present, these were used to the fullest extent; where they were not, smaller stones and earth were used; and on the lower stone-free parts of the gentle 4° slope only earth and sand were used. Long walls, running from the hill at the back of the gardens towards the beach, consisted of all three materials in different sections. Clearly, the purpose of the walls was more than just a convenient place to put stones cleared from the garden plots. They may have also assisted with the down-slope drainage of cold air, thus providing warmer growing conditions, particularly in the South Island where the extreme southern limit for kumara growing is reached.

Some gardens were divided into rectangular plots rather than long strips, as at Titirangi in the Marlborough Sounds. The walls running across the 7° slope also formed the scarps of terraces, the purpose of which is not clear unless it was to retain moisture. Elsewhere, on steeper ground, terraces were sometimes formed to facilitate the preparation and cultivation of the ground.

Other features commonly associated with garden walls include pathways marked by rows of placed stones on either side and mounds of stones and earth. Such mounds are usually thought to be associated with the growing of gourds. One mound excavated at Titirangi had contained much organic material in the centre; presumably this had been a compost providing both nutriment and perhaps warmth for plants growing on top. Similar methods are still used today to grow pumpkins and marrows.

Another feature, not necessarily associated with walled gardens, is modified soils, and there are a number of areas recorded where fine gravel has been mined and spread on the ground to enhance the properties of the soil. Perhaps the best known of these is in the Waimea County of

Prehistoric varieties of kumara tended to be long and thin. An early type (left) is here compared with a modern variety (right). Both can be grown successfully in North Canterbury, but further south the shorter growing season leads to poor and unreliable crops.

Stone walls at Wiri, Auckland (below left). Many prehistoric horticultural areas are easily recognised because of low stone mounds or the walls that divided garden plots. Usually local available material was used — at Wiri the extensive mounds and shelters were made of volcanic rock.

Fine gravel (below) was often mined so that it could be added to the soil to improve its suitability for growing kumaras. In some parts of New Zealand, as here in Taranaki, extensive hollows left from prehistoric gravel mining are still clearly visible.

Nigel Prickett

57

Tasman Bay, near Nelson, where it has been estimated there are over 400 hectares of 'Maori gravel soil'. Both here and at Motueka, charcoal and ash also appear to have been added to the soil. Other well-known areas of modified soils are in the Waikato and in southern Taranaki. Besides promoting good drainage, improving water retention and increasing the friability of the soil, the gravel and charcoal mulch also increased the soil temperature to the extent of advancing by up to a week the beginning of the growing season — an important consideration in the cultivation of what are essentially tropical plants.

The prehistoric Maoris worked up garden soils using digging sticks, and such sticks are not infrequently found in swamps during drainage operations — it is possible they were placed there to prevent the wood from deteriorating by drying out, cracking and becoming brittle. These digging sticks are usually about two metres long, with a sharpened point at one end and sometimes with a simple carved design at the other. In use, a shaped wooden 'footrest' or step was bound on to the digging stick about 30 centimetres from the pointed end to enable foot pressure to be used to force the stick into the ground. The use of wooden adze-shaped implements is also recorded, and the wear marks on some stone adze heads have the appearance of having been caused by digging in the ground rather than by wood working.

Another common feature of prehistoric horticulture was the kumara storage pit. In most parts of New Zealand kumaras, whether for food or 'seed' for the next season's crop, need to be specially stored during the colder months to prevent them becoming 'frosted'. The pits built to store the kumaras are often found near the garden wall complexes, and vary in size and shape between regions. Best known is the bell-shaped *rua*, which has a large circular chamber underground entered through a small opening which would have been closed with a wooden door; some excellent examples of these occur in

An artist's reconstruction of the preparation of ground for horticulture — the bush is being cleared, stones are piled up in a boundary wall, and the area is being made ready for planting kumaras. With no mechanical assistance, and no metal tools, the labour involved was considerable; even so, some large areas of ground were modified for horticulture. Much of the work was accompanied by rituals which undoubtedly provided a stimulus for such strenuous toil.

the Taupo district where they have been dug into the hardened volcanic ash. A similar design, dug into the side of a cliff or scarp slope, has a more cave-like appearance. Elsewhere, a rectangular pit was dug and provided with a roof (as mentioned on pages 17-18 these are sometimes confused with dwellings).

Besides introduced plants a wide range of indigenous species was also used for food, although there is for the most part considerably less archaeological evidence for this. Fibres of bracken fern roots (*Pteridium esculentum*) have been identified in human faeces from archaeological sites, and areas where land has been cleared to promote the growth of this fern have been recognised. Pollen analyses from dated swamp deposits show a marked increase in bracken fern during the period of Polynesian occupation, and it is likely that areas of forest were cleared by burning to encourage the growth of this species. There are many accounts by early European observers of the use of fern root as a staple diet in both the North and South Islands.

Fruits of several different trees were used for food and the seeds or kernels, including hinau (*Elaeocarpus dentatus*), tawa (*Beilschmiedia tawa*) and karaka (*Corynocarpus laevigatus*) have been found in sites where preservation conditions have been particularly good or where they have been lightly burned in a fire (even slight charring enhances their resistance to rotting in the ground). Remains of large earth ovens in South Canterbury and Otago also indicate the widespread cooking of cabbage tree roots (*Cordyline australis*) in these areas, where, notably, the kumara could not be cultivated. The slow cooking of these roots produced a sugary substance.

Despite the problems encountered by the earliest Polynesians in New Zealand in adapting their introduced plants to the new conditions, horticulture was widely practised at the time of European contact. The adoption of the more cold-resistant 'white' potatoes of the Europeans allowed the Maoris to extend their gardening activities over the whole of the country, and their produce played an important part in the early European settlement of New Zealand.

Geoffrey Cox/BM

Hunting and Fishing

*T*HROUGHOUT the country are many tens of thousands of middens — prehistoric rubbish dumps of shells, bones and the other occupational debris of daily life. These provide a valuable account of the great variety of food animals that were being caught and consumed in the past. Some of these could have been obtained quite simply — shellfish and crayfish, for example, could be collected by hand although 'prisers', scoops and traps were also used; the domesticated dog required only killing and butchering. Others needed special equipment and techniques to harvest them from the forest and the sea. Interestingly, although midden analyses tell us that the prehistoric Maori had a varied diet, particularly in the first few centuries of occupation, most archaeological evidence we have of the implements they used relates to fishing; we know very little about how they hunted.

Fish were caught principally using hooks and lines, nets, spears, and both portable and structural traps. Midden bones indicate that a variety of fish were caught, including those whose habitat was well out at sea and which must have required a canoe to catch them. There are surprises: kahawai bones, for example, are rare in South Island coastal sites in areas where this species can easily be caught today, while those of barracouta, which can be caught using the same method, are quite abundant.

Fish hooks are commonly found on sites of all ages throughout the country. Three main types of prehistoric fish hooks are evident, each with numerous variations, designed for different purposes or to suit the whim of the maker; often a subtlety of design is peculiar to a site or locality. For example, a distinctively designed fish hook point has become known as the 'Oruarangi Point' because of its predominance on the Oruarangi site near Thames; and on the East Coast of the North Island, a small U-shaped hook design with internal barbs on both the point and the shank is generally thought of as an East Coast type. To modern eyes, accustomed to the fine steel fish hooks of today's anglers

prehistoric designs often look ineffective. Yet it must be remembered that, within the restrictions imposed by the available materials, these were developed over centuries when livelihood or even survival depended upon their efficiency.

During the early centuries when moa bone was readily available, bait hooks were commonly made in one piece — sawn, chipped, or chiselled from a leg bone and finished off by grinding with sandstone files. Moa-bone hooks were usually not more than about five centimetres long but some were occasionally made up to 15 centimetres long. Often the centre of a U-shaped hook was removed by drilling a series of small holes through the bone and then knocking the unwanted piece out; sometimes the bone did not

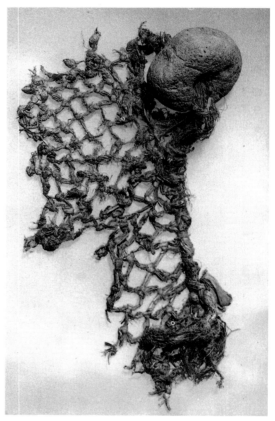

Fragment of a flax fishing net (right), from Moa-bone Point Cave, made from New Zealand flax (*Phormium*) with a pumice float attached. More commonly, wooden floats would have been used, but these rarely survive in archaeological contexts.

A massive nineteenth-century weir (below) across the Patea River, Taranaki, used by Maoris to catch eels. The weir diverted migrating eels to channels where they were caught in basket-like traps. Similar constructions were doubtless used in prehistoric times.

break along the line of holes as intended, as the numerous broken 'tabs' in archaeological sites testify. In some places the centre of the hook was chiselled out, or bored out with a single large hole. In early times, most one-piece hooks were not barbed, the common design having an inturned point instead; these are sometimes called 'rotating' hooks from the belief that the hook would have had to rotate to impale and hold a fish. In some areas, however, barbed hooks were used concurrently with those having an inturned point. At the 500-year-old Tai Rua site in North Otago, where over 50 per cent of all fish hooks were one-piece varieties, one in 12 of these was barbed.

In later sites the hooks tend to be both barbed and made in two pieces, typically a bone point lashed to a curved wooden shank. This doubtless developed out of the difficulty in obtaining large pieces of bone once moas became extinct. (Sometimes sub-fossil moa bone was dug out of swamps, and sometimes human skull bone and whale jaw bone were used, although neither of these had the density of moa leg bone.)

Although numerous wooden shanks for two-piece hooks have been found in cave sites throughout the country, the best-preserved specimens are those collected at the time they were being used. Some are V-shaped, and were formed from a branching twig; others are sub-circular or U-shaped and appear to have been made from a twig that was bent into shape while it was young and flexible and then allowed to grow to the required size. These usually had a groove (at the end opposite the line attachment) on to which a sharp bone point, usually barbed, was bound with fine flax twine. Sometimes these points were made from the canine teeth of dogs.

Trolling hooks had straight shanks of stone, bone, shell or wood, to which a bone point was fitted. They were probably used without bait and were pulled through the water in such a way as to make predatory fish, such as barracouta and kahawai, mistake them for potential food. On some early moa-hunter sites, distinctive triangular-sectioned stone 'minnow' lure shanks are found along with specially shaped bone points that were lashed to them. These stone lures appear to have gone out of fashion about 500 years ago, when they were replaced by wooden-shanked hooks in which the bone point sat in a hole near the end. Such trolling hooks were used well into the nineteenth century when a metal nail was substituted for the bone point.

One of the common ways of removing the centre portion when making a one-piece fish-hook from bone was to drill a series of holes around the inner margin and then knock the unwanted piece out.

Geoffrey Cox/BM

One-piece fish hooks (below left) of bone and shell. The two larger hooks illustrate the 'inturned point' variety and are made of moa bone, as is the unfinished example or 'tab'. The smallest example has barbs on both the point and shank legs.

Two-piece fish-hooks (below) for use with bait usually comprised a barbed bone point lashed to a curved wooden shank. Trolling hooks had a straight shank of stone, bone, wood or shell, and were used without bait.

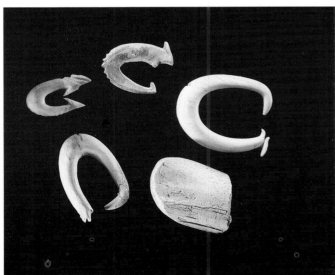

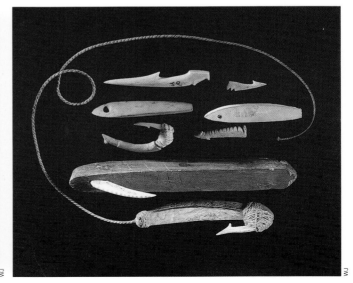

Boultbee described Maoris still using such hooks to catch barracouta in 1826:

> The Baracoota season had now commenced and we had an abundance of these fish; the roes of which only, we ate, preserving the fish and drying them in the sun for a future period. As the manner of catching Baracoota is singular I will describe it to you. The fishers are provided with a rod of about 12 feet long, at the end of this a line of 3 feet length is fastened, to which is attached a narrow and flat piece of wood about 5 inches long, in this piece, a seal's tooth, a nail or some other sharp thing, is fixed with the point upwards so as to form a hook. The end of the rod is plunged in the water, and kept moving round in a quick manner, so as to cause a strong ripple, the fish seeing the agitation of the water, and the brightness of the hook, mistake it for a shoal of small fish, and voraciously snap at the hook, which never fails to penetrate through their jaws; as fast as the fisherman throws in his fish, he continues working his rod and line about, as long as a fish is to be caught; sometimes they will load a canoe in two hours with fish. The women are kept busily employed at this season, drying the Baracoota which are cut open and hung on racks for the purpose.

Besides the stone and wooden lures, shell and bone lures were also used throughout the prehistoric era. In moa-hunter times, solid lures were occasionally made of thick mussel (*Perna*) shell — doubtless a substitute for the pearl shell lures used on many Pacific islands. Later, especially on the East Coast, paua shell (*Haliotis*) was used, but it needed to be backed with wood to give it sufficient strength.

Evidence of the fishing lines used dates from late prehistoric times when the lines were mostly made of two-ply twisted flax fibre, and it seems likely that this form of cordage was developed fairly early. Set nets, on the other hand, seem to have sometimes been made of thin strips of unprocessed or only partly scutched flax leaf. However, nets are seldom found on archaeological sites, except for a few that have been found in caves. One such net from Banks Peninsula was 40 metres long, and some of immense length have been referred to in ethnological publications. In set net fishing, it is normal to use floats to hold the net upright in the water. As few have been found we presume that they were mostly made of wood or seaweed, but one found in Moa-bone Point Cave was of pumice and still had a piece of a net fragment attached to it.

Both fishing lines and nets were used with sinkers. In their simplest form these were just a stone with a groove cut or chipped around it to hold the line; more elaborate varieties, including those with a hole chipped through for attachment and those with ornamentation, are known from some areas.

For freshwater species such as whitebait and eels, small portable traps made of basketry were used. Larger structural traps were made of stakes and were deployed across streams and rivers. These eel weirs are best known ethnographically and appear similar to those still used in some areas today.

Eels were also caught using spears made of

Tidal fish trap (right) off Onawe Peninsula, Canterbury. Although we don't know exactly how these large stone enclosures functioned, it is thought that fish entering the enclosure at high tide were unable to escape when the tide receded.

One of the numerous eroding shell middens (below right) on Ninety Mile Beach, Northland; a prehistoric rubbish dump of burnt and unburnt tuatua shells.

Seals were a popular food in prehistoric times and their numbers had already been considerably depleted by hunting prior to the arrival of European sealers.

Rod Morris

John Coster

multiple tines of sharpened wood. Ethnographic records reveal that a favourite method of catching eels at Lake Ellesmere and other coastal Canterbury wetlands was to dig 'dead-end' ditches on the seaward side of the lake or swamp. When migrating, the eels would swim down the ditches in an attempt to reach the sea, and would then be easily caught.

Despite the abundant evidence in middens relating to the moa, little is known as to how they were hunted. Bone harpoon heads have been found on moa-hunter sites, sometimes in areas where moas were butchered, and the obvious inference is that they were used in hunting moas. They are designed to have a line attached to the head, which was also attached to a wooden shaft. When thrown at the prey, the head became embedded in the animal, but detached itself from the shaft to prevent it breaking. The prey could then be 'played' or retrieved by the line.

It is often thought that these harpoons would have been used for hunting sea mammals such as porpoises — as they must have been in the Marquesas and other islands where similar harpoons occur. However, the use of porpoises for food was common throughout the prehistoric period in New Zealand and it is unlikely that this method of hunting sea mammals would have

been coincidentally abandoned on the extinction of moas. It also seems unlikely that harpoons would have been used to catch seals, as it would have been much easier simply to knock the seals on the head while they were ashore, much as European sealers did to vast numbers in the early nineteenth century.

Small birds were caught with another type of harpoon, often referred to as a bird spear, the bone heads of which are common on later sites, although they were in use at all times. This type was longer and much narrower than the moa-hunting harpoon head, and typically had a series of barbs along one side. In use, it too was lightly attached to a wooden shaft, but the lengths of such shafts in museum collections indicate that they were hand-held rather than thrown. Only rarely is there any means for attaching a line — presumably because of the difficulties a line could cause amid forest vegetation.

Birds were also caught with snares, and some elaborate methods using feeding troughs and highly carved perches — numbers of which occur in museum collections — have been recorded. A distinctive and not infrequently found artifact on late sites is a ring made of bone or stone (usually nephrite). It is said to have been used to tether a tame kaka which decoyed wild kaka close to the hunter for capture.

Bird spears (left). Bone points with multiple barbs were lightly tied to long wooden poles, and once the bird was speared, the point came free from the pole to avoid breakage.

Moa eggs from South Island moa-hunter sites (far left). These have had the contents extracted through a small hole so that the shell could be used as a water container. Presumably the shell was fitted with a wooden stopper and carried in a flax bag, although no remains of these have been found.

This small moa (below) found at the Kaupokonui site appears to have had its neck wrung. Only the legs have been removed for food and the remainder cast aside.

Food Preparation

Julie O'Brien/CM

Birds were sometimes preserved in fat in kelp bags which were then protected with bark strips and bound into flax containers.

ARCHAEOLOGICAL remains pertaining to food preparation are the most widespread evidence of prehistoric human activity in New Zealand; although some foodstuffs were eaten raw when they were gathered, most required cooking to make them palatable.

It was Joseph Banks in 1770 who first described the cooking methods used:

. . . simple as their food is their cookery as far as I saw is as simple, a few stones heated hot & laid in a hole, their meat laid upon them & covered with hay, seems to be the most difficult part of it; Fish & Birds they generally Broil, or rather toast, spitting them upon a long skewer, the bottom of which is fix'd under a stone, & another Stone being put under the fore part of the Skewer, it is raised or lowered by moving that stone as the circumstances may require; the fern roots are laid upon the open fire, until they are thoroughly hot, & the bark of them burned to a Coal, they are then beat with a wooden hammer over a stone which causes all the bark to fly off & leaves the inside consisting of a small proportion of a glutinous pulp, mix'd with many fibres which they generally spit out after have suck'd each mouthfull a long time. . . .

Methods such as these were probably used during the whole of the prehistoric period, although this cannot be confirmed from the archaeological evidence. We do know, however, that the use of hot stones was widespread. The desire to steam or otherwise cook food with the aid of heated stones must have been very strong. Where stones were not locally available they were sometimes carried several kilometres from a suitable source — as much as 20 kilometres to one North Canterbury site. Stones that have been burnt and broken in the process of cooking food

are both durable and distinctive; in many areas they remain after all other signs of occupation have disappeared. And sometimes the hard inedible parts of food items, such as bones and shells, also remain to provide some indication of what was being cooked.

Although the deep earth oven or 'hangi' is popularly believed today to have always been the principal cooking method of the Maoris, archaeological evidence suggests that it may not have been used as frequently in the prehistoric period as is supposed. Generally, just a small hollow was scooped out of the ground, and a fire made in it upon which stones were heated. When the stones were hot enough, food was placed upon them (presumably protected from burning and dirt by being wrapped in leaves) and soil heaped over the top to retain steam and heat. The degree to which stones used in ovens are broken suggests that water was sprinkled on them to produce steam, which would have been more effective than relying on direct heat and the steam produced from the moisture in the food.

Nevertheless, it is the deep earth ovens which usually provide the most spectacular archaeological evidence of cooking, particularly when they have been infilled fairly rapidly after use and as a result the contents are well preserved. It was large deep ovens which had been used for cooking moas that Julius Haast investigated at Rakaia in 1869. One such oven in the same area, which was investigated in 1972, was two metres in diameter and 75 centimetres deep in the centre. It contained burnt broken stones, charcoal and moa bones, and the soil into which it had been dug had been stained by the heat of the fires.

Despite the relatively common occurrence of these ovens throughout the country, their scarcity, or even complete absence, on some sites

Although this photograph was taken as late as 1907 at Wahi Pa, home of the Maori King, the activities portrayed, and the elevated food platform and cooking area, as well as the houses, reflect earlier times despite the very obvious European influence on dress and utensils. Note the bell, probably used to indicate the meal was ready. The platform upon its rough, natural tree supports, and the fairly simple houses, are probably far more typical of everyday prehistoric Maori life than the elaborately carved examples so often pictured.

Auckland Weekly News

indicates that food was also cooked directly on open fires — a view supported by Banks's description of the use of spits to 'toast' both fish and birds.

Besides oven stones and charcoal, probably the most frequently occurring evidence of food preparation is the great quantity of shell 'middens' found coastally right around New Zealand. (Midden is a common archaeological term which comes from the Danish word *mø-dding*, a dunghill, but which commonly means a rubbish heap. It should more correctly be 'kitchen-midden' as used for food remains.) There are so many shells in some middens (some at Karamea, others at Kairaki, were 'mined' this century to produce poultry grit) that the shellfish could not all have been consumed at one time; nor is there always associated evidence of cooking. Many of these middens instead indicate that shellfish was collected and preserved by drying for later consumption. After the extinction of many bird species and the reduction of the seal population, the resources of the sea must have become very important.

Fish were also preserved by drying and smoking. A 600-year-old archaeological site investigated at Purakanui, on the Otago coast, was found to be a specialised fishing camp for the catching and processing of red cod and barracouta in particular. It was estimated that something like 400,000 kilograms of flesh had been obtained there, much more than could have been consumed by the likely resident population at the time. It seemed likely that much of the catch was preserved for later consumption elsewhere. Such circumstantial evidence is probably the best archaeological affirmation we are likely to get of the practice of preserving fish by drying, although there are numerous descriptions of it virtually up to the present day. Edward Shortland, wrote of 'a few women drying fish on the scorching sands' in South Canterbury in 1844, and Alfred Reynolds referred to the sun-drying of cooked barracouta, strung out between thirty-foot-high poles in eastern Otago some time later.

The Maoris also preserved birds, usually by 'potting' them in their own fat in baskets, gourds or bags of kelp, but most were probably caught and cooked directly, the smaller species just over or in an open fire, as also were many fresh fish.

A staple foodstuff recorded in the late eighteenth and early nineteenth centuries was the roots of the bracken fern (*Pteridium esculentum*) which were dried and then pounded with a wooden beater to produce a paste that was either sucked from the fibrous material or made into cakes. At Kairaki, 15 kilometres north of Christchurch, two large flat water-worn greywacke stones were found in a small site that was occupied just after moas had become locally extinct. Such stones do not occur naturally in this locality and it is thought that they were probably brought here for the purpose of pounding fern root. Similar stones have been found on other sites; Maori ethnologist Peter Buck considered them a required part of kitchen equipment.

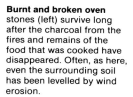
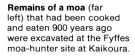

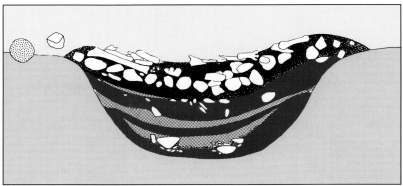

Remains of a moa (far left) that had been cooked and eaten 900 years ago were excavated at the Fyffes moa-hunter site at Kaikoura.

Section cut through a midden of toheroa shells (far left below) on the inland dunes of Ninety Mile Beach. This one has been radiocarbon dated to 480 yrs BP.

Burnt and broken oven stones (left) survive long after the charcoal from the fires and remains of the food that was cooked have disappeared. Often, as here, even the surrounding soil has been levelled by wind erosion.

Cross-section of an earth oven (below) excavated at the Redcliffs moa-hunter site, Banks Peninsula. It had been used on several occasions, principally for cooking moa meat. Its large capacity indicates that it was intended to serve many people.

John Coster

CM Coll.

Canoes and Watercraft

*O*UR ideas about the canoes used in the prehistoric era tend to be dominated by the descriptions given by people like Cook and Banks and by the often detailed drawings of the artists who accompanied them. These earliest European observers, particularly the artists, were most impressed by the spectacular carved war canoes which frequently greeted them as they approached New Zealand shores. The description given by Captain du Clesmeur, who accompanied Marion du Fresne on his ill-fated expedition of 1772, is typical of its period:

> *Their pirogues or canoes are of great beauty. I have measured some that were 70 feet in length by 8 feet in width, and made out of a single piece of timber . . . The stern and the prow are ornamented with two pieces of carving; that on the stern is about 12 feet in height and 2½ inches in width. It is open-worked and painted red like the canoe itself. Above this board is a sort of plume of black feathers.*

It is this type of canoe that today is popularly associated with the prehistoric Maori. Yet a variety of watercraft were used — most of them smaller than the large single-hulled war canoes. For example, the double canoe, favoured in East Polynesia, remained in use in New Zealand until at least the 1840s. The very earliest description and drawing of a canoe we have — that of Abel Tasman in 1642 — is of this type.

A number of other early visitors, including Cook and Banks, also described double canoes in use — all of them in the south; one of the latest observations was made in Akaroa Harbour on Banks Peninsula, by the survey ship *Acheron* in 1849, nearly 200 years after Tasman's visit.

There are also various passing references to outriggers and smaller fishing canoes used in coastal waters. These seemed to be mainly

unornamented except for a carved bow piece, often in the form of a stylised human head.

Watercraft were also used on inland waterways — the lakes and rivers — although these are seldom described by the early European visitors, who rarely ventured inland from the coastal regions. The simple dugout, hollowed from a tree trunk, was the most common craft used; it was sturdy and durable and many remained in use until well into the period of European settlement. On broad, calm-flowing rivers such as the Wanganui, they were invaluable for the transport of goods — by European and Maori alike. Some were even adapted this century to have an inboard motor fitted and one redoubtable old dugout was reputedly powered by a Buick Straight-8 engine!

But on swifter, more treacherous rivers, particularly those of the South Island, the 'mokihi' or reed craft was favoured when it became necessary to cross a river. A mokihi with two occupants features in one of the South Island's best known rock drawings, and Edward Shortland left a graphic description of its construction and use on the Waitaki River in January 1844: 'Large enough to carry himself and wife, with two of my natives, myself and all our baggage.'

Shaped like a canoe, the mokihi was made from tapering bundles of raupo or flax stalks, all bound together and secured with flax — the finished craft being 'remarkably buoyant [although] impossible to guide unless in calm weather'. After launching, it was carried downstream on the swift current for several miles

Remains of a canoe (right), reputed to have been used by Te Rauparaha in the 1830s, continue to serve a useful purpose. Wattie Watson of Arapawa Island displays a piece that he discarded while making fence posts from part of the hull. Another section of the hull has been preserved in the Canterbury Museum.

An unfinished canoe hull (below) lies on the slopes of Mount Fyffe, Kaikoura, where it was abandoned over 150 years ago. Several other unfinished canoes in this area have been destroyed by bush fires.

before it could be safely brought ashore on the opposite bank. It was then abandoned, its purpose fulfilled.

Although we are basically dependent on historic records for what we know about watercraft in use from the seventeenth to the nineteenth centuries, a number of canoe pieces have been archaeologically recovered. Like most wooden artifacts dating from the prehistoric era, these are mostly small and were preserved in swamps or caves. Some pieces are obviously quite early and so provide some insight into changes in canoe design and decoration. From North Island swamps come two fascinating bow covers. A dragon-like figure from Doubtless Bay is at once distinctly Polynesian in style yet clearly an early stage in the development of the 'manaia' figures of classic Maori wood carving. A bow cover from a Waitore swamp is decorated with a 'punched' pattern of double spirals — one of the earliest known examples of this characteristically Maori design — plus decorative notching typical of the archaic period.

Another unique bow piece is among pieces of a small canoe recovered from a swamp at Jacksons Bay in South Westland. Although minus ears, the head is clearly that of the Polynesian dog or kuri — an appropriate effigy as the kuri was a regular canoe traveller, described by Joel Polack in 1838 as 'constant compagnon du voyage in the canoe . . . viewing with head erect the passing scenery.' All of these carved pieces were probably special features of individual craft and it is possible that they were deliberately secreted in swamps for safekeeping.

Other finds have included outriggers, as well as bailers and paddles. Moncks Cave in Christchurch (*see page 44*) yielded one each of all these items, almost certainly stored in this small coastal cave for safekeeping between trips.

A few canoe hulls have been located in archaeological contexts in different parts of New Zealand. Totara was the most commonly used timber and is remarkably durable, even when exposed to weathering. For many years two partially completed totara hulls lay in the forest on the slopes of Mt Fyffe, behind Kaikoura, nearly 500 metres above sea level. Others in the same general area were burnt when the land was cleared for farming. Why they were abandoned we will never know. Perhaps the Ngai Tahu craftsmen who began them were victims of Te Rauparaha's raids on the area.

Some other interesting relics, reputed to be parts of a canoe which belonged to Te Rauparaha himself, were being 'recycled' as recently as 1978. Long after that redoubtable warrior's raids in the south, the canoe was found abandoned at the Maori village of Ngakuta on Arapawa Island in the Marlborough Sounds. The sound timber of the hull was eventually cut up and used as fence posts.

Despite the relative paucity of their remains in an archaeological context, watercraft of all kinds were of vital importance to the Maori people for travel, transport and food gathering for the whole of the prehistoric period, and it was only the advent of the more sophisticated European whaleboat that led to the eventual abandonment of those of prehistoric design.

An artist's impression of a mokihi, a type of reed raft-canoe used on fast-flowing South Island rivers. The swiftness of the current made it impracticable to take water craft upstream, but quickly constructed mokihi were useful for travelling downstream or across rivers.

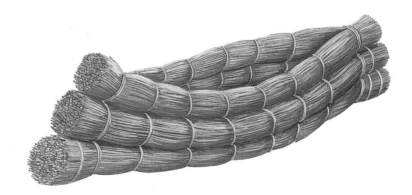

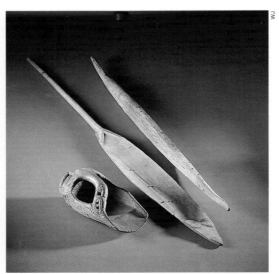

An early canoe stern-post (far left) from Okains Bay decorated with carved single spirals and originally coloured red. At some stage it had split in two and was repaired by lashing cord through two small holes near the top edge.

A wooden bailer, a repaired painted paddle, and an outrigger float from a small canoe, all from Moncks Cave, Banks Peninsula (left). Early European accounts only rarely mention the use of outriggers in New Zealand waters.

Clothing and Textiles

*A*LTHOUGH the original Polynesian migrants introduced the paper mulberry tree to New Zealand, barkcloth never attained the popularity it had elsewhere in the Pacific, and there is no evidence that it was actually used for clothing in this country. In fact, because of its perishable nature, very little clothing that was worn in prehistoric times has been found in archaeological sites. Yet suitable clothing must have been essential for comfort and welfare, if not survival, in the colder parts of New Zealand. It seems likely that skins of the larger animals, particularly moas, would have been used but no proof of this has been found, and it is possible that difficulties in treating the skins made it impracticable for them to be used whole.

The most important archaeological item of clothing to have been discovered is a cloak in a cave burial on Mary Island in Lake Hauroko, Fiordland (*see page 95*). The burial has a radiocarbon age of about 300 years, making the cloak the oldest complete article of clothing to have been found in New Zealand.

The Hauroko cloak, as it is known, is about 85 centimetres wide and nearly 120 long, and comprises a coarse fabric made from dressed flax (*Phormium tenax*) to which narrow strips of feathered bird skin had been attached when the cloak was being made. Most of the feathers were red-brown kaka (*Nestor meridionalis*) relieved with an occasional tuft of green kakapo (*Strigops habroptilus*), and although much of the cloak is now denuded, it was once completely feathered on one side. A fur collar was produced using a strip of dog skin along the top edge and the cloak was probably held in place by a drawstring around the neck. During the burial the cloak had been draped around the body with the feathers

on the inside, and although this might have had some ceremonial significance, it seems as likely that it reflects a practice observed in 1769 where dog-skin cloaks were worn with the hair outside for ceremonial occasions but with the hair inside when warmth was the more important consideration.

Cloaks collected by the first European visitors — 100 or more years later than the Hauroko burial — usually have a basically similar fabric construction, but with finer warps (the horizontal threads) and with the crossing wefts much closer together, giving a much smoother finish. Many have no feathers, but where they are present they have been inserted individually rather than as strips of skin.

The earliest European description of clothing comes from Tasman who reported that the people he saw in Golden Bay in 1642 were mostly bare above the waist — this comment though must be qualified by the fact that it was only an expeditionary force he observed on this occasion. Fortunately, from the latter part of the eighteenth century better descriptions emerge and from these it is evident that the most common articles of clothing were two rectangular pieces of fabric tied around the shoulders and waist. The fabric was made of New Zealand flax and had long projecting ends of thin strips of flax leaf on the surface. Joseph Banks, a scientist on Cook's first expedition, wrote in 1770 that:

The common dress of these people is certainly to a stranger at first one of the most uncouth and extraordinary sights that can be imagined. It is made of the leaves of the Flag . . . which are split into 3 or 4 Slips each, and these as soon as they are dry are wove into a kind of Stuff between netting

This group, photographed in the 1870s by Herbert Deveril at the Waipahihi hot springs near Taupo, shows a mixture of traditional and European clothing. The chief Te Rangitahau in the centre favours traditional dress, probably for reasons of ceremony or prestige. An interesting aspect is the degree to which many of the group, including the women, are unclothed — such semi-nudity became uncommon following Christianisation.

and cloth, out of the upper side of which all the ends, of 8 or 9 inches long each, are sufferd to hang in the same manner as thrums out of a thrum mat. Of these pieces of cloth 2 serve for a compleat dress, one of which is tied over the shoulders and reaches about their knees, the other about the waist which reaches near the ground; but they seldom wear more than one of these and when they have it on resemble not a little a thatched house.

Twenty-five years later John Savage observed:

. . . when they are seated, or squatted down their figure very much resembles a large bee-hive, super-mounted with the head of a New Zealander.

Sometimes they went nearly naked, the men wearing only a belt around the waist from which hung a string to which the end of the penis was tied; the women wearing a short apron or 'bunch of grass or Plants' fixed to a girdle to conceal the pubic area.

Besides the very serviceable and apparently rainproof clothing described, cloaks were also made without tags or thrums; these were referred to by early observers and examples occur in early collections. Such cloaks were often ornamented around the edges, and were occasionally decorated or even covered with feathers, as was the Hauroko cloak. Border decoration was provided using coloured threads in the flax fabric

to form various geometrical patterns, mostly oblique to the warp and weft of the garment.

Some early descriptions also refer to cloaks made of whole dog skins, but this is most likely a mistake — the standard dog-skin cloak in ethnological collections is made of very tightly woven flax fabric with narrow strips of dog skin attached so as to give the appearance of a whole skin (Banks refers to this in his journal). The dog-skin strips appear to be dried rather than tanned leather, and they were probably used in preference to larger pieces to give the cloak a flexibility not obtained from dried skins. The Maoris appear to have never developed a really successful method of curing skins and, although at least one cloak of trimmed whole skins is known, such usage may well have been a post-European development.

The techniques of weaving and plaiting have survived to the present day — indeed articles such as the kete or flax kit have continued to be made and are regularly used in some parts of New Zealand. And although European clothing

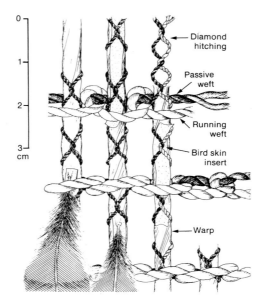

The 300-year-old Hauroko cloak (left) was made of dressed fibres of New Zealand flax with inserts of feathered bird-skin. The weaving process involved hand twisting and twining and was quite unlike the process or the product of European loom weaving.

Although cloaks such as this (below left) are commonly referred to as rain capes, and this was undoubtedly one of their uses, early records indicate that they were the common dress of the people. This example is made from a combination of kiekie and flax fibre and some of the tags have been dyed for ornamental reasons.

This photograph taken at the beginning of the twentieth century shows Pai Kanohi of Tuhoe wearing the common dress of prehistoric times. Today this form of clothing is usually referred to as a rain cape. The containers in front of the house are large gourds covered with woven flax for holding preserved birds.

was rapidly adopted by the Maori people, cloaks too continued to be made in limited numbers, to be worn as a mark of social status or for ceremonial purposes. The greatest changes were in the material from which they were made, with cotton candlewick and coloured wools replacing the traditional vegetable fibres which took so long to prepare; the feathers of introduced birds — domestic poultry and pheasants — also feature prominently on many cloaks held in museum collections.

In the last two centuries traditional Maori clothing fashions have undergone some interesting changes. The dog-skin cloak, which once denoted rank, stopped being made once the Polynesian kuri gave way to European dog breeds, and has how been replaced by cloaks of kiwi (*Apteryx*) feathers. And two distinctive items of clothing worn today by performers of Maori cultural items, the piupiu flax skirt and the decorative head-band, are both comparatively recent innovations.

Although several different plants were used in the manufacture of fabrics, flax was the most important: besides clothing, it was also used for cords, nets, bags and mats. Often the wide flax leaves were simply slit into thin strips and left unscraped with the epidermis or outer skin intact. In this form it was plaited into mats and bags, tied to form fishing nets and used to make sandals, all of which have been found in archaeological contexts and were also collected by early Europeans. Where finer cordage or thread was required for high-quality cloaks or fishing lines, flax fibre was manufactured by peeling the epidermis off each side of the flax leaf using a shell. (The same method is used by craftspeople today, and with the right technique — and practice — a skilled operator can become highly proficient at this seemingly laborious task.) The fibre was then washed, scraped and sometimes pounded or scutched to produce the required softness and, when dry, rolled into single or two-ply cords.

One of the most important archaeological discoveries of recent times was made in 1983 when the remains of a 400-year-old back pack made of plaited flax strips were found in an inland Canterbury rock shelter. No such artifact had been found before, nor had any been referred to by European observers, yet it was of a highly developed design, basically similar to the frame packs used by modern trampers. The pack comprised a circular wooden frame over which a large drawstring bag, 73 centimetres in diameter and 36 centimetres deep, was fitted. Two plaited shoulder straps were sewn through the back of the pack on to the frame for carrying, and there was padding inside to prevent hard or sharp objects digging in to the wearer's back. Inside the pack were a woven pouch and the fabric for another slightly smaller back pack of the same design. All had been plaited from thin strips of unscutched flax leaf using a simple under-and-over twill pattern.

Although early European travellers often employed Maoris to carry their provisions and equipment overland, there is no record that framed packs like this one were used; instead,

The attractive chequer-board effect of this early twentieth-century cloak (right) was achieved by inserting a pattern of pigeon, kaka and tui feathers into a shaped flax fibre base. The feathers of the border are kiwi.

This *c.* 1920 postcard (below) of guides at Whakarewarewa highlights the prestige bestowed on the kiwi feather cloak.

loads were transported in flax kit bags hauled with the aid of carrying straps. For some reason the 'frame pack' did not continue in use and may have had only a local distribution.

Sometimes flax sandals were worn during overland journeys and several have been found in archaeological sites such as the Irongate Cave in southern Marlborough, the Big Dog rock shelter in South Canterbury, and Moa-bone Point Cave near Christchurch. These were simply and quickly made from thin strips of flax or cabbage tree leaf, and were discarded when the sole wore through. In 1844 Edward Shortland recorded in his diary:

This evening, Huruhuru made me a pair of sandals, such as are in common use among these natives. They are called 'paraerae', and are made either with the leaves of the flax-plant, or of the 'ti' [Cordyline australis]. The latter are preferable, being much the toughest. Mine were a pair with double soles called 'torua', calculated to endure several days' walk along a beach, which is so destructive to shoes. They no doubt owed their invention to the necessity of protecting the feet from the snow and the sharp prickles of the small shrub tumatakuru [Discaria toumatou], which is very common on the plains, and often lies so much hidden in the grass, that you first become aware of its presence by your feet becoming wounded by it.

Although textile items are rare on archaeological sites, small bags and pieces of fabric made of thin strips of flax leaf plaited in both twill and check patterns have been found in a number of cave sites throughout the country. Recently, part of a mat was found in an old swamp when a ditch was being dug through it. Mats were probably used on the floors of dwellings for sitting or sleeping on, and may have also been used for covering food when cooking in earth ovens. This particular mat comprised wide strips of flax leaf plaited together in a check pattern; some of the strips had had the epidermis scraped off half their width. The scraped parts had become stained black from the swamp mud, while those parts with the epidermis intact remained unchanged, producing a pattern on the mat. The dyeing of scutched flax in swamp mud has been well recorded ethnographically and was widely used for decorative purposes, but this is the first record of a pattern being formed by dying only half the strip of leaf.

Fragment of a flax mat (left) preserved in mud near the mouth of the Tentburn, Canterbury. It exhibits a previously unknown decorative process in which half of some strips of flax have been stripped of the epidermis to allow them to become stained black by the mud.

The remains of a framed Maori back pack (below left), dating back some 400 years, were recently found in an inland Canterbury rock shelter. It is very similar in principle to modern frame packs used by trampers.

An artist's impression of the Canterbury back pack and flax sandals in use.

Geoffrey Cox/BM

CONTINUED growth of the population put an increasing pressure on the food resources that were readily available, and led to the widespread destruction of forest and the avifauna that lived in it. Of particular economic importance was the depletion of the coastal seal colonies and the decimation and eventual extinction of the moas and other large, easily caught birds. All this happened about 500 years ago and led inevitably to a major change in staple foodstuffs with resultant modifications to lifestyle and settlement patterns.

No longer was it possible to roam freely over the countryside hunting game and, although there would initially have been 'pockets' of moas still to be found, these would soon have been exploited. It became necessary instead to depend to a far greater extent on vegetable foods — particularly kumara and fern root. This in turn led to groups of people laying claim to selected areas of land and establishing permanent settlements on them, both to provide validity to their claim and to ensure that it was respected by neighbouring groups. What itinerancy persisted tended to be confined to within a discrete territory, and only extended into other groups' territories during hostilities.

Permanent villages now became essential, particularly in areas where kumara horticulture was practicable. The warmer half of the year would be spent in preparing the ground, planting the tubers, tending to the growing plants and harvesting the crop. And for most of the remainder of the year the tender kumaras were stored in underground pits, both for food and as 'seed' for the next year's planting. To leave either the growing crop or the stores unattended would be tantamount to inviting a raiding foray from a neighbouring settlement. In many places — for example, Auckland and Clarence — permanent village sites are found close by the remains of extensive gardens.

It also became expedient to situate a village on higher ground so that any approaching enemy force could be easily detected and the village better defended. Within a few centuries the ultimate development in defensive strategy had become the Maori fort or *pa*, in which artificial terraces, ditches, walls and palisading contrived to protect the resident community, its chattels and its stores of food.

When Europeans first arrived in New Zealand they found people living in fortified pas, in unfortified villages and in temporary accommodation. Not as much is known about the relationship between these modes of living as might be expected, largely, we suspect, because the advent of Europeans disrupted the normal lifestyle. Understandably, people may have retired to a pa when the visitors appeared, and may also have flocked to the European ships to trade artifacts and food for the coveted metal tools and perceptibly superior fabrics, once their fears were allayed.

Like their ancestors, the classic Maoris made temporary use of rock shelters and shallow caves where these were convenient, but they now no longer occupied the inland rock formations that had earlier proved so useful to hunting parties. Around the coast, however, fishing parties still often took shelter in eroded hollows in rocky cliffs. Sometimes a cave provided more permanent shelter; at Teviotdale, North Canterbury, a woman lived alone with her dog for some years in a small cave (*see page 92*). It seems likely, however, that hers was an abnormal situation; the woman had left her family group to live alone once her health, particularly her inability to eat normal foods, made her a liability to her community.

This photograph, taken in the 1870s, shows a fairly conventional Maori house, made of natural materials — light stakes, brushwood, and reeds. It is probably not greatly dissimilar to many used in prehistoric times; unfortunately, structures such as this are never preserved archaeologically.

Not surprisingly, temporary shelters have left very little archaeological evidence of their form or structure. There is ample evidence of where people have camped, where they have left behind shell middens, artifacts and the remains of their fires. Often on small temporary sites, archaeological investigations reveal marks in the ground where stakes have been, and at least some of these stakes may have supported makeshift shelters. Other sites contain no such clues, and there must have been many thousands of other camps from which all occupational evidence has long since vanished.

When James Cook was in Queen Charlotte Sound in 1777, Maoris came from adjacent bays, motivated by curiosity and a desire to trade (Cook had been here several times before). They quickly erected temporary shelters in Ship Cove, and later Cook described what happened:

> It is curious to see with what facility they build these little temporary habitations: I have seen above twenty of them errected on a spot of ground that not an hour before was covered with shrubs & plants. They generally bring some part of the Materials with them, the rest they find on the spot. I was present when a number of people landed and built one of these Villages: the moment the canoes landed men leapt out and at once took possession of a spot of ground, by tearing up the plats &c or sticking up some part of the framing of the hut . . . These temporary habitations are abundantly sufficient to shelter them from the wind and rain, which is the only purpose they want them for.

Across the bay from Ship Cove was an island pa — Cook called it *Hippah* — deserted on this occasion. On his first voyage seven years earlier, however, the small pa of 32 or 33 houses held upwards of 200 inhabitants. Besides the steep rocky sides of the island it was additionally fortified with:

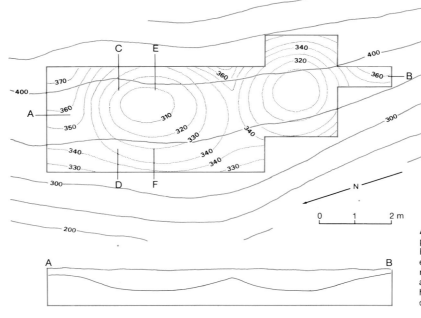

Plan and sections of the excavation of a double dwelling site on the large Peketa Pa in southern Marlborough. The blue contour lines represent the present surface and the black lines, within the excavated area, the two hollowed out areas over which the shelters had been erected.

An artist's impression of the pair of dwellings on Peketa Pa, remains of which were excavated in 1976. This reconstruction is based on archaeological evidence and historical observations of other such dwellings.

PEKETA PIT HOUSE

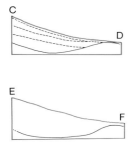

roof

Julie O'Brien/CM

A reconstruction of a cross-section through the larger unit of the double dwelling. All that was left of the roof were the charred remains of branches; there were holes in the floor where uprights had been anchored.

Geoffrey Cox/BM

. . . strong posts or sticks drove into the ground, & those interwoven with long sticks in a horizontal direction, & then filled with small brush wood with one place two feet square where was a wooden dore, so that only one man could get in at a time & that on his hands and knees & of course easily destroy'd if at war.

And it was noted that 'they have here places for doing their necessary occasions at each end of the place without their houses.'

Cook and his companions believed that the Maoris normally lived scattered along the shores and retired to the 'Hippah' in times of threatened danger — a view supported by the deserted dwellings, somewhat more substantial than the 'temporary habitations' of Ship Cove, around the various small bays they visited.

It was the fortified villages of the Maoris that attracted the attention, even admiration, of the European explorers. Besides the Queen Charlotte Sound Hippah, descriptions and illustrations were made of pa sites elsewhere from the late eighteenth century. These provide useful additional details to add to the information obtained from archaeological research.

Although hill forts occur in other parts of Polynesia — as they do in other parts of the world — the Maori pa appears to have developed in New Zealand in response to a growing need for a defensible area in which to live. Although attempts have been made to document this development from archaeological

research, these have been based largely on radiocarbon dates of unknown reliability obtained from the remains of timber posts buried in the ground. Such dating is suspect for two main reasons. Radiocarbon analysis measures the time that the dated sample stopped growing — an inner part of a tree trunk may be several centuries older than the growing leaves, twigs and bark, and hence have a much greater age than the pa that was built from it. As well, most of the dated samples are of charcoal, which can give erroneous dates.

In some parts of New Zealand the archaeological landscape is dominated by pa sites; there are areas where every suitable hill seems to have been modified by some sort of prehistoric earthworks. The distribution of such pa sites roughly correlates with the distribution of the classic population so that they are, for example, common in Auckland and parts of Taranaki but relatively infrequent in the South Island and rare south of Banks Peninsula.

One early pa site which was dated from midden shells rather than wood or charcoal is Peketa in southern Marlborough. It is a good example of the simplest type of defence, which relied on natural features rather than artificial structures to deter enemies.

Peketa is said to have been built by the Ngati Mamoe people about the time that the Ngai Tahu started coming into the South Island from the North in the seventeenth century, and this age is supported by limited radiocarbon dating. The whole site occupies two steep-sided

At the height of Maori occupation, One Tree Hill pa must have been a populous centre — as were many of the pas which topped Auckland's volcanic cones. This artist's reconstruction is based on the archaeological evidence of ground modification still obvious today on the slopes of One Tree Hill, together with our general archaeological and historical knowledge of the lifestyle of the pa Maoris.

Geoffrey Cox/BM

spurs and part of the hillside between them — a total area of nearly two hectares. Because of the steepness of the spurs, small terraces were cut into the hillsides and the tops flattened off to provide level areas for dwellings and other domestic activities. Today the site is partly covered with patchy bush which has probably become established since it was abandoned, but there is a marked incidence of ngaio trees growing on the outer edges of the terraces, and it has been suggested that they were deliberately

planted there, perhaps to act as anchoring points for ropes to help haul goods and people up to the living areas.

Until a few years ago large water-worn greywacke stones could be seen where they had been placed on the terraces, presumably to throw or roll down on to any unwanted visitor approaching from below. The defence of the village was largely dependent on the steepness of the hillsides, and struggling up the steep slope in the face of boulders being hurled down would

The Auckland volcanic cone known as One Tree Hill has been modified over most of its area by a complex of living terraces, storage pits and other earthworks, and remains today as a spectacular example of Maori pa construction.

Strong point

Living terrace

Pits

0   100m

CRATER

CRATER

CRATER

Caroline P...

have been a formidable task. The only artificial fortification on the pa was a low wall which divided the smaller spur off from the rest of the site, and it is thought that this was a later addition rather than part of the original plan.

Activities in other parts of the pa site included cooking food and burying the dead (*see page 94*). On the hill slope between the two spurs some circular pits had been dug into the hard though fractured rock; at least one of these had been lined with clay, presumably for use in storing water.

Details of one of the Peketa dwellings were obtained when one of the hillside terraces was excavated in 1976. A shallow oval pit, 4 × 3 metres in size and 30 centimetres deep, had been dug into the terrace and a roof — indicated mainly by the charred remains of light branches and a couple of stake holes — had been built over it. There was no fireplace, either within this shelter or on the terrace outside it, but adjacent to it was another smaller pit which had presumably been roofed in much the same way. Occupational material left within the larger 'pit house' indicated that it was used to shelter people (rather than stores), but a nephrite adze head had been cached under a paua shell and a forequarter of dog had been left in it when the site was abandoned.

The large size of Peketa and the amount of terracing and levelling that had been carried out indicate that it was designed to hold a large number of people. That people actually did live in it is indicated by the quantity of artifacts and food remains they left behind; it was not occupied only during siege, since they were able to carry out food-gathering operations, including deep-sea fishing, when they lived there. That it was involved in warfare is suggested by the sudden departure of its occupants. The attack appears to have succeeded and the pa was burnt down. Subsequently, erosion filled in the pits and a major slip took a large part of the site away.

Although natural features — steep hillsides, cliffs and swamps — were used for defensive purposes well into the nineteenth century, increasingly artificial structures were built, particularly walls, scarps, ditches and palisades. Where an earthen wall was used, a ditch was often dug immediately in front of it, the soil from the ditch being used to build the wall. Although a deep ditch in this position would add to the effective height to the wall, this was not always considered to be an important factor. In some sites, ranging in age from 150 to 400 years, soil was simply scooped up without making a deep ditch. In others the ditch occurs *behind* the main defensive wall. Although palisading would seem to be most effective if placed on top of the wall, both excavation and historical observation indicates that in at least some pa sites, heavy palisade posts were erected at the base of the wall on the inside.

Although there are considerable regional differences and a wide range in the way these artificial fortifications were deployed, a pa site at Kauri Point, near Tauranga, provides an example of ditch and wall (often called ditch and bank) defenses. Apparently associated with the pa were an adjacent terraced hillside and a unique swamp 'shrine' containing a number of wooden combs (*see page 89*). The defended area was roughly a rectangle about 29 metres by 75 metres in size, two sides of which were protected by a steep bank into Tauranga Harbour and the other two by a double ditch and wall structure. Here was a low outer wall, then a ditch, followed by a larger wall, another ditch, and then a steep scarp to the relatively flat interior of the pa. Excavations showed that the fortifications had been modified on at least two occasions since they were first built and that there had also been earlier undefended occupation of the site.

The interior features of pa sites vary as much as their defensive works. Inside Kauri Point, for example, were a number of rectangular

A cluster of storage pits (below right) associated with extensive horticulture, a hilltop pa and a village site at Clarence Bridge, Marlborough.

At Opotiki on D'Urville Island (below), a complex of sites includes the archaeological remains of walled gardens, pits, middens and occupational areas.

pits that had been filled in, some of which had been dug through earlier filled-in pits. Some of these were interpreted by the excavators as house pits and others as store pits. (When it subsequently became unfashionable to believe in house pits, it was suggested that all might be storage pits.)

On other sites evidence of above-ground houses has been obtained. They were rectangular in shape, usually defined by post holes (some still containing the remains of posts, which were often squared slabs of timber) marking the walls. Nearly all of these houses had but a single room, although there was sometimes an open porch in front. Larger buildings often had a centre post to support the ridge pole — indicating an inverted V-shaped roof — and some had a stone-edged fireplace.

At Takahanga Pa, Kaikoura, a house has been excavated that was similar to some of those depicted by nineteenth-century painters. It was rectangular, oriented north-south, and was roughly 3 × 5 metres in size with a porch on the northern end. There was a single doorway between the porch and the main area, approximately in the centre of the front wall, and a single fireplace inside, not far behind a centre post. The walls had been built of slab timber posts, and there was a ditch around three sides to trap water dripping off the eaves. Although it had been rebuilt on at least two occasions, the size and shape had not changed much. The last time it had been occupied was after European contact, but before European settlement of the area.

A surprising number of pa defensive works appear to be incomplete or badly designed for effective defense. As well, there is little direct archaeological evidence of the widespread prehistoric fighting that the large number of fortified villages throughout the country might suggest. If, however, fighting was largely conventionalised (*see* Weapons and Warfare) the defensive earthworks may have been designed primarily to provide a suitable setting for challenges and somewhat formalised conflict. The introduction of firearms in the early nineteenth century, however, provoked a marked change both in the concept and aims of warfare and in the design of pa fortifications. Earthworks that had been developed in response to a highly conventionalised warfare with hand-to-hand fighting were woefully inadequate against weapons that could maim or kill at a distance. Such a change was clearly demonstrated at the Takahanga Pa during excavations in 1982. Originally, in pre-European times a wall had been built with a central gap to provide an entrance way, which was lined on both sides with light palisading. With the advent of firearms which could shoot straight through the gateway, an L-shaped extension of the earthen wall was built around the opening, making it impossible for attackers to shoot into the interior of the pa.

A spectacular ridgetop pa, Ruahihi (far left), on the Taranaki coast. The summit of the ridge has been levelled into five platforms separated by defensive ditches. The very steep sides of the ridge would have provided natural defense, although like many such sites, access to water must have been difficult during any prolonged attack.

The foundations of a small house (left) with a front porch, sliding door, and central fireplace were revealed by excavation at Takahanga Pa, Kaikoura, in 1980. It appeared to have been rebuilt several times without deviating noticeably from its original, very typical, design.

'View of Patea Pah and River' by Charles Heaphy (below), probably in the 1860s. Many early European visitors were impressed by how pa defences combined natural features, such as cliffs, with palisading.

Nigel Prickett

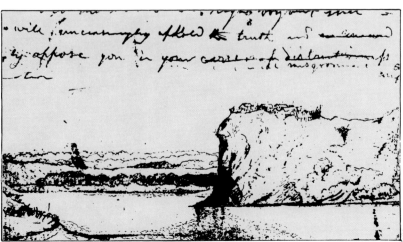

AIM

Weapons and Warfare

ONE of the most commonly reported characteristics of the New Zealand Maoris at the time of early European contact was their fierce and warlike nature. Had Tasman not had such a hostile reception in 'Murderers Bay', this country may well have become a Dutch colony, while incidents such as the cannibalism by Maoris of a boat's crew in Queen Charlotte Sound during Cook's second expedition, and a similar occurrence in the Bay of Islands during Marion du Fresne's 1772 visit, almost certainly stopped New Zealand from being used by Britain to establish a convict colony — Australia, with its more easily controlled Aborigines, being chosen in preference.

This reputation of the prehistoric Maoris for warring incessantly is apparently supported by the great number of pa, or fortified village, sites that can be seen throughout most of the country. They are among the most dominant and easily identified features of the archaeological landscape, and the enormous amount of labour and effort which must have been expended in their construction merely emphasises their importance to the society which developed them.

The Maori weapons of war were described in detail — and collected in quantity — by early European visitors, adding weight to the premise that war was an important and regular activity during the prehistoric period. Weapons included short 'clubs' manufactured from wood, bone and stone, and longer wooden items such as staffs and spears. All these seem to have been used almost entirely for hand-to-hand fighting; the Maoris had no knowledge of bows and arrows, and even spears do not seem to have been used as throwing weapons.

The shorter hand weapons or patu, although often referred to as clubs, were not generally employed as such. Secured to the wrist with a thong, they were used as jabbing or thrusting weapons; the sharpened end inflicting severe wounds. John Boultbee, a sealer in the south of New Zealand, described a skirmish with the

Maoris in which one of his boat's crew was killed with a patu. The victim was '. . . covered with gory blood and his temples cut across with some sharp weapon, so that his eyes were started.'

Patu were made in a variety of shapes, the best known and most spectacular being the greenstone mere or mere pounamu. The mere is the most simple patu in shape, having a smooth spatulate-ended blade, with the butt or knob at the end of the handle simply ornamented with curved parallel grooves. Other forms of patu (commonly made of wood) were the kotiate with a broad flat blade, notched on both edges to give it a fiddle shape, and the wahaika, on which one edge of the blade could be smoothly curved like a mere or notched like a kotiate, while the other edge displayed a stylised human figure. The butts of both the kotiate and wahaika were also carved, sometimes to represent a human head. Patu were also distinguished by the material of which they were made — for example, those made of stone other than greenstone were called patu onewa, those of whale bone, patu paraoa.

Although there is evidence that the classic patu shapes developed in New Zealand from more parallel-sided forms, wide-bladed examples in whale bone and wood have been recovered archaeologically in the Society Islands.

Longer weapons were usually made of wood (a few of whale bone are known); these too were used at close quarters for quick strokes and thrusts. The most elaborate of these was the taiaha, which probably developed along with an increased interest in wood carving. The pointed end was a tongue protruding from a human mouth, the other end was a flattened striking blade. It was decorated with dog hair and feathers.

Many of the more beautiful and elaborate weapons were highly valued personal possessions and often became family or tribal heirlooms. It is

Patu hand weapons (right), showing different shapes and materials — wood, whale bone and stone.

The decorated ends of two taiaha and a tewhatewha (far right). These weapons, generally between 1.4 and 1.8 metres in length, were used in display more than actual combat.

recorded that even in the era of musket warfare, the redoubtable Te Rauparaha still went into battle himself carrying only a greatly prized taiaha.

Despite the abundance of historic evidence relating to Maori warfare, archaeological evidence for its occurrence throughout the prehistoric period is remarkably sparse. Although fortified pa are numerous, most are of relatively recent origin; a few date back to 300-400 years ago but they are unknown for at least the first 500 years of human occupation of the country. Anyway, the presence of fortifications is not itself evidence of actual warfare — only of preparations for defence in the event of war. Many pa, particularly in the South Island, appear never to have been actually occupied.

Weapons, so abundant in early historic New Zealand, are extremely rare on prehistoric archaeological sites, including pa sites. Although those of wood, and even bone, might not have survived except in certain conditions, stone artifacts would last unchanged at least for the thousand or so years that man has been in New Zealand. But these too are seldom found archaeologically — especially from very early

sites. A patu made of pumice was recovered from the Whakamoenga cave site near Lake Taupo and fragments of stone weapons, mostly patu onewa, have been found on a number of sites in both the North and South Islands — all of them belonging to the later or classic Maori period. A greywacke patu onewa was recently found in the sea off Hippa Island, opposite Ship Cove in Queen Charlotte Sound, and another off Kaikoura Peninsula; presumably they were lost off canoes, and perhaps are evidence of skirmishes at sea.

There are also a few patu which have been found in isolation rather than on an archaeological site. Some of these, such as a very long black stone weapon with laterally projecting knobs found near Oxford in Canterbury, are quite unlike any others known. Because the Oxford example was not located on a site, there is no evidence of its age, and it is often considered that it must be archaic — of a style that had ceased to be made by the time Europeans arrived. (The same reasoning has been applied to other deviant forms.) However, if this was so, it is surprising that no stone weapons have turned up on any known early sites.

Takahanga Pa, Kaikoura, was reputedly attacked and sacked by Te Rauparaha in 1830. The excavation of this gateway in 1982 was a unique opportunity to check the historical record by using archaeology. This plan (right) indicates the position of the main palisade posts and the lighter stakes of the gateway. The modified passageway allowed safe egress as well as protection for those within the pa. Despite the Maoris' familiarity with traditional hand-to-hand fighting, they were able to respond quickly and effectively to the requirements of musket warfare.

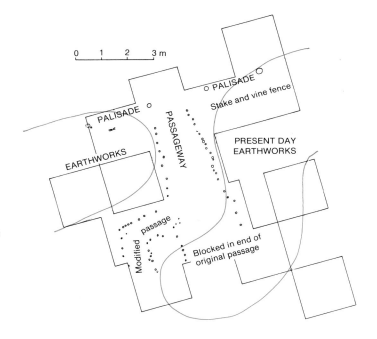

0 1 2 3 m

PALISADE

PALISADE

PASSAGEWAY

Stake and vine fence

PRESENT DAY EARTHWORKS

EARTHWORKS

Modified passage

Blocked in end of original passage

An artist's reconstruction (below) of the defended gateway at Takahanga Pa; the light stake and vine fence is continued from the passageway along the front of the main palisades which were set behind the earthworks. (South Island pa defenses were not usually elaborately carved.) The small house in the background is a reconstruction of that which was excavated upon the same site and which bore evidence of having been occupied well into the European period.
The photograph (below left) clearly shows the burnt stumps of the fence stakes which defined both an original straight-through passageway, and a later 'hooked' modification to one side. Burnt bracken, used as tinder, a broken patu, a musket ball, and human remains, all served to verify the story of the raid.

Julie O'Brien/CM

All this may be evidence that there was no large-scale inter-tribal warfare in the early period in New Zealand. (It would not preclude violence between individuals, or even small groups.) It could also be that there was a quite different form of warfare in which fortified positions and stone weapons were not used. On balance, however, it seems likely that warfare was virtually absent, being unnecessary in a society which seems to have had a largely itinerant way of life and a population that must have been fairly thinly spread throughout the country for some centuries after first settlement. Only later with the extinction of species such as the moa and the loss of large tracts of forest was there greater competition for resources. Certainly, the spread of agriculture with its associated permanent villages, the increasing value placed on greenstone, and the growing concentration of population, particularly in the northern parts of the North Island in the late prehistoric period, must have created more likely conditions for inter-tribal discord.

While it is certain that there was some warfare in New Zealand, at least in the later prehistoric period, we cannot be sure of its frequency or intensity, nor of the number of people killed in such engagements. (One of the other comparative rarities in New Zealand archaeological sites is the remains of people who have died violently.) We can be quite sure, however, that there was a great upsurge in fighting with the advent of the musket. Those who possessed muskets could kill at a distance and without any risk to themselves. Furthermore, quite small parties so armed could overcome very large groups armed only with traditional weapons. It was the possession of muskets, coupled with his own abilities as a strategist,

which allowed Te Rauparaha and his chosen warriors to decimate and demoralise the numerically greatly superior Ngai Tahu forces in Canterbury and Marlborough in the early 1830s. Hongi Hika made equal depredations among the tribes in northern New Zealand. During this period of inter-tribal musket warfare, traditional pa sites were sometimes modified to better suit the new style of fighting, while the defenses on others, such as Onawe in Akaroa Harbour, were specifically constructed with musket attacks in mind, although still retaining many traditional features.

One aspect of prehistoric life which also seems to have increased with the advent of the musket is cannibalism. There is slight archaeological evidence that this may have occurred at times during the whole of the prehistoric period, although it is not always easy to determine this from the remains found on sites; the effects of cremation upon a human body, for example, may be mistaken for those of cooking it for consumption. But cannibalism was definitely being practised at the time of Cook's

Elevated vantage points (right) were frequently utilised as defended positions. The summit of this small volcanic lahar at Parapara has been greatly modified by terracing, defensive earthworks, and pits.

Te Heuheu's old pah of *Waitahanui, Lake Taupo,* handcoloured lithograph after the original by George Angas. Although the pa had been deserted for some years when Angas depicted this scene, it shows the extent and scale of the fortifications still in use in the nineteenth century. Note that the warriors in the foreground are carrying muskets.

first visit in 1769; the name Cannibal Cove in Queen Charlotte Sound was given by Cook because it was here that he and his men obtained their first indisputable evidence of this practice among the Maoris.

As with warfare, we cannot be sure how frequent cannibalism was in prehistoric times, nor the reason for its practice; Sir Joseph Banks was informed that some of those eaten, whose remains he saw in Queen Charlotte Sound, had been killed as a result of a tribal skirmish.

However, we do know that along with the increased killing, which occurred during the musket wars, went an enormous increase in cannibalism. Early European eyewitness accounts tell of the mass consumption of human flesh by

Te Rauparaha and his men subsequent to his 1830s raids on the Ngai Tahu; in one instance he used a European ship to convey many baskets of human flesh, obtained in a raid on a pa at Akaroa, back to his own stronghold on Kapiti Island. It is suggested that the reason for this increase is that prior to European arrival inter-tribal warfare and associated activities were largely ritualised. This would have resulted in much less killing — possibly only a few individuals — before the encounter was broken off with honour satisfied on at least one, and possibly both, sides. Ritual would also account for the lack of archaeological evidence of large-scale battles as well as the ornate and formalised nature of many Maori weapons.

The earthworks of many Maori pas are of a type commonly referred to as 'ditch and bank', as seen on this well-preserved site at Pukewaranga. Excavations at several pas have shown that the associated palisading was not necessarily on the top of the bank or wall. A great deal of labour was involved in constructing earthworks such as these by hand with the aid of only digging sticks and flax baskets.

Nigel Prickett

Kaiapohia, the paramount pa of the South Island Ngai Tahu people, from a historic plan made in 1870. Both natural and artificial features were used for defense, although these were insufficient to deter the musket-bearing Ngati Toa, under Te Rauparaha, who sacked and burnt the pa in 1831.

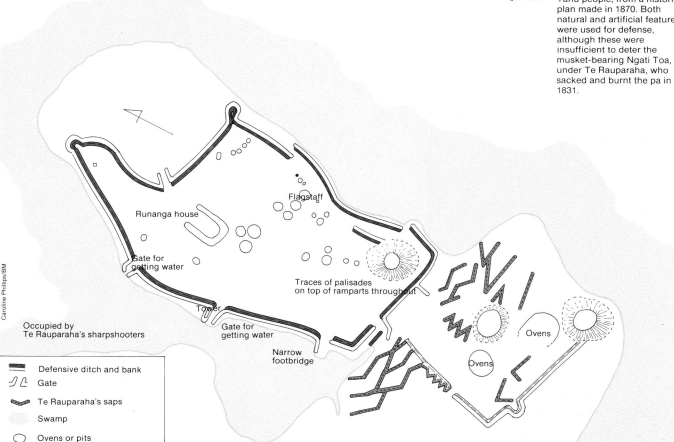

Caroline Phillips/BM

Runanga house

Flagstaff

Gate for getting water

Traces of palisades on top of ramparts throughout

Tower

Gate for getting water

Ovens

Narrow footbridge

Ovens

Ovens

Occupied by Te Rauparaha's sharpshooters

Defensive ditch and bank

Gate

Te Rauparaha's saps

Swamp

Ovens or pits

Classic Arts

THE spread of agriculture, tied to its seasonal plantings and harvesting, and the accompanying development of more permanent settlements now allowed more time to be spent on activities not strictly related to the needs of survival. Much of what we know about the arts, as practised by the prehistoric Maoris, dates from this later or classical period and reached what some consider to be the acme of its expression in the elaborate ornamental wood carving that today dominates most museum displays. Permanence meant that carvings could be larger, more elaborate and complex than those made when the population was partially itinerant. These now found expression and form in the carved meeting houses, war canoes and storehouse fronts familiar to most New Zealanders today. Interestingly, most of the work still in existence dates from the nineteenth century and was done with metal tools. Nevertheless, it does to a large extent reflect the designs and traditions of the late prehistoric era.

One of the best historical accounts we have of wood carving comes from Sydney Parkinson, who in 1769 wrote:

The men have a particular tafte for carving: their boats, paddles, boards to put on their houfes, tops of walking fticks, and even their boats valens, are carved in a variety of flourifhes, turnings and windings, that are unbroken; but their favourite figure feems to be a volute, or fpiral, which they vary many ways, fingle, double, and triple, and with as much truth as if done from mathematical draughts: yet the only inftruments we have feen are a chizzel, and an axe made of ftone. Their fancy, indeed, is very wild and extravagant, and I have feen no imitations of nature in any of their performances,

unlefs the head, and the heart-fhaped tongue hanging out of the mouth of it, may be called natural.

Many specimens were collected by the early European visitors, and important examples of the more portable eighteenth-century carved wooden artifacts are now held in museums worldwide. These include trinket boxes (*waka huia*), bird snare supports, hafts for ceremonial adzes (*toki pou tangata*), door lintels and other parts of buildings, and sternposts and bow pieces of canoes.

Generally, the ornamentation used on these late wood carvings comprises highly stylised figures and conventionalised patterns, and differs from many of the earlier carvings in its predominently curvilinear style.

As in the earlier rock art, the most commonly depicted forms are human beings, although normal anatomical proportions are not adhered to — in this respect they follow a convention adopted elsewhere in Polynesia. It has been suggested that the deliberate avoidance

This ornately carved monument (right) to Te Wherowhero's favourite daughter, at Raroera Pa, was recorded by the artist G. F. Angas. It is typical of the complex wood carvings executed with the advent of metal tools — in this example an old bayonet.

Waka huia (trinket boxes) (below right) were made to hold personal ornaments, particularly those relating to the head. Many were symbolically decorated in prehistoric times, although some which were made for trade with Europeans were carved elaborately merely for aesthetic reasons.

Some of the most ornate carving of the late prehistoric and early historic period can be seen on war-canoe bow pieces (below). These often featured elaborate openwork spiral designs or pitau linking the full-bodied figurehead to the body of the canoe.

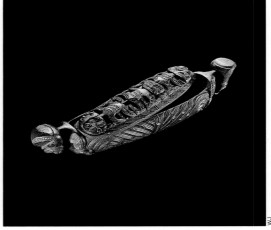

of realism may be because the human forms represent deified ancestors and gods. The figures nearly always have flexed legs and usually have flexed arms, although one arm may go to the mouth or the pubic region. Commonly, only three fingers are portrayed on each hand with the thumb projecting backwards, and the eyes may be inlaid with eliptical or round pieces of paua (*Haliotis*) shell. A tongue protruding from a figure-of-eight shaped mouth is also a characteristic feature. The human form is carved both frontally and in profile, the latter being stylised to produce what is known as a 'manaia' figure, and which appears to have developed from half a frontal figure. In these, the mouth (which derived from half the figure-of-eight shape) often has a beak-like appearance, suggesting a bird-headed man. Another development of the human form is the 'marakihau', in which a single elongated leg forms a tail-like appendage to the body. In many carvings, the stylised human figures themselves are in turn decorated with curvilinear motifs, including double spirals. The double spiral features in many carvings, particularly the more elaborate bow pieces of war canoes, and there has been much speculation as to its origin with suggestions ranging from diffusion from Melanesia — and even from the Mediterranean — to it being developed from the shape of a young unfolding fern frond. However, in rock art there appears to be a progression over time from concentric circles to single spirals, and then to double spirals; it seems unlikely that the wood carving design has a different origin — the double spiral almost certainly evolved in New Zealand.

Early European accounts indicate that the most prominent place for carved wooden figures was on, and in, important buildings. Many elaborately carved meeting houses and storehouses were erected in the nineteenth century. The meeting houses had intricately carved bargeboards, threshold planks and entrance lintels; the wall posts were of wide flat slabs of timber, exposed on the interior, carved in stylised human forms named after ancestors, and exposed rafters were usually painted in red, black and white patterns; storehouses on raised piles sometimes had the whole front surface covered with ornamental carving. (Such carved houses were often lined with interior *tukutuku* panels of naturally coloured or dyed reeds, flax and grasses. These do not survive archaeologically and are known from ethnographic accounts.)

Although the introduction of metal tools undoubtedly led to this efflorescence of ornamental wood carving, some very elaborate work using stone tools on prehistoric war canoes was reported by early European visitors. Most spectacular were the tall sternposts and the bow pieces, intricately carved in open fretwork designs from single pieces of wood.

In contrast to archaeologically recovered wood carvings of the early period, most of which are small, some quite large pieces of classic carving have been recovered from swamps and caves, almost all in the North Island, where they have been preserved in dry or anaerobic conditions. These have included some very ornate pieces, particularly lintels and other house parts. Most had obviously been deliberately placed where they were found, probably for security. This was certainly so with the elaborately carved bone chests which were placed in caves, especially in the northern part of the North Island.

This storehouse or pataka stood at Maketu in the Bay of Plenty, where it belonged to the Arawa chief Te Pokiha Taranui, otherwise known as Major Fox. The house was built in the 1870s, after the introduction of steel tools, and is unusually large and ornate, combining European construction methods and corrugated iron roofing with traditional Maori art forms. The carving of the large figure over the door represents Tama te Kapua, traditionally the captain of the Arawa canoe. Other ancestors are commemorated in the carved panels.

*'They hung to them
by Strings many
very different things
. . . in short
everything they
could get which was
either valuable or
ornamental . . .
Besides these the
women sometimes
wear bracelets and
anklets made of
bones of birds, shells
etc . . .'*

JOSEPH BANKS, 1770

The remains of stone tools, the carved objects themselves, and the chips of wood that are sometimes found on sites reveal the processes used in prehistoric woodworking. There is little evidence that wood was ever sawn (although saw-edged flaked stone blades do occur on sites). Instead, the principal instrument used to shape a piece of wood was the adze. These were produced in a variety of shapes and weights for different purposes. Some had a wide cutting edge and are presumed to have been used for the same purposes as the European steel adze, for cutting with the grain to reduce the size of a piece of wood and produce a relatively flat surface. Others had a relatively narrow cutting edge, and with proportionately more weight behind each blow would have been effective in cutting across the grain. Narrow-edged adze heads are more common on early sites, whereas chisels occur more frequently on later sites, indicating that changes took place in woodworking methods, and hence in the designs that were being produced.

The preferred timber for carving was totara (*Podocarpus*) — it is durable and has a structure that allows it to be cut cleanly both with and across the grain.

Ethnographic evidence indicates that the chisel blade was hafted to a wooden handle set in line with the blade; there is, somewhat surprisingly, no evidence of handles being set at right angles to the blade as was done with adzes and tattooing chisels. These records also indicate that in use the end of the handle was struck with a wooden mallet, but it is inevitable that much fine work was done solely by hand pressure. Experimental work with such chisels has shown that those made of nephrite can produce results very similar to those of modern steel chisel blades but it takes about three times as long. Blades of softer stones such as argillite that were mostly used in earlier prehistoric times are not so suitable for intricate design work, since they cannot take such an acute bevel or sharp edge and become blunt more quickly. It is likely that the elaborate curvilinear designs were developed only after the increased use of nephrite tools from about 400 years ago.

Personal ornaments, like wood carvings, had been made in New Zealand since the early period of Maori occupation. Similarly, they had undergone many stylistic changes and modifications so that by the time the first Europeans arrived, many of the personal ornaments favoured during the early period (*see pages 48-49*) had ceased to be made or worn (although some basic types persisted for the whole of the prehistoric period). It is, of course, easier to change the design of a purely decorative object than it is to modify a utility item such as an adze head, the basic form of which is controlled by its function.

Most ornaments were still manufactured

The ornately carved gateway at Maketu Pa, shortly after the pa had been occupied by the Ngati Pikiao tribe of the Arawa confederation. This is one of the earliest photographs of Maori carving and was taken by the artist John Kinder in 1865.

from shell, bone, ivory and stone, but the principal stone used for ornaments was now pounamu (greenstone or nephrite). Pendants, both for the neck and particularly for the ears, predominated while necklaces or bracelets — consisting of a number of separate units strung together — had become less common. Nor, it seems, were shells in their natural form so often used, although teeth, now including those of humans, were still popular.

Once the means had been developed to work pounamu, it was increasingly used in ornament manufacture, particularly so with the onset of European trade. It has even been suggested that the best known of greenstone ornaments, the hei tiki, was not a truly prehistoric ornament at all, or was at least very rare in pre-European times. But this is an exaggeration; it is described by a number of early writers, including Banks who observed in 1770 that the men 'often had the figure of a distorted man made of the green talk [talc]'. Monneron, who accompanied De Surville in 1764 had noted that the Maoris wore around their necks 'a kind of image made of stone resembling a jade. This image seems to be squatting on its heels.'

Such descriptions confirm that the hei tiki was not only worn in pre-European times but that its usage was widespread and perhaps not uncommon. Ear pendants of greenstone seem to have been even more popular, particularly the straight variety or kuru, some reaching

considerable lengths. There was also a wide variety of other greenstone pendants — some rare or unique. Among the more common were stylised fish hooks (hei matau) and small adze heads and chisel blades that had a hole drilled through them so that they could be suspended around the neck.

Although most of the more ornate ornaments held in museum collections are clearly of post-European origin, there are many which are definitely prehistoric. Some have been found on archaeological sites, particularly in the South Island, but as fortuitous discoveries rather than the result of deliberate excavation. On the other hand, the simpler greenstone pendants are not infrequently excavated during archaeological excavations in both the North and South Islands. Although most of the sites on which they occur are of late prehistoric age (and some were still occupied during the early European period), others date back 400 years, indicating that greenstone ornaments were being worn soon after they were able to be manufactured.

(Continued on page 88)

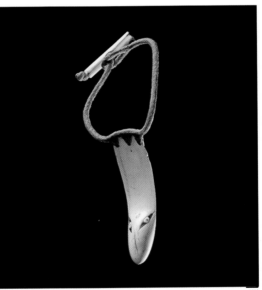

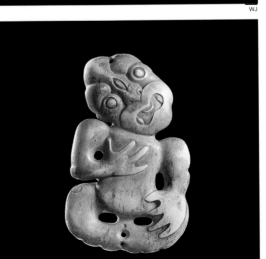

This rei puta (pierced ivory) ornament was collected during Cook's visits to New Zealand. Both in style, and in its use of a sperm whale tooth, it more closely reflects the ornaments of the early Polynesian period in New Zealand, and undoubtedly evolved from the wearing of drilled, but otherwise unmodified teeth. The distal ornamentation is a simplified human face.

The Heads of six men natives of New Zealand . . . by Sydney Parkinson (centre). Early artists liked to depict this sort of elaborate personal decoration and their work may give a distorted view of the extent to which it was employed at a daily level.

A delightful example of the well-known hei tiki, executed in ivory, rather than the more usual greenstone. Although found on Banks Peninsula, the style suggests it originated in the North Island.

GREENSTONE

*The most common is a kind of stone, of a green which is sometimes pale,
sometimes milky, and sometimes quite bright . . .*
LIEUTENANT POTTIER DE L'HORME, *St Jean Baptiste, 1769.*

GREENSTONE, known to the Maoris as pounamu, and technically called nephrite, is today the best known of the stone materials used in prehistoric times. It certainly excited the attention of early European visitors, who often referred to it as green 'talk' (talc) or jasper, and particularly noted its use for ornaments and weapons. Perhaps because of such attention it is now commonly assumed that greenstone was always used by the Maoris for their most valued artifacts. Archaeological evidence, however, indicates that although they were aware of it, and even made some use of it in the early period, greenstone did not come into widespread general use until quite late in the prehistoric era. The simple reason for this is that the flake technology used for working fine-grained stone in the early period was unsuitable for working greenstone satisfactorily.

Nephrite is an extremely hard and tough stone with a structure made up of closely matted crystal fibres, and as such is not amenable to controlled flaking. Flaked nephrite artifacts are known from a number of relatively early sites and it is clear that the early Maoris recognised its desirable features of hardness and beauty, and persisted in their attempts to find a suitable method of working it. (Nephrite should not be confused with the much softer green mineral, bowenite, called tangiwai by the Maoris. It was much more easily worked, but of little value for tools, being primarily used for ornaments.)

A site where early attempts had been made to manufacture adze heads from nephrite was discovered near Kowhitirangi in Westland in 1969. Here hundreds of waste flakes were scattered over a working area which also yielded a number of crudely shaped and ugly adze head 'blanks'. Such results must have been dispiriting to craftsmen accustomed to working with rocks such as argillite and basalt.

It is not surprising that this working site was in Westland as this is one of the main sources of nephrite. The early Maoris are hardly likely to have begun to transport the raw material any distance around the country before it was of any great use to them. Nor is it likely that they ever gathered much of their nephrite from the actual rock source — usually in rough mountainous terrain. Their technology did not allow them to cut very large boulders of such a tough material and they were almost certainly restricted to small boulders, cobbles and pebbles gathered from streams and beaches.

Eventually, and probably not more than about 400 years ago, a technique for working greenstone was perfected. Instead of flaking, the greenstone was sawed into shape using narrow-edged pieces of abrasive stone such as sandstone. The 'teeth' of the saw or abrader were sharp angular grains of sand. The process was sometimes aided by sprinkling loose grains of a hard sand, such as quartz, into the cut once it was commenced, while water

was added to prevent clogging and to allow the 'teeth' to 'bite' more cleanly. Opposing 'scarf' cuts were frequently made on both sides of a slab of greenstone until they nearly met, when the two portions could be broken apart with a sharp blow.

With objects such as adze heads, chisels and meres, which have a relatively simple shape, the basic outline was relatively easily achieved by sawing to a suitable shape a piece of greenstone of appropriate thickness — often a water-worn cobble, although sometimes a slab might be sawn from a larger boulder in the first place. The object was then ground down into its final shape, using a hoanga or grindstone, and then polished using finer rock.

Items with a lot of surface detail such as the hei tiki were also sawn initially to achieve the basic shape, and

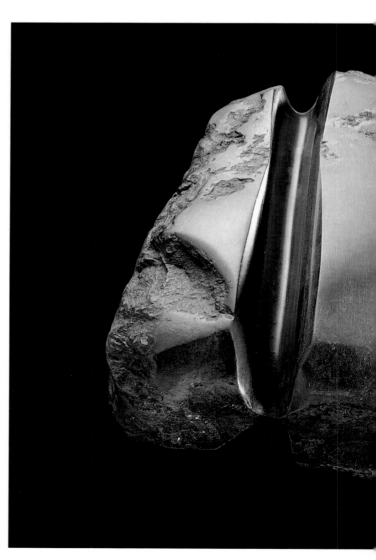

then the features were ground into the surface using smaller and finer abrasive tools. Abrasion was also used for drilling holes in greenstone ornaments to allow them to be suspended, and also in meres to take a thong so that it could be attached to the wrist. For this simple cord drills were used with abrasive stone drill points. Sand and water were also used in this operation and, in the manner of scarf cutting, conically shaped holes were drilled from opposing sides to meet in the middle.

Working greenstone took a long time and it has even been suggested that it might have taken several generations to produce a large mere or particularly ornate hei tiki. However, this is not supported by the observations of Charles Heaphy, who in 1846 saw Maoris working greenstone at Teremakau on the West Coast:

The process does not appear so tedious as has been supposed; a month sufficing, apparently, for the completion of a meri out of the rough but appropriately shapen slab.

Heaphy's observations are borne out by modern experimental work using Maori stone-working techniques.

The most suitable method of shaping greenstone was by 'scarf cutting' with an abrasive stone. This block of stone from Okains Bay shows an adze head partly cut out. More often, however, the raw material was in thinner or smaller pieces of stone that did not require so much laborious work.

Hei matau — an ornament or amulet in the shape of a stylised fish hook. This beautiful 131 mm high specimen came from the shores of Lake Ellesmere. When obtained last century it was thought to be a 'greenstone implement for cutting hair'.

Clearly, greenstone was highly esteemed by the Maoris in the later prehistoric period, filling the place which is accorded to gold in European society. This persisted into historical times when the main stimulus for Te Rauparaha's devastating raids on the South Island was his desire to obtain adequate supplies of this highly prized material, unobtainable in the north. The upsurge of intertribal warfare which arose during the latter half of the prehistoric period may also be attributable in part to the same desire to obtain a neighbour's greenstone as part of the spoils of war. (There are many stories of villagers hiding their greenstone in a swamp or other hiding place when faced with attack.)

Items of relatively indestructible greenstone, finished or unfinished, sometimes broken, even pieces of unworked raw material, are found on archaeological sites all over the country, although in greatest abundance in those sites where artifacts were manufactured — usually in the South Island.

One of the richest manufacturing sites was Murdering Beach in Otago, which was 'dug' systematically (as well as archaeologically investigated) for at least a century. Augustus Hamilton, who was thoroughly familiar with the collections from that site, estimated that by 1900 three and a half hundredweight (178 kilograms) of worked nephrite and 'near-nephrite' had been removed from Murdering Beach — certainly the largest concentration to have been found of any site — with a remarkably high proportion of fine and varied ornaments.

More recent investigations suggest that the specialised industry on this site, although started in prehistoric times, reached a height of production after 1800 when there arose an unprecedented demand for such items to exchange for European goods. The European interest in greenstone artifacts — particularly the hei tiki — resulted in increased manufacture of such items for trade all over the country. Ornament manufacture was also greatly assisted from this time by using European lapidary techniques, while the advent of metal axes and chisels, as well as muskets, vastly superior to those tools and weapons of nephrite, no doubt released quantities of stone which would otherwise have been used for weapons or implements.

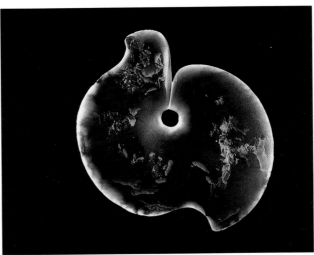

Ornaments of shell, bone and ivory are also not infrequently located on archaeological sites. They include hei tiki and other elaborate pieces as well as the simpler forms of neck and ear pendants. One of the more interesting ivory ornaments is the rei puta (pierced ivory) which is a tongue-shaped pendant made from a sperm whale tooth cut lengthwise; the distal (pointed) end was usually decorated with carving of facial features, particularly eyes. These were being worn at the time of Cook's first visit and Banks described them as 'the tooth of a whale cut slauntwise'. Parkinson also recorded them in his drawings, while Cook collected a fine example which is still in existence. These must have developed from the use of whale teeth for pendants which was popular throughout the Pacific and in early New Zealand (*see page 49*). Two of these have been recovered from archaeological sites, both of relatively late age. A complete specimen was found on Oruarangi Pa, near Thames, in the 1930s by a private collector, while the distal end of a rei puta, with inset greenstone eyes, was excavated archaeologically from a small pa site at Clarence in the South Island (*see page 15*).

The teeth of humans, dogs, seals and sharks were also commonly worn as pendants during the late prehistoric period. Writers such as Banks also recorded Maoris wearing feathers, small bird skins, moss and wood, particularly as ear ornaments. For obvious reasons these do not survive long and none have been recovered archaeologically but that does not mean that they were not worn frequently in the pre-European era, perhaps during most of the prehistoric period.

A quite different ornament was the head comb or heru. Some combs were made of separate pieces of wood, which formed the teeth, and were bound together at the top. One-piece combs were made of whale bone or wood and were worn decoratively in the top knot rather than having a strictly utilitarian function of holding the hair in place. Both kinds have been found on archaeological sites, although seldom in complete form. Bone combs, both complete and fragmentary, were recovered along with the rei puta from Oruarangi Pa, but the most important archaeological discovery was that of a whole series of wooden one-piece combs from a swamp at Kauri Point Pa. These seem to have been deposited over about 200 years for what were probably ceremonial reasons.

Cloak pins, fashioned like large needles and often curved, were generally made of bone or ivory. These too are not uncommon on archaeological sites. Although sometimes regarded as ornaments they had a primarily utilitarian function.

Another typically classic art form was tattooing. The most common archaeological evidence of this is the special type of tattooing 'chisel' found on sites. (These also occur on early sites, but are

Chisels (right) were used for applying decoration to both flesh and wood. The toothed examples on the left were for tattooing, those on the right for fine wood carving.

Body and limb tattooing (below right) was not as common as facial tattoos, although examples were recorded by several early European visitors, including D'Urville. From *Voyage de la Corvette Astrolabe*.

An early photograph (below) of an unidentified man with a facial tattoo or moko.

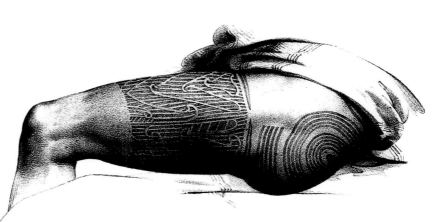

the only evidence we have that this art form was practised in the archaic period.) Tattooing chisels were nearly always made of bone, in both early and late sites, and had a serrated cutting edge like a small comb with very short teeth. This comb was fixed at right angles to a wooden handle like that of an adze. Black pigment was applied to the teeth, they were pressed against the skin, and driven in by the other end of the comb being tapped with a light mallet. Descriptions and sketches made by early European visitors indicate that Maori men were often tattooed on various parts of the body, particularly the face and thighs, but women on the lips and chin only. Dried male heads that were collected in the early decades of the nineteenth century provide a good record of tattooing patterns in use at that time, although with many of these relics the tattooing was done or enhanced just before or even after death to increase their sale value. These show a predominance of curvilinear designs, although there are reports of rectilinear designs as well.

Another art form practised by the prehistoric Maoris was music and archaeological evidence of this is supported by the observations of the early European explorers.

One of the earliest historical records comes from Captain de Clesmeur, who accompanied Marion du Fresne on his ill-fated 1771-73 voyage:

We have only seen three kinds of musical instruments in this country, of which one is a sort of trumpet which can be heard a very long way off. I can bear witness to this, having heard its sound the day we burnt down the first village. They have also a species of flute, made in two pieces, bound well together, into which they blow at the thick end. The smaller end and three little holes are closed with the fingers, and serve to vary the tones a little. The third instrument is almost the same, but is much smaller; into this they blow with their noses.

As his account implies, trumpets were probably used more as signalling devices than as musical instruments, and would have been sounded at the first sign of danger. These included a large wooden trumpet measuring up to two metres long, a shell trumpet using the trumpet shell, *Charonia*, and a short wooden flutelike bugle also referred to as a flageolet.

Flutes were made of both wood and bone (and in later centuries from human bone). Although it is unlikely that wooden flutes would survive, bone flutes have been found on sites dating back several centuries. One from a pa site traditionally known as Te Raka-a-hine-atea in North Otago, which was occupied in the late eighteenth century, is made from a 130-millimetre length of albatross wing bone, and has three holes drilled along one side. (There is also a small hole at one end, presumably to allow the flute to be suspended on a string.) Similar flutes from other sites are often decorated with series of diagonally incised lines. Blowing across one end and stopping the holes with the fingers produces a variety of notes. While it is possible for a skilled 'flautist' to produce European tunes on such flutes, the spacing of the holes shows that they were designed to produce notes at closer intervals than the usual European scale.

A short flute, usually of wood and often intricately carved, was also used. It generally had three holes like the flute described, but with the end curved round at right angles. These are often called 'nose flutes' in the belief that they were played with the nose — which they can be, although much better control can be achieved with the mouth. Some writers have referred to these as 'whistles', but they can actually produce very pure flute-like tones.

Three different varieties of Maori 'flutes' are illustrated here: the koauau, a simple tube of bone open at both ends and pierced with finger holes; the pu torino, made of wood with a sound opening in the middle of the upper surface; and an elaborately carved whistle-flute, often referred to as a nguru or nose-flute.

A difficulty when trying to portray the physical characteristics of the prehistoric Maori is that direct comparisons with present-day Maoris are largely invalid. There has been much intermarriage with other races, and a radically changed environment, different culture, new foods and improved living conditions would all have had on impact in the last 200 years. So we are almost wholly dependent upon the limited observations of the earliest European visitors, and the almost equally limited archaeological evidence, to try to put together a picture of just what the Maoris looked like.

Although Abel Tasman was the first European to record a description of the Maoris, it was Joseph Banks who provided more pertinent details on the 'Indians' as they were then called (the term 'Maoris' did not come into general use until the late 1830s). He described the men as being about the size of the larger Europeans, stout, clean limbed and active, fleshy but not fat, vigorous and nimble with much strength, and having firmness and agility in their movements; the women were rather smaller than European women, and were more lively, airy and more laughter-loving than the men. They appeared to have very sound health and had little or no disease.

The references to height must be seen in the context of that time. We have no accurate record of the stature of the average European then, although undoubtedly it was much less than today. Nevertheless, from the limited data available, an estimate of about 165 cm can be made for European men of Cook's time. By comparison an average height of 168.3 cm was obtained by an army surgeon, Arthur Thomson, in 1859, when he measured 147 'better fed' adult Maori men, while in 1919, Peter Buck measured 400 Maori soldiers who claimed to be full-blooded, obtaining an average height of

170.9 cm. Although these were small, non-representative groups, the results suggest that there may have been an overall increase in height between 1859 and 1919, probably resulting from a more regular food supply, better living conditions and medical care. By extending this argument back into the prehistoric period a figure of 167 cm is a likely estimate of the average height of Maori men at the time of Cook's arrival, some 20 mm taller than the Europeans.

No early measurements are available for Maori women, but several observers noted that they were noticeably shorter than men. The average female is generally about 6 per cent less in height than the average male; a study of Hawaiian Polynesians early this century showed that the difference was 6.2 per cent. This is in keeping with the observations of Banks and others, and a suggested average height for prehistoric Maori women is about 156.6 cm.

Once an average living height has been estimated for a race of people, formulae can be devised from which individual stature can be calculated from one or more limb bones where skeletal material is available. Although only limited studies of this sort have been done on material recovered from burials — today always undertaken with the consent and often interest of the local Maori community — there have been some interesting results. For example, Canterbury people appear to have been taller than those living in Marlborough, and both groups were generally taller than North Islanders.

As well as giving information on height, the general size of skeletons and the muscle attachment sites on the bones confirm the early reports that the prehistoric Maori men were relatively tall, well-built, active people. The length of their legs in proportion to their bodies

Woman of New Zealand and *Man of New Zealand*, both by William Hodges, the artist on Cook's second voyage (1772-1775). The tendency of some of the European artists to romanticise their subjects means that their work is of limited value to researchers today. In this portrait of a warrior in ceremonial dress, the spectacular is emphasised at the expense of the ordinary. Beards were unusual in full-blooded Maoris.

was shorter than that of Europeans, and there is a tendency for the long bones — particularly the femur — to be slightly bowed.

Skulls have long been a favourite topic of study, and although some different conclusions have been reached in the past, there is no doubt today that the shape of the Maori skull is typically Polynesian with, of course, a range of variation in individuals. Two of the Maori skull's best known features are the pentagonal shape when viewed from behind and the 'rocker jaw', a term that describes the curved shape of the bottom of the mandible, which often allows the bone to 'rock' when placed on a flat surface; a European mandible tends to be flat or concave on the bottom. While the percentage of 'rocker jaws' has been quoted as about 80 per cent for Polynesians, the distinctive curved shape is present in a higher proportion of mandibles, even although they may not actually 'rock'. (There is no skeletal evidence of any non-Polynesian people having lived in New Zealand in prehistoric times.)

Philip Houghton, who has made a detailed study of human skeletal remains, has noted how occupational activities sometimes resulted in actual skeletal changes during a person's life. A groove sometimes present on the clavicle (collar-bone) appears to have been caused by this bone being forced down on the upper surface of the top rib. As well, an area for ligament attachment on the under-side of the bone is often roughened through it having been subjected to considerable strain. It is most likely that these effects have been caused by consistent paddling of canoes. Dr Houghton has found that the grooves occur on both male and female skeletons from the early prehistoric period but only on males from later

centuries, suggesting that there was a change in male and female roles, perhaps related to the development of warfare in later times.

Most people today expect to live 'three score and ten' years. In the past the average life span was much less than this. Bones and teeth provide invaluable clues on how long prehistoric people lived, about aspects of their health, certain diseases and misadventures, and even the size of their families.

The expected times of eruption of both deciduous and permanent teeth from infancy to adulthood are widely known, and more precise data on the probable ranges for both tooth eruption and development are readily available. From puberty to about 30 years is the main period for the fusion of the various bone epiphyses — on the long bones of the limbs, for instance, the small cap-like epiphyses become joined to the ends of the bones in a fairly regular progression. Together, the evidence of the teeth and of epiphyseal union provide good indicators of age during the first three decades of life. For older people the amount of wear on the biting surfaces of the teeth can also give an indication of how long they have been exposed, but as this is largely affected by diet, its use has to be restricted to within a group having the same living conditions.

Studies of the remains of prehistoric New Zealanders from throughout the country have shown that on average adults did not live much longer than the early thirties. With somewhat limited medical knowledge, they suffered far more from the effects of accident, disease, and sometimes malnutrition than is commonly realised.

A sketch by J.A. Gilfillan entitled *A settler bartering tobacco for potatoes and pumpkins.* Those carrying backloads may be slaves and, if so, their depiction here appears accurate and is reflected in contemporary accounts. The European, however, is shown here disproportionately tall in relation to the Maoris — probably for compositional reasons.

Hocken Library

91

It is harder to determine how many people actually reached adulthood because relatively few children's bones have been preserved, both because they are softer and do not last so well in the ground, and because the burial of children tended to be undertaken with less care than for adults. An analysis of burials associated with a small Wairarapa community, however, indicated that half of them died within the first few years of life. Similar results have been obtained from Hawaii, and this is in keeping with the 50 per cent or higher infant death ratio noted from Europe in past times.

During childhood, if a person is subjected to severe disease or malnutrition, a faint line of 'arrested growth' may be left in the long bones of the arms and legs and can be detected by X-ray examination. As a rule, these Harris lines, as they are usually called, do not occur frequently in the bones of adult prehistoric New Zealanders, indicating that they had a relatively healthy childhood. It could also suggest, however, that only the healthy survived.

An interesting aspect of tooth wear is that in the early centuries of occupation, birds (including moas) and seals were plentiful for the relatively small human population, and the peoples' teeth were generally sound without caries, abscesses or undue wear. At the Wairau Bar settlement 600 years ago, the majority of residents retained all their teeth, which were in excellent condition and showed only little or moderate signs of wear. Later, however, more people had to share much diminished food resources, and greater dependence on harsh, gritty foods like fern root and shellfish from sandy beaches resulted in very worn teeth in adults. The first molars often

became dislocated sideways because (it has been suggested) of the habit of pulling pieces of fern root sideways through the mouth to extract the edible starchy component of this fibrous material. Sometimes a tooth lying almost sideways in the jaw continued to be used so that the roots, normally protected through being embedded in the jaw, also became worn. The dislocation and the wear often led to abscesses in the jaw and to loss of teeth. Quite apart from the effect on general health that would have been caused by jaw abscesses, the lack of effective teeth must have severely affected a person's ability to survive, especially when the principal foodstuffs required much chewing, biting and scraping. One woman living at Teviotdale in North Canterbury did manage to survive a number of years after the loss of her lower molars and pre-molars, and her remaining teeth becoming so worn as to be of little use. She had had several children, her elbows and knees had become arthritic, and she spent the final years of her life in a cave with only a dog for company, existing on a diet of mussels taken from the nearby rocks. Both she and the dog suffocated when bush surrounding the cave entrance was burnt. Her remains were found, curled up on her bedding with the dog alongside; she was just 30 years old.

It was possible to tell that the Teviotdale woman had borne children from the presence of small pits alongside joints in the pelvis. These were caused by the softening and loosening of ligaments towards the end of pregnancy to allow the pelvis to open up slightly during childbirth. The presence of these pits is a clear sign that the pelvis belonged to a woman who had a

In the nineteenth century
Maori portraits were a favourite subject of photographers who would sometimes 'add' facial mokos to their subjects to increase the commercial value of their photographs. These two portraits of unidentified Maoris appear authentic however.

pregnancy, and the nature of the pitting can give some indication of the number of children borne, although there is, of course, no way of testing the accuracy of this indication in a prehistoric population. Studies suggest that it was common for women to bear three or four children. Actually, given the likelihood of a fairly high infant mortality and the fact that the population did achieve a reasonable rate of growth, four to five births per woman is more likely.

About the time of European settlement it was commonly noted that what were fairly minor or childhood ailments for Europeans sometimes had a drastic effect on the Maoris. They had no resistance to diseases such as measles, with the result that large numbers of them died. The reason for this is generally thought to be that these common diseases require a fairly large human population in which to survive; the figure of 6000 which has been suggested for measles, for instance, is much higher than the initial settlement population in New Zealand or that of the islands from which they came. Even if such diseases had been present, it would be difficult to find archaeological evidence for them because they would not have affected the bones or teeth, which are usually the only parts of the body to survive. What we do find are the indications of degenerative conditions that affect particularly the vertebrae of the lower back or the joints of the arms, legs and jaw. It is unusual not to find some 'lipping' of the lumbar vertebrae in a mature adult. Less common are conditions like the erosion of a North Canterbury girl's vertebrae which could well have been due to cancer — Harris lines indicated that she had suffered ill-health during the year prior to her

death, which is consistent with the time a malignant tumor would have been giving trouble.

With limited medical knowledge, people would have suffered continuously from ailments and conditions which today are easily treated. There are many examples of broken bones that have healed satisfactorily, although often the alignment is far from perfect and may have caused at least some discomfort. In others, breakages were inadequately treated and did not heal at all. A young man from Banks Peninsula had suffered a break just above his knee; the break had joined, but the end of the bone was at right angles to the shaft instead of being in line with it. He would have been unable to use his leg.

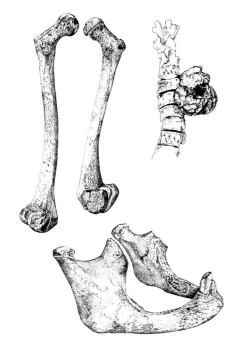

Julie O'Brien/CM

Reconstruction of a man (far left below) whose remains were found at Washpool, Wairarapa. This individual died nearly 500 years ago when he was about 45 years old, by which age most prehistoric people had advanced osteo-arthritis and few if any teeth. Drawing by Linden Cowell.

Archaeological evidence (left) of some of the hardships and problems of prehistoric life. A massive kidney stone alongside a young woman's vertebrae. Lower jawbone of an elderly woman who had lost all her teeth but one. The right femur of a young man which had broken; although the break healed, the end of the bone joined at right angles to its correct position making normal walking impossible.

In this 1974 excavation (below) at Takahanga, Kaikoura, a number of Maori burials, including the remains of a woman with a massive kidney stone (above), were found.

Linden Cowell/NM

93

Disposal of the Dead

LIKE other societies throughout the world, the prehistoric Maoris treated the disposal of their dead according to traditional customs and beliefs. The archaeological evidence of these disposal methods — which include burial in the ground, deposition in caves and sometimes cremation — indicates that they differed in a number of ways from those recorded by ethnologists. Disposal of bodies by water (at sea or in spring holes) is referred to traditionally and historically, but this has not been investigated archaeologically.

Although the relationship between archaeologists and the Maori community varies throughout the country, it is not uncommon for archaeologists to have opportunities to examine bones of the prehistoric dead with the approval, and often the interest, of Maori leaders. These bones, which may be uncovered through erosion or in the course of residential, commercial or national development, are invaluable for what they can tell us about the people of the past, providing clues to aspects of their state of health, certain diseases, and how long they lived.

Many ground burials have been excavated in New Zealand, some as the result of deliberate searches but most following accidental discovery. All have been relatively shallow, generally not more than 50–60 centimetres below the surface. Comparative studies also reveal that there were two main burial positions. Usually the body was placed in a folded position with the knees brought up against the chest. The folded body was put in a shallow grave, often lying on its left side, but sometimes with the head upright. Occasionally personal ornaments have been found with the remains; a cloak-pin in the area of the neck or chest can with reasonable certainty be taken to indicate the former presence of a cloak around the body. Red stains and pieces of red ochre show that at least part of the body, particularly the face, was sometimes painted before burial. This custom of folding the body before burial appears to have been prevalent throughout the whole prehistoric period. Six 'crouched' skeletons studied by Julius Haast at Sumner in 1873 were surely of moa-hunter age, as was that found at Fyffes, Kaikoura, in 1857. Most of the burials at Palliser Bay were also folded. Nevertheless, most crouched burials are

of a later period, as for example, those at Motutapu Island, Auckland, while at Takahanga, Kaikoura, they date to the earliest European period.

In many early prehistoric burials, however, the body was laid out full length, sometimes with the knees slightly flexed. A number in this position were excavated from the moa-hunter site at Wairau Bar in the 1940s. A typical example was that of an 'elderly' man (aged about 40 years) who had been placed face down in a 50-centimetre-deep grave with his head and feet turned to the left. One arm lay under his chest, while the other, with a bracelet of seven tooth-shaped units carved from moa bone, lay at his side. There was a necklace of 23 similar units around his neck, and a moa egg and four adze heads had been buried alongside. Radiocarbon dating has shown that he was buried about 650 years ago.

Some burial sites show that bodies have subsequently been removed, either wholly or in part. On Mt Wellington a shallow grave on a living terrace contained only a few remaining bones. The outline of a later pit showed that the rest had been removed, possibly for reburial or to obtain bones for manufacturing items. One grave that was investigated at Kaikoura was completely empty; at some time after burial the bones had been dug up and burnt nearby. Similar examples of digging up and burning bones have been found at Peketa, south of Kaikoura, and at Birdlings Flat, near Banks Peninsula; in some of these only part of the skeleton was removed, the remainder being left in the ground. No evidence of the burning of bones has been found at any very early site.

An interesting aspect of ground burials is that most of the graves for which we have good records are in the immediate vicinity of where people were living. Cave burials, on the other hand, were usually located at least a short distance away — doubtless because the people rarely lived in caves. (An exception was in Moa-bone Point Cave where a young man had been buried in the deep deposits of sand and midden refuse in the floor of the cave which had been occupied on and off for over 600 years. This was to all intents and purposes a ground burial which happened to be inside a cave.)

Human remains in caves fall into two categories. Many are 'secondary' burials, comprising bones only. The body appears to have been given an initial ground burial to allow the flesh to decompose, after which the bones were removed and placed in a rock cleft or cave. This method seems to have been common, particularly in the northern parts of New Zealand although examples are known from throughout the country. The practice was recorded from an early site at Palliser Bay in the Wairarapa where the bones of four children and an adult had been deposited in a cleft and it was still being observed at the time of European contact.

Sometimes, however, the whole body was

The two main burial positions adopted were folded and prone, the latter being more common on early sites. Artifacts and occasionally food items were sometimes buried alongside the body.

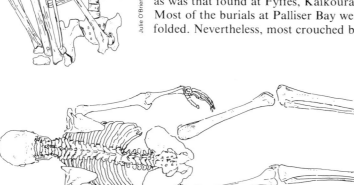

Julie O'Brien/CM

placed in a cave, and a good, though perhaps uncommonly elaborate, example is on Mary Island in Lake Hauroko. The body of a woman in her twenties had been propped up against some stakes in a sitting position on a low seat, her knees up to her chest, looking out of the cave's small entrance across the lake. She had a cloak of flax and feathers around her, and had been bound in position with lianes. Less elaborate cave burials have been found throughout New Zealand, and although some (as at Lake Taupo) have attracted a great deal of attention from a morbidly interested public, very few have been subjected to archaeological investigation: those that have been investigated date to within 200 years of European settlement.

In the early 1800s there was a well-developed trade with Europeans in dried human heads; surviving examples can now be found in museums throughout the world. In archaeological contexts, skulls have been found which have been modified in a manner consistent with the heads having been preserved, indicating that the drying of heads was a prehistoric custom. One was found in a burial cave in North Canterbury. Here, the body of a 30-year-old man had been propped up in a similar position to that of the Mary Island burial, looking out of the cave opening. His head had been cut off, dried, and then replaced on the body.

Evidence of a dried head being kept separate from the body was found in a small cave at Raupo Bay, Banks Peninsula, in 1935; this was of a 20-year-old woman. There were slight

In the late prehistoric period cave burial became more common with remains often being placed in relatively inaccessible, though none-the-less prominent, sites such as this crevice part way up a rock cliff on Banks Peninsula.

haematite stains on the region of the face, forehead and lower jaw. With it were two pendants, one of ivory and the other of greenstone, and six red-painted carved wooden panels which fitted together to form a box.

Similar carved or plain boxes which would have been suitable for holding bones have been found elsewhere in New Zealand, but in the north of the North Island a different form was used. These were commonly hollowed out of one piece of wood, usually had a fitting lid, and were typically carved in the form of a stylised human figure — most are females and it has been suggested that these represent the Maori goddess of death. They were used for storing disarticulated bones and usually placed in caves; all appear to be of late prehistoric age.

Artist's reconstruction of the burial of a moa hunter at Wairau Bar, based on the evidence of archaeological research. This site has become known for the number of burials there, but it was nevertheless primarily a workshop and general living area.

Geoffrey Cox/BM

III. The European Period

The First Europeans

*T*O the best of our knowledge the first non-Polynesians to visit New Zealand were Abel Tasman and his crew. This Dutch navigator, commanding the ships *Heemskerk* and *Zeehaen*, arrived in New Zealand waters in 1642, and although he never landed in New Zealand he did have a disastrous offshore encounter with the Maoris at Mordenaers Bay (Murderers Bay, now Golden Bay) in the north of the South Island, in which four of his men were killed. As far as we know, he left no physical trace of this visit although there is an apocryphal story about a musket discovered in the Nelson area, and reputed to be the one lost by Tasman in his clash with the Maoris. Unfortunately, no one has ever actually been able to produce it for inspection.

What he did leave for the world was the first written account of New Zealand's existence, with a description of a large high-lying land and its inhabitants. He also indirectly bequeathed to it what has been its internationally recognised name for over 300 years. As a result of Tasman's discoveries, the cartographer Blaeu was able to fill in some of the large gaps in the hitherto unknown southern ocean. In about 1648, on a map of the world, he marked the new islands, naming them Zeelandia Nova — New Sea Land after the Dutch province of that name — nowadays we call it New Zealand.

The best known of the early Europeans to arrive in New Zealand was the Englishman James Cook, who paid three visits between the years 1769 and 1777. Cook's voyages to New Zealand and the South Pacific were to be a combination of scientific observation and exploration. Cook himself, the scientists and artists who accompanied him, and many of his

officers and men left for us a comprehensive picture of the Maori people and the land that they inhabited at a time when they had not apparently been subject to any outside cultural influence for 7–800 years. It is against the records of people like Banks and Solander, the Forsters, Parkinson, Hodges and Webber, as well as Cook that we measure many of our archaeological observations today.

Cook landed in New Zealand on numerous occasions and in a number of places; his favourite spot being the sheltered waters of Ship Cove in Queen Charlotte Sound. Like Tasman, Cook also had problems with the Maoris, with deaths on both sides, but on the whole the relationship seems to have been amicable, of benefit and interest to both parties.

Unlike Tasman, Cook left considerable evidence other than written records of his visits to New Zealand and deliberately introduced a variety of vegetable plants and some animals —

This sketch made during Tasman's visit to New Zealand depicts the Dutch encounter with the Maoris in 'Mordenaers' Bay; (the letter 'C' indicates the Zeehaen's boat which is under attack). It is of considerable interest in that it depicts a double canoe in the foreground and also shows something of the dress and hairstyle of the people.

the most successful being a line of pigs, now feral and popularly called 'Captain Cookers'.

Among the archaeological evidence of Cook's visits there is still visible at Dusky Sound in Fiordland the clearing on 'Astronomers Point' made in March 1773 so that the scientists could set up their instruments and accurately fix the geographical position of New Zealand 'by the coelestial Observations . . . Occultations of the fixt Stars & Planets . . .' On this point the stumps of the trees felled by Cook's men can still be seen, preserved by a covering of moss and fern roots.

Cook also left various items, including medals struck to commemorate his second voyage, at Cascade Cove in Dusky Sound. One of these medals was found by John Boultbee in Dusky Sound 53 years later in 1830. Another turned up in a large Maori village site at Murdering Beach in 1863, while yet another was found at Katiki in North Otago.

Cook also distributed these medals in Queen Charlotte Sound and several have been found in the Marlborough Sounds area. Tree stumps, carved initials, and garden areas have also been reported from Ship Cove in Queen Charlotte Sound, and although there is no real evidence that these originated with Cook and his men, they are generally attributed to them.

In 1835 Joel Polack, while travelling in the Tolaga Bay area, was presented by the Maoris with 'two spike nails originally given by Te Kuki [Cook] to the natives of Turunga'. These were tribal treasures and presented to Polack as a mark of appreciation. He described them as

. . . one a five inch spike without any head . . . the other was a six inch spike with a small projection on the head . . . they have an antique appearance and had been used by the natives as chisels for carving.

Besides these relics left by Cook, he also made unsurpassed collections of Maori ethnological material as well as natural history specimens, still in existence today.

When Cook first sighted New Zealand on 7 October 1769, he was only a matter of weeks ahead of the Frenchman Jean-Francois-Marie de Surville in the *Saint Jean Baptiste*. De Surville sought to beat the British in claiming new territory in the Pacific but his voyage was something of a disaster. When he arrived in Doubtless Bay in Northland on 17 December 1769 (while Cook was lying off the north coast), he had already lost 60 of his crew from scurvy. And then within a few days the *Saint Jean Baptiste* was struck by a storm and crippled by the loss of her rudder. Although de Surville and his crew were assisted in many ways by the Maoris (many of them may not have survived without that help), de Surville seems to have made little attempt to understand them, and even kidnapped the local chief in revenge for a minor incident, the result of a misunderstanding. After

Two views (left) of Ship Cove in the Marlborough Sounds separated in time by more than 160 years. Upper: the drawing by the Russian Mikhaylov, made during Bellinghausen's 1820 visit, shows considerable artistic licence since although the setting is clearly Ship Cove the Russians reported that they saw no Maoris there. This greatly reduces the sketch's historical value. Lower: the same site in 1982.

James Cook distributed a number of medals (below) to the Maori people during his second voyage, 1772-1775. These were made of brass and struck by Matthew Boulton, an engineer, to commemorate the voyage of the *Resolution* and *Adventure*, which are depicted on one side — the other has a head of George III. Those shown were found at Katiki Beach, North Otago, and Arapawa Island, Marlborough Sounds.

this they sailed for Peru taking their hapless captive with them. Within a matter of weeks both the chief and de Surville were dead.

Apart from three anchors lost in Doubtless Bay during the storm (two of which, weighing 1½ tonnes, have been recovered) there remains no physical evidence of their brief visit to New Zealand and probably the main thing they left behind was a strong sense of wrongdoing and mistrust within the Maori village which had befriended them.

The wealthy adventurer Marion du Fresne with his ships the *Mascarin* and the *Marquis de Castries* was another Frenchman who visited New Zealand at this time. He sighted Mount Egmont on 25 March 1772, between Cook's first and second visits. Like Cook and de Surville, Marion du Fresne planted vegetables. He also seems to have treated the Maoris with considerable tolerance. Despite this, men from both ships became victims of an unexpected and apparently unprovoked massacre; Marion himself was one of the first victims.

We will never know the real reason for that sudden attack: it has been suggested that it was an act of revenge for the actions of de Surville in the same general area a little over two years earlier, or Marion and his men may have violated unknowingly some local custom. In any event, the *Mascarin* and *Marquis de Castries* sailed from New Zealand waters shortly after the massacre, apparently leaving no archaeological trace of their visit.

By the early nineteenth century there was already a substantial population of European inhabitants who had been arriving since within a

few years of Cook's publication of his findings. Sealers commenced their operations in Dusky Sound in 1792, and were followed by two Spanish ships which visited the Sound in 1793. At the same time bay whalers and kauri timber traders in the north kept up a steady contact with the Maoris, and the first missionaries arrived in 1814.

So far we have considered only those early non-Polynesians of whose visits we have a definite record. The possibility exists, of course, that New Zealand was reached by other people who left no record — perhaps at a much earlier time, or even in the 127 years between Tasman and Cook. Several unexplained objects found in New Zealand have given rise to such speculation.

One of these is the so-called 'Spanish' helmet, of a style dated to about 1580, now housed in the National Museum, Wellington. Details of its finding are sketchy; reputedly, it was dredged up from Wellington Harbour, although there is no real evidence that this is so, nor evidence of its existence in the museum prior to 1904. Yet its discovery has raised the question as to whether or not New Zealand might have been visited by Spanish explorers prior to Tasman's visit in 1642. There are, however, several problems associated with this as a theory, when based on the finding of this helmet alone. The helmet is of a standard 'international' type which might have been worn in many places in Europe, including England. There is no evidence at all that it is Spanish — it is simply an iron helmet of a very common type for its period. As well, there is no evidence of it having been in the sea for any length of time, as if it had been lost in

The death of Marion du Fresne in the Bay of Islands in 1772 (below right), by the French painter Charles Meryon. Paintings such as these owe more to the imagination and Romantic ideals of the artist than they do to fact and, unlike the work of artists who accompanied Cook, are not intended to record accurately what was seen. The depiction of the Maori pa as a Greek temple was undoubtedly influenced by Dumont d'Urville who had earlier drawn an analogy between Greek and Maori architecture. (The Greek/ Maori analogy was also noted by the artist Augustus Earle, who likened his meeting with the chief Hongi, to a 'passage of Homer'.)

Arapawa Island (below). Cook got his first view of the South Island when he climbed Arapawa Island. He left a cairn on the summit of the island but attempts to locate it have been unsuccessful.

these waters towards the end of the sixteenth century.

Another unusual item to find its way into our National Museum last century was a cast bronze ship's bell. Like the helmet, the exact details of its discovery are unclear, although it was reputedly found by the Reverend Colenso in the interior of the North Island. The inscription on the bell is in a script which was originally identified as Tamil (a race of people from southern India) and translated as *MOHOYIDEEN BUKS SHIPS BELL.* (There have been subsequent suggestions that it may in fact have been cast in Java rather than India, and there have been alternative although similar translations of the inscription.)

It, too, has been used to suggest that others, of whom we have no record, may have reached New Zealand in the past. Julius Haast, examining Maori rock drawings at Weka Pass in 1876, thought he could see a strong resemblance between some of the drawings and the characters on the bell. He suggested that a Tamil ship had been wrecked on the New Zealand coast some time in the past and that 'one or more of the wrecked mariners of Indian origin were saved, and [that] these paintings were executed by them'.

As with the helmet, there is unfortunately no evidence to show how the bell arrived in New Zealand — it could have been brought by a European ship early last century. Similarly, Haast's theory is rather negated by the fact that no one else has ever been able to see the similarity he noted between the Tamil script and the rock drawings.

This relic, known as the 'Tamil Bell', was bequeathed by its discoverer, William Colenso, to the National Museum. An accompanying note claimed he had found it in the 'interior of the N. Island in 1836'. Although he reputedly wrote a 'long and interesting history' of the bell's discovery, unfortunately no such manuscript has ever been located and the bell's origins will probably always remain shrouded in mystery.

Like the Tamil Bell pictured above, the origins of the so-called 'Spanish Helmet' have also given rise to a great amount of romantic — and generally unfounded — speculation. There is no record of its existence in the National Museum prior to 1904 — nor any real evidence that it was actually recovered from Wellington Harbour — or indeed that it is of Spanish origin. One supposition is that it was part of a suit of armour gifted to a Maori chief — another that it may have formed part of a ship's ballast.

Sealers and Whalers

*F*OLLOWING the initial period of European contact, the first Europeans to regularly visit New Zealand were the sealers and whalers. Archaeological evidence shows that both seals and whales were hunted around New Zealand from the earliest times of Maori occupation, and from historical records we know that the first European sealing gang to work the New Zealand waters was from the whaleship *Britannia* at Dusky Bay in 1792. In the 34 years from then to 1826, when the industry declined, hundreds of thousands of fur seals were killed on the southern coasts and offshore islands of New Zealand.

The legacy of those years is found in today's depleted seal population and in the geographical names the early sealers left behind. As one example, Captain John Grono of Windsor, New South Wales, explored much of the west coast of the South Island; Milford, Caswell, Bligh, Nancy and George Sounds were named by him, the names stemming both from his native South Wales and his ships.

Sealing in New Zealand was mainly an extension of the Australian sealing industry, bringing the South Island into the commercial ambit of Australia — particularly after the Tasmanian fur seals had been hunted out. The Governor of New South Wales supported sealing in New Zealand waters, encouraging the industry to become a staple export producer for the new colony.

Gangs were put ashore along the southern coast or islands with a few provisions and were left for months, sometimes years, with orders to kill and skin the seals and to sort and peg the hides in readiness for when their ship returned to pick them up. The sealers usually lived in tents or flax huts which, when abandoned, left little occupational evidence. Some sealers sheltered in the caves along the coast. One of these in

Fiordland, called Grono's Cave, after the sealing captain who used it, preserved such artifacts as boots and a knife as well as the reason for it all, a cache of sealskins in reasonable condition. It is not known exactly when they were put there. Grono scratched on a piece of slate a record of one visit, probably in 1823. In Grono's Cave, as in others, there are also traces of earlier Maori visits.

Sealing lasted in New Zealand roughly from 1803 until it virtually ceased in the mid 1820s when the seal colonies were wiped out.

New Zealand whaling began when British whaleships visited the country in 1792 and 1793. As with sealing, the new Australian colonials and Governor King strongly supported whaling from the colonies both by British and local ships. British ships almost exclusively hunted sperm whales, prized for their byproducts: sperm oil itself, spermacetti for candles, and ambergris for perfume. Sperm whales were found in every ocean; those off New Zealand were exactly the same as those off Scotland or Spain.

Whaling from Australian shores, and deep-sea whaling from Britain, developed into shore whaling from New Zealand in the late 1820s. Shore whalemen hunted the humpback and southern right whale which migrated past New Zealand shores annually, proceeding north past the eastern coasts of both islands, and were hunted from boats as well as ships.

The first shore-based station was established in 1829 at Te Awaiti, a sheltered bay inside the Tory Channel, and was the forerunner of 113 such stations which operated during the next 135 years. They stretched from Parengarenga Harbour in the far north to Preservation Inlet in the far south, the biggest concentrations being in Northland, Bay of Plenty, Poverty Bay, Hawke's Bay, Cook Strait, Banks Peninsula, Otago Peninsula and Foveaux Strait.

Initially the shore stations survived only under the aegis of the local Maori tribes. The whalers usually took Maori women as wives and lived under the protection of the tribe; in return they traded in European goods when the supply ships visited. In this way whale station housing soon began to affect Maori housing, as the chief Tuhawaiki's house at Ruapuke illustrated. Whaling houses are credited with introducing Maoris to the fireplace and chimney, door and window. Typically, a house had one large room with a couple of windows and with most of the walls taken up by bunks. A long table stood on the pounded clay floor. Whale vertebrae became stools.

Shore whalemen hunted the whales from boats similar to those used from whaleships. Once the boats had secured their quarry, the dead whales were towed back to shore, winched on to the beach, and then began the slow process of flensing and mincing the blubber into smaller pieces or 'bible leaves' before it was pitched into trypots whose bases had been plastered or pugged in. Once the oil had been extracted by

A shore whaling station somewhere on the east coast of the North Island sometime in the first two decades of this century. Needing little capital and equipment, such stations were quickly established and as easily abandoned, leaving little occupational evidence of their activities.

boiling, it was bailed into large storage tanks called coolers, and from there poured into barrels.

By all accounts an overpowering stench pervaded the stations and monstrous amounts of bone and meat remained when whales weighing many tons were despoiled and stripped of blubber. As such, whale bones are today the most common and often the most visible archaeological evidence of shore stations. Bones littered the immediate vicinity of the stations, often heaped into huge piles. Occasionally, they were utilised for other purposes: at both Fyffe's and Te Awaiti bones were used extensively as fence posts and also at Te Awaiti as the studs (uprights) for the boatshed. George Fyffe built one of the wings of his house using whale vertebrae as piles. At Peraki, Banks Peninsula, a farm road passes over a culvert made of whale jawbones.

And yet today, apart from such bones and a few houses, usually rebuilt beyond period recognition, little obvious occupational evidence remains of the stations on the surface. Some of the equipment, such as flensing knives and trypots, has found its way to local museums, while the whalers' personal possessions — their clay pipes and scrimshawed whale teeth — are held in public and private collections. Of the stations themselves virtually nothing remains: usually only traces of foundation material, the plastered bases for trypots and ferrous deposits where oil barrel bands have rusted. In part, such rapid disintegration can be explained by the fact that many of the early stations were haphazardly built from materials at hand — the boathouse at Island Bay, Banks Peninsula, for example, was made from the staves of old oil casks.

By the early years of this century many of the early stations had ceased to exist. By 1900 all that remained of Johnny Jones's station at

Waikouaiti, Otago, were bone fragments, two trypots, two settling tanks and a capstan. In 1843 Te Awaiti had been a prosperous community of some 25 buildings; today none of the original buildings survive, and all that is evident are a few fence posts of whale ribs and a few rusting iron implements.

It remains for archaeology to tell us more about this, the earliest period of European occupation in New Zealand. Until now, however, the bias of archaeological research has favoured pre-European sites so that only a few surveys, such as at Kapiti, have been completed, and where excavations have been undertaken, it is invariably because the stations were adjacent to earlier Maori sites. Unlike the missionaries, who were prolific chroniclers, whalers were often illiterate or poorly educated. Nevertheless, there is some good, historical, documentary evidence of their activities and their observations tended to be less biased than those of the clergy. And yet despite the attention of some historians, without archaeological investigation our understanding of how the early shore whalers lived will remain incomplete.

Nigel Prickett

The plastered side wall (left) of a trypot foundation, Kapiti Island.

At the end of an era — Te Awaiti station (below) in 1910, just six years before it finally ceased operations. Then only a few derelict buildings remained on the foreshore amid the huge piles of whale bones.

Canterbury Times

Traders and Missionaries

John Wilson

CONTACT between the Maori people and the earliest Europeans to frequent New Zealand's coasts — sealers and whalers — was generally intermittent and restricted to a few places. Among the first Europeans to come into sustained contact with the Maoris were traders and missionaries — traders generally preceding the missionaries by several years. The Maoris' wish to acquire various European goods — nails, axes, blankets, tobacco and, above all, muskets — enabled the traders, in return, to acquire foodstuffs, preserved tattooed heads and, most importantly, flax, items for which there were markets in Australia or Europe. The preparation of flax fibre was labour intensive and many Maori hapu shifted their settlements and mobilised their resources to cut and scrape flax because the only way to secure the muskets, which had become a key element in tribal warfare, was to have copious supplies of dressed flax ready when traders called.

Initial contact between European traders and Maoris was intermittent, with traders merely calling into bays or harbours, picking up a cargo and sailing away again. Gradually, a few began to settle ashore and from the second decade of the nineteenth century European traders were living ashore in the North Hauraki Gulf, the Waikato Heads, Mahia, Mokau and the shores of Cook Strait up to Kapiti Island.

But these early resident traders have left little archaeological record of their presence. There were no trading stations as such, where European traders lived in settlements distinct from those of the Maoris. Rather, the traders became assimilated into the Maori communities, often taking Maori wives and adopting local customs. Consequently, the only archaeological evidence for their settling ashore is the presence of European trade goods — clay pipes, nails, axe heads, metal fish hooks and glass — on the sites of Maori settlements.

Unfortunately, there have been no systematic excavations of sites where early European traders are known to have settled. The occasional finding of European items on or adjacent to Maori settlement sites remains, so far, the extent of archaeological evidence for the presence and activities of the early traders.

One of the most profound results of this early trade, however, was the use of muskets in tribal warfare, for which there is archaeological evidence. Thus, at Takahanga Pa, Kaikoura, in a thin layer above layers of pre-European occupation, was found, along with bits of bottle glass, a well-preserved musket ball probably fired during Te Rauparaha's 1830 raid on Kaikoura. Analysis of a human skeleton found in dunes at Waikanae showed that the individual had been wounded by a musket ball in the right thigh. The musket ball, flattened by the impact, was found with the skeleton. The person survived some months after the injury, but the musket ball remaining in the body tissue caused infection which eventually resulted in death. The skeleton probably dated from the period 1820–1840 when Te Rauparaha and his allies seized the Kapiti Coast from its previous occupants, then quarrelled among themselves. Te Rauparaha established himself in the area primarily to be able to trade with the Europeans then frequenting the Cook Strait area.

Buried with the individual at Waikanae was a clay pipe, another of the trade items Maoris were keen to obtain. However, similar clay pipes were popular with whalers and the remains of such pipes in archaeological sites can be evidence of the presence of whalers rather than of exchange of goods between Maoris and

The mission station on Ruapuke Island, Foveaux Strait. Little now remains of the building, and excavations of the site have provided little information not already documented.

Europeans. These clay pipes can often be dated in various ways, from the diameter of the stem bore or makers' marks, for example, and when more excavations are done at places where traders settled ashore or traded with the Maoris, the presence of clay pipe fragments will help pinpoint dates more accurately.

Besides muskets and ammunition for them, the Maoris were most anxious to obtain from European traders the metal tools and implements that were more efficient than their own stone equivalents. Items like axes and nails have been discovered incidentally at sites where early trading exchanges apparently took place. Thus, just outside the Huirapa Gateway of the Kaiapohia Pa north of Christchurch has been found, along with stone tools, the metal blade of a plane which had been modified to serve as an adze head.

Traders gathered primarily on the coasts, like the whalers and sealers who preceded them. Missionaries were often the first Europeans to penetrate far inland. Between 1814 and about 1860, more than 100 mission stations were established throughout New Zealand. Many were short-lived and abandoned a few years after they were founded.

Mission activity among the Maoris began with the establishment in 1814 of a Church Missionary Society station at Oihi, on the northern shore of the Bay of Islands, next to the populous Rangihoua Pa. From there, missionaries gradually spread inland in Northland and then southwards to other parts of the North Island. The first truly inland mission station was that established at Waimate in 1831. Stations were founded at Kaitaia in 1835 and Kaikohe in 1845. In 1838 the Roman Catholic Bishop Pompallier arrived and soon established his mission headquarters at Kororareka (Russell). By the 1840s mission activity extended across Cook Strait to the South Island, Maori converts often preaching Christianity in advance of European missionaries.

Archaeology has as yet not contributed significantly to our knowledge of life on, or the development and decline of, New Zealand's mission stations. The missionaries were prolific writers of letters and reports and many kept detailed diaries. Such abundant documentation seems to make archaeological excavation of mission sites unnecessary. In addition, some buildings have survived, including two mission-related buildings at Kerikeri, the mission houses at Waimate and Tauranga and the building erected as a printery for the Catholic Mission at Kororareka. This building, now known as Pompallier House, was subsequently used as a tannery — an aspect of the building's history only recently clarified as a result of excavations.

What excavations of mission stations that have been conducted to date have for the most part been only cursory or coincidental. For example, the first mission station in New Zealand, at Oihi in the Bay of Islands, was established next to the large Rangihoua Pa. Pa and mission station were both abandoned in the 1830s. Limited excavation on the site of the mission station has confirmed details about the location and use of certain buildings and structures, including a sawpit to which there were only obscure references in the written record. Rangihoua Pa has attracted more archaeological interest, however, than the Oihi mission station.

Even where a mission building is still standing, as at Waimate, archaeology could play a role in unravelling the station's history. The mission house is the only building to have survived of a sizeable mission village. There were once other houses, a watermill, a printing works, blacksmith's and carpenter's shops, barns and sheds. Archaeology may one day clarify the location of, and activities at, parts of the station of which no trace now remains above the ground.

The Waikanae mission station, at Kenakena, was established by young Ocatvius Hadfield in 1840, but abandoned later in that decade when most of the local Te Atiawa returned to Taranaki. The substantial church that had been built at Kenakena fell into disrepair. Its remains were eventually buried in drifting sand. In 1961, however, the remains were uncovered when the ground on which the church had stood was being prepared for subdivision and details about the structure not mentioned in any written sources were discovered.

And in the far south, limited excavations on Ruapuke Island in Foveaux Strait have added to the knowledge about the mission station founded there by Johann Wohlers in 1844. Very little remains above the ground of the buildings of Wohlers's mission and although photographs of them exist and the documentary sources are voluminous, excavation again provided small or corroborating detail not recorded at the time.

A musket ball found during an archaeological excavation of the main gateway earthworks of Takahanga Pa, Kaikoura. It probably relates to an attack by Te Rauparaha in 1830. The introduction of muskets by Europeans promoted a new type of warfare, requiring different defensive strategies.

Originally built as a printery for the Catholic mission at Russell, Pompallier House is one of the few missions still standing, and is presently administered by the Department of Conservation.

The First Gaol: Archaeology in the Central Business District of Auckland

Simon Best

THE settlement of Auckland came into official being in September 1840. At that time the rolling hills of the area were covered in scrub and fern, with larger trees in the gullies. No permanent Maori settlements are recorded but the sites of two pa are known from Land Court records: one on the soon to be defunct Point Britomart, and the other on the site of the town hall.

The European settlement grew quickly, from tents and raupo whares to wooden buildings with brick chimneys to brick buildings, spreading from an initial area between Mechanics Bay and Freemans Bay up the Queen Street watershed and out along the surrounding ridges.

Activities that took place on the outskirts of the settlement were quickly over-run as the place grew, the replacement activities themselves often succumbing to other pressures as the character of the area changed. Although wells were dug and street levels raised in those early days, it was not until the last quarter of the century, when basements began to be added to buildings, that the original ground surface was disturbed to any great extent.

In certain areas of Auckland a stratified record of the European settlement is still preserved. Salvage excavations over the past few years have covered such diverse sites as an 1842 bakery, a half-finished 1845 fort, an 1852 brickworks and, most interesting of all, the site of the first gaol and courthouse in New Zealand.

In the heart of the Auckland Business District, on the block bounded by Queen, Derby, Elliott and Victoria Streets, had stood from June 1840 to the mid 1860s the guardroom, courthouse, cell-blocks, hard-labour yard, stocks and gallows of the early colony. Sited then on the outskirts of town beside the Waihorotiu Creek, this was a place where an individual could be locked up, tried, sentenced, hanged and then buried. Six executions are recorded, with the bodies interred on the Queen-Victoria Street corner.

In 1987 this site became the focus of a major archaeological excavation; scheduled for construction on the site was a 21-storey building, the underground part of which would effectively remove all traces of the ground surface which had existed for possibly thousands of years. A time limit of nine days, later extended to 12, was put on the excavations by the developers. The

Auckland Projects Office of the New Zealand Historic Places Trust organised the project, and provided most of the excavation team from their staff, together with some volunteers.

When the site had been cleared of existing buildings down to the basement floors it resembled a huge square concrete-based pit, with basalt retaining walls along the sides. Across the centre of this, running north-south from Victoria Street West to Derby Street, was Theatre Lane, now some four metres higher than the basements on either side.

This last area became the main target for excavation — it was thought that the original ground surface probably existed only under this, and the developers were wary of the concrete basement floors being broken to any extent since they were required both to support their machinery and to hold in the street retaining walls. Five small areas outside Theatre Lane were, however, examined to look for the prison well, the two gaolers' houses, the courthouse, and also to find the Ligar Canal (built where the Waihorotiu Creek had originally flowed). Machinery was used both to break the concrete in these areas, and to remove about 300 cubic metres of fill from between the two retaining walls of Theatre Lane.

When finally excavated, the six-metre-deep prison well showed evidence of having been deepened from an original three metres. Archival research showed that this had happened prior to 19 June 1844, owing to contamination from decayed vegetable matter. The remains of three metal buckets were found in silt at the base of the well, presumably lost while being used and all with fragments of rope still attached.

Beneath the fill of Theatre Lane, which itself contained various artifacts ranging from chamber pots to door locks, was found part of a cell-block foundation, the prison kitchen, and the hard-labour yard, together with some of the cobbles broken there by the leg-ironed prisoners.

At that time the Waihorotiu Creek still flowed alongside the gaol, and the section of the creek that has been excavated was found to be lined with basalt blocks, with no European material beneath them but with layers of silt and refuse on top. Historical research has found that the original creek had been enlarged and lined with stones in 1845, after successive floods had overflowed the banks, carrying away the gaol fence. Lying on these stones, close to where the gaol kitchen had been, was found a collection of animal bones and tin containers.

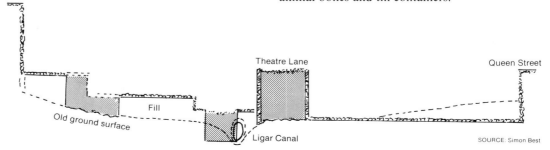

An east-west cross section of the site, showing the old ground surface and the excavations. The Waihorotiu Creek bed lies directly under the Ligar Canal drain.

Elliott Street

Theatre Lane

Queen Street

Old ground surface

Fill

Ligar Canal

SOURCE: Simon Best

The bones are mainly those of cattle, with some sheep and pig. Analysis of the butchering evidence indicates that the cheaper cuts are present: neck and blade chops, short ribs, and fore and hind shanks, probably for use as soups and stews. Two of the sheep bones seem to have been chewed; a letter from the Sheriff of Auckland to the Colonial Secretary in 1844 complains of the large amount of bone in the meat for prisoners — apparently their diet did not improve!

With the bones was a tall pot, with a base designed for sitting on a stove and showing evidence of having been heated, a dixie and three food tins. Along with other refuse such as cutlery and pottery were many discarded boots and shoes. Complaints about the quality of imported footwear can be found in the Colonial Secretaries' correspondence for the first few years, along with the mention that in 1844 Governor Hobson ordered a trial sample of footwear from a Mr Price at Pakaraka near Waimate, made of New Zealand leather. These, at 9/6d each, and furnished with hobnails, were to be issued to the hard-labour prisoners. The

footwear in the mud may include some of these, which may have been the first such made in this country.

Evidence for activities carried out just south of the gaol fence was also found in the creek. The city pound had functioned next to the courthouse, with unclaimed dogs being either poisoned or hanged. The remains of eight dogs were found in the mud, two with their leather collars in place. Analysis of the bones shows that two of these may possess characteristics of the Maori dog, kuri, possibly the earliest recorded instance of such a cross.

Beneath the level of the gaol earlier beds of the Waihorotiu Creek were exposed as foundation work for the new buildings progressed, with reminders of other and earlier settlers in the area. Under the stone lining by the cell-blocks were Maori wooden digging implements, a shell midden and a fragment of woven flax. The shells, mainly scallops and cockles, gave a C14 date of about AD 1400.

Beneath this again was a deposit of leaves, bark, twigs and branches, lying at the base of the first creek bed. Perfectly preserved, this has not only provided information on the environment of the Queen Street watershed, but has also told us, through C14 dating of the leaf litter itself, that this material fell into the creek almost 800 years ago, at about AD 1200.

At that time a small creek with a white sand base, with freshwater mussels on its bed, flowed down the Queen Street gully through a forest which included totara, rimu, matai, pohutukawa, rewarewa, puriri, mahoe, hinau and maire. Down on the forest floor a small animal gathered the fallen seeds of the forest giants and nibbled them for their kernels. These rat-gnawed seeds were preserved along with the leaf litter and indicate as clearly as a human footprint that the Polynesians had landed, and were active in the area, possibly even hunting moas in what is now the Central Business District of Auckland.

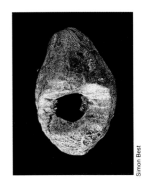

Nearly 800 years old, this rat-gnawed hinau kernel is one of many from the base of the earliest bed of the Waihorotiu Creek, and tells us that man was nearby.

The prison well (left) was originally only 3 metres deep but when the water became contaminated the well was deepened to almost 6 metres. A 'privy' sited only 2½ metres away would not have helped sanitation.

A section of the basalt foundation (below left) for the debtors' cell block, together with the external covered drain.

A view of the excavation from the north (below). The remains of Theatre Lane run across the middle of the block; to the left is the Courthouse area and to the right the gaolers' house sites.

Shipwrecks:
The
Problems of
Marine
Archaeology

Mike Bradstock

IN the 200 years of continuous European contact New Zealand has had a long history of shipwrecks. Many wrecks have resulted from difficulties encountered with the country's geography — its often inclement weather and the long coastline, much of which offers little shelter and even today remains imperfectly charted. The rugged New Zealand landscape has also meant that until recently it was more practical for both people and goods to travel around the coast by that ready-made (if somewhat hazardous) highway, the sea. As a result, well over 2000 ships have been lost in New Zealand waters — and shipwreck even today is no rare event.

Yet this very rich part of New Zealand's heritage has until recently been rather neglected, and it was not until 1976 that legislation came into force protecting shipwrecks — long after the more accessible ones had all been looted by souvenir hunters and scrap-metal salvors, and there is still very little policing done of the Historic Places legislation of 1975. In fact, at present there still are no known, and readily accessible, intact wrecks around New Zealand; all have received some attention from amateur 'salvors' and their most significant artifacts are scattered in private collections throughout the country and overseas. They are not even formally catalogued or recorded, let alone photographed and subjected to proper preservation measures.

This is unfortunate because shipwreck sites more than most other archaeological sites encapsulate a moment in history when a wide cross-section of objects relating to that time suddenly become lost. For ships are the homes of their crew (and passengers, if any), and as such contain most of the impedimenta of everyday life with nothing saved because the loss is usually sudden and unforeseen. The ships usually also have cargoes and equipment which can later become of archaeological interest. The only ships that, when wrecked, do not become tomorrow's

archaeological sites are those which are salvaged or so broken up and scattered by the elements that, to all purposes, they cease to have existed. Age and decay add to this process, but even so some of New Zealand's oldest known wrecks remain recognisable. They provide material links with the past and evidence of how tangible objects — including the ships themselves — were constructed, operated and used.

The barque *Endeavour*, lost in 1795 in Dusky Sound, is New Zealand's oldest shipwreck — indeed the only known European wreck to pre-date the nineteenth century. It is also closely associated with two other 'firsts' in New Zealand history: the first, though temporary, European settlement, and the first Australasian shipbuilding using native timbers, both events taking place in Dusky Sound between 1792–99.

Soon after the *Endeavour's* arrival from Port Jackson in 1795 it sank, still showing partly above water, at its moorings in a sheltered inlet, where the fittings and much of the timbers were stripped for other uses. Thereafter, the wreck lay forgotten until its rediscovery in 1963 by a party from the survey ship *Tui*. The vessel's outline could clearly be seen in the shallow water, and wooden beams, fragments of copper sheeting and a millstone were recovered. Later visits to the wreck revealed no trace of the clearly apocryphal greenstone it was reputed to be carrying as ballast, but history records that two of its cannon had been lost while being transported ashore, and in 1984 these were finally located, during a filming expedition, by Kelly Tarlton. Using a highly sensitive metal detector called a proton magnetometer, he found the two cannon lying side by side in 20 metres of water. One was totally buried by 188 years of progressive sedimentation from off the land and its very existence could only be confirmed by excavation; the other protruded from the bottom, with a conger eel living inside the barrel.

On 28 July 1840 *HMS Buffalo* was driven ashore at Whitianga, Coromandel Peninsula, when a strong north-easterly arose while it was anchored. Launched at Calcutta in 1813 as *Hindustan*, HMS *Buffalo* was purchased by the Royal Navy (a sixth rater of 589 tons) in the same year. It made three voyages to New Zealand; on the last it disembarked a contingent of the 80th Regiment along with Governor Hobson's wife, three servants and four children. It then proceeded to the Coromandel Peninsula to cut kauri spars. It was there that it was wrecked.

Reconstruction by Gainor Jackson

This search was by no means straightforward: even in so remote a location there were a number of false alarms, caused by other metal items on the sea bed, before the actual cannon were found. This is a problem for salvors and marine archaeologists that becomes worse in busy shipping lanes where there is much metal jetsam as well as debris from wrecked ships.

Kelly Tarlton also located what are the earliest confirmed marine relics of European contact: de Surville's anchors in Doubtless Bay. De Surville's vessel *St Jean Baptiste* lost three anchors during its 1769 visit, when it was nearly driven on to rocks during a fierce storm while at anchor. Reconstructing the incident from the ship's log, Tarlton determined that the ship had about 300 metres of cable out, and so determined that the anchors had to lie that distance offshore from the rocks, in a direction determined by the north-east wind direction at that time. However, because of an error in transcription of the original chart, the search was fruitless for some years until a check against the original chart

revealed they were searching in the wrong place; it was also found that the magnetic variation of the *St Jean Baptiste's* compass and the wind direction were both different from what had previously been believed. With this new information, the first anchor was quickly located, and the second shortly afterwards just 100 metres from the first. Then, by triangulation from the positions of these two anchors, Tarlton was able to work out the location of the third with remarkable precision.

Two of the anchors have now been raised, and their restoration has provided a challenge for modern technology. Iron objects when brought to the surface after long immersion in sea water are prone to acceleration of the corrosion that began in the water, and to combat this an electrolytic preservation treatment was used. This involved placing the anchors in a caustic soda bath and connecting them into an electrical circuit as cathodes, in a process akin to electroplating. This caused the chlorides from the salt, which had infiltrated the decaying iron, to migrate slowly out of the metal. After thorough

A reconstruction of *HMS Buffalo* as it would have appeared 30 years after it had been wrecked. Because it was exposed to both the tides and the weather, the process of disintegration would have been more complete and rapid than if the ship had sunk. Only the more durable timbers remained: the keel, the inner ceiling, the diagonal sheathing and the iron straps. Today only fragments of the keel and lower frames survive buried in sand where they are denied oxygen.

Reconstruction by Gainor Jackson

Both *HMS Buffalo* **and the** *Edwin Fox* (overleaf) were East Indiamen, built by the East India Co. in Calcutta, 1813, and Bombay, 1853, respectively. Massively timbered often of teak, these squat ships proved extremely durable and several gave service for over 40 years. Despite the use of iron for hull construction for small craft early in the nineteenth century, most shipyards persisted with wooden construction and multi-skinned hulls and iron straps. Below is a cross-section and profile showing the construction of a typical East Indiaman.

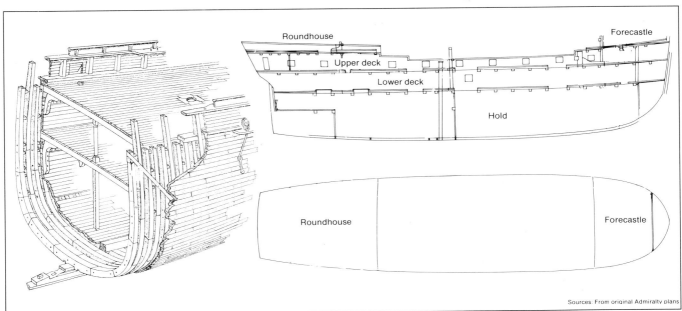

Roundhouse

Forecastle

Upper deck

Lower deck

Hold

Roundhouse

Forecastle

Sources: From original Admiralty plans

washing and drying, the anchors were coated in resin and displayed — one at the National Museum and the other at the Far North Museum in Kaitaia, where a room was specially built for it.

The gold of the *General Grant*, wrecked at the Auckland Islands in 1886, is the subject of much speculation among treasure seekers. It also presents some special problems apart from the harsh conditions of the wreck site, as the ship (or ships) that have been searched have so far eluded positive identification. The syndicate undertaking the seventh serious salvage attempt found this particularly frustrating. Its efforts in the early 1980s were concentrated on a wreck site within a cave close to the presumed sinking. During storms, boulders inside the cave roll about and have greatly broken up the remains of whatever ship lies there. Because the *General Grant* was supposed to be carrying spelter (zinc), a method for testing the bottom sediments for traces of the metal was investigated but was abandoned because the results would have been inconclusive. More useful was the discovery that mechanical parts of the ship, such as pipes and screw threads, were built to metric measure and that floor tiles found were of French manufacture. This raised the likelihood that the ship was built in France, not the USA, and was thus definitely not the treasure ship. The discovery of a fragment of the ship's bell was tantalisingly inconclusive, as the only legible fragment of writing on it was part of a letter or numeral which could be a J, Y, or 9. This gives credence to the theory that the wreck was actually the *Anjou*, a French ship wrecked in the area during 1905. The mystery seems to be solved by the 1985 discovery of a small plaque bearing the name 'Nantes' — where the *Anjou* was built — but this leaves the future of the *General Grant* an open question.

The *Wairarapa*, lost with 121 lives in 1894, was wrecked when it steamed at full speed into the northern cliffs of Great Barrier Island. The dent caused by the impact is still visible in the cliff. This ship too has been commercially salvaged with explosives, and picked over by countless souvenir hunters. Its accessibility underscores the problem of marine archaeology that has grown with the increased popularity of recreational skin diving. Although much of the hull still remains in large pieces, the site has not been systematically excavated or even a comprehensive site plan completed. However, many fine artifacts from the vessel have found their way to the Shipwreck Museum at Paihia, giving a glimpse of this particularly splendid relic from the twilight of the Victorian era. Even purely functional fittings on this ship were beautifully fashioned, such as a rope pulley with ornamental spokes, and there is a superb brass balustrade from the purser's office. Reflecting the ship's role as a luxurious passenger vessel, there is fine silverware, including a gravy boat, a teapot, three-legged cake tray and cake knife, all elaborately patterned in the Victorian style.

And yet it is doubtful whether the recovery of such artifacts is itself archaeologically significant. Their value lies more in their romantic appeal, their association with often tragic events. What defines most such artifacts is their *commonality* and, as such, they differ little from similar items found in museums and collections worldwide. Nevertheless, when seen as a whole — for example at the Shipwreck Museum at Paihia — they may show trends not otherwise immediately apparent. Silver cutlery recovered from wrecks show one such development through the nineteenth century from the large and obviously hand-made to the

Despite its former role as a convict and immigrant ship, the *Edwin Fox* (below) had become a floating cool store by 1885. Refrigeration machinery was installed first in England, and then at Port Chalmers boilers from the wrecks *Lyttelton* and *Northumberland* were added to power steam winches so that frozen carcasses could be offloaded on to outward bound ships berthed alongside.

By 1905 when this picture was taken (right), the *Edwin Fox's* days as a cool store were over and it had become a coal hulk in Picton. Trucks on rails now operated through holes cut in the topsides.

finer, smaller and less individual. Bottles show a similar progression, from hand-blown to machine-made. Changing fashions in emblems on crockery are also apparent: fragments from the *Tararua* have the Union Steam Ship Company's name in an oval scroll pattern, but those from the *Wairarapa* have the name backgrounded by a flag.

Of more significance are those items recovered which help identify a wreck or denote something of the original ship's construction. On some wreck sites, such as the Greymouth Bar where there are many wrecks in close locality, it is only by determining the age of an artifact that a wreck can be positively identified. Usually such dating is corroborated by historical records. Overseas, especially in the Mediterranean, where wrecks may be several thousand years old, C14 dating is often used to determine the age of organic material, but because of the variation in the dates obtained this method is impractical for New Zealand where most wrecks are less than 200 years old. Even if a reliable dating could be obtained from its timbers the ship might have been many decades old when it sank and the date obtained would relate to the date when the tree was cut. Sometimes a ship was constructed from older ships that in turn could have been constructed from the timbers of an even older vessel.

A more reliable method of dating a ship is from the shape of its hull, the method of construction and the means of propulsion. During the nineteenth century there was a progression from sailing ships made almost entirely of wood, to composite vessels made of timbers with iron frames (after the 1860s) to iron-clad sailing vessels and eventually steamers. Sometimes more specific dating can be obtained. After 1825 treenails (wooden pegs, used to fasten the planking to the frame of the ship) were turned on a lathe rather than shaped by hand. From that date also, all anchors were cast in one piece, whereas before they had been hand-forged from several pieces of iron; stocks, though, continued to be made of wood until the middle of the century, when they were replaced by iron.

And occasionally archaeology can be used to substantiate the historical record. In the 1960s the salvage operation on the *Elingamite*, lost at the Three Kings in 1902 with the loss of 45 lives, recovered the ship's bronze propeller blades, enabling a long-standing question to be settled: were the ship's screws still turning when she struck? This query had been raised at the 1903 inquiry and never satisfactorily answered, but was relevant in assigning blame for the disaster. The jagged edges of the blades vindicated the ship's master more than 60 years later.

Although little proper archaeological work has been done on our wrecks, there is hope that new technology will enable the deeper, as-yet-untouched shipwrecks to be discovered, properly excavated and restored. Recently a remote-operated vehicle (ROV), which operates like a tethered mini-submarine with camera, lights and a grappler, has been used to photograph and examine the wreck of the *Niagara*, a large (13415 tons) mail/passenger steamer which lies in water too deep for conventional salvage techniques. Such technology may see this and other important wrecks brought to light again.

By the 1950s (below left) upper deck beams still remained; it was here that both convicts and immigrants were accommodated. In 1967 the hulk of the *Edwin Fox* was beached near Picton and abandoned.

A view (below) inside the *Edwin Fox* taken in 1988 shows the keelson timbers and iron straps. Lower deck beams are seen above. Recently, a restoration society has refloated the hulk and towed it back to Picton waterfront where restoration is progressing.

Fortifications of the New Zealand Wars

Nigel Prickett

FROM the 1840s to the early 1880s European military forces in New Zealand were engaged in a series of campaigns aimed at ensuring the supremacy of British law and government and securing land for settlement. Major campaigns were fought in the Bay of Islands district (1845–46), North Taranaki (1860–61 and 1863–66), South Taranaki/Wanganui (1865–66, 1868–69), Waikato (1863–64), East Coast (1865) and Bay of Plenty (1864, 1867).

Until the final guerilla phase in the Ureweras and central North Island the various campaigns were largely fought around fixed positions, or fortifications. Pakeha fortifications were designed to provide campaign or battlefield security, while Maori fortifications were designed to invite and repulse attack — to inflict heavy loss on the enemy at small cost. In many North Island districts defensive works of the New Zealand Wars are among the most important features of the archaeological landscape.

The Maoris and British took into the wars considerable experience in the design, construction and defence of their fortifications. Maori experience was based upon hundreds of years of pa building, the previous few decades of which involved musket warfare among the tribes.

Among changes brought about by musket warfare was the need for fortifications to be out of range of higher ground. Pa were now situated to give defenders an all-round field of fire rather than having precipitous but obscured approaches as formerly. Bastions jutted out to cover the sides; zig-zag trenches prevented an attacking party from firing down their length. Defenders who once occupied elevated platforms to gain a height advantage over the enemy now dug themselves down in hidden trenches and tunnels.

The British brought with them the ancient European art of military engineering, on which textbooks were written and professionals received both theoretical and practical training. More specifically, the small earthwork or wooden defences which were employed in New Zealand had their origins in earlier frontier warfare in North America and elsewhere. They were sometimes thrown up in battlefield situations but more commonly in a garrison role where success was measured not by their having withstood an attack but by no attack having been made.

Maori fortifications of the New Zealand Wars were much more powerful and complex than their European counterparts for one simple and over-riding reason: theirs had to withstand artillery fire whereas British or colonial fortifications did not.

This became apparent in the first major campaign, the so-called 'War in the North', which revealed both the sophistication of Maori defensive positions and the inexperience of British commanders in New Zealand conditions. The chief Kawiti built fortifications at Ohaeawai and Ruapekapeka which proved embarrassing to the attacking force's battle plan, which consisted of an artillery bombardment to create a breach which could then be entered by a storming party.

At Ohaeawai two palisades were constructed to defend the pa: a light outer palisade or pekerangi covered with flax screens obscuring the major defence of puriri logs sunk 1.7 metres into the ground and reaching three metres above it. Protection was also offered by a trench located just inside the inner defence. Some 1.7 metres deep, the trench had firing steps cut in the side, enabling the defenders to fire from the inner palisade without exposing themselves.

In order to bring maximum fire to bear on the British assault force, Kawiti also abandoned the traditional fighting platform — an easy target for artillery fire — in favour of salients projecting from the perimeter of the main palisade. In this way flanking fire could be brought against an enemy trying to penetrate the pekerangi.

The most innovative development at Ohaeawai was, however, the anti-artillery bunker. Buried deep underground, these dugouts

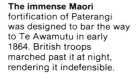

The immense Maori fortification of Paterangi was designed to bar the way to Te Awamutu in early 1864. British troops marched past it at night, rendering it indefensible.

HBAG & M

or rua were capable of accommodating 15 to 20 men, and were roofed by timber beams, earth, and fern (Evidence of this type of bunker can still be seen at Ruapekapeka).

The artillery bombardment of Ohaeawai lasted a week, during which the Maori defenders were quite content to sit out the bombardment underground, and only emerged to man the rifle pits when the final attack came on 1 July 1845 Although the pa contained only 100 warriors, the British assault force of 250 troops was easily repulsed, leaving 110 casualties behind. Maori losses numbered between one and 10 killed.

Fifteen years after Ohaeawai and Ruapekapeka, the British army showed it had learnt nothing when the 40th Regiment was repulsed at the twin pa of Puketakauere and Onukukaitara, near Waitara in Taranaki. Here the fortifications consisted of two small earthworks and stockades and outlying trenches

and rifle pits which barred the approach of an attacking force. The advancing troops did not get near the central positions.

The First Taranaki War of 1860–61 also saw the first major use of field fortifications by the British. These were of three basic forms: redoubts, stockades and blockhouses. Redoubts were small earthwork fortifications defended by a two-metre-deep ditch and a 2.5-metre-high bank; they were generally designed for one or two companies, approximately 1–200 men. The Taranaki landscape contains several fine examples of redoubts of various forms including the classic form: a square with all four sides defended by bastions at two corners, and the so-called 'New Zealand redoubt' with bastions at all four corners.

In later campaigns much use was made of redoubts either in a frontier role, preventing enemy incursions, or in an attacking role when

An aerial view of what remains of the twin pas of Puketakauere and Onukukaitara. None of the trenches and outworks still exist and only the mounds forming the inner defenses are still visible, though partially destroyed by quarrying.

Nigel Prickett

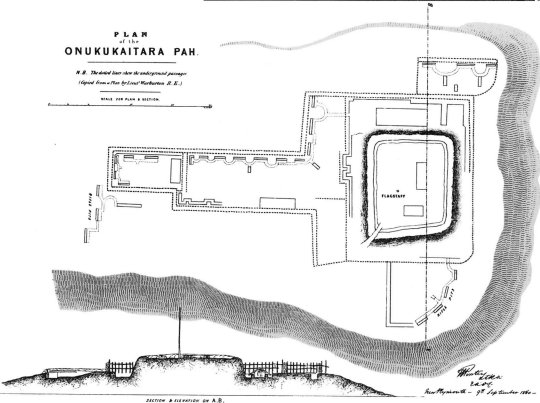

PLAN
of the
ONUKUKAITARA PAH.

N.B. The dotted lines shew the underground passages
(Copied from a Plan by Lieut' Warburton R.E.)

SCALE FOR PLAN & SECTION.

FLAGSTAFF

RIFLE PITS

New Plymouth — 9th September 1860—

SECTION & ELEVATION ON A.B.

Onukukaitara was typical of the modern pa — a rapidly constructed defensive work which because it had no strategic importance could be easily abandoned. The pa was built in June 1860 by Te Atiawa and Ngati Maniapoto warriors. This plan and section drawing was prepared after the Maori force had evacuated the pa and British troops had occupied the site as a signal station. Designed to withstand artillery bombardments, the pa was also surrounded by trenches and rifle pit outworks (not shown here) while bastions jutted out to cover the sides.

111

they were thrown up to protect a line of advance. The Waikato War provides examples of both. From the Waikato River to the Firth of Thames the Surrey, Esk and Miranda redoubts were established to prevent a Maori advance towards Auckland. At the same time a series of redoubts was established up the Waikato and Waipa Rivers to protect communications as the troops struck into Waikato territory.

Some redoubts occupied positions previously held by Maori pa. Examples are at Meremere and Rangiriri where the later fortifications take an unusual form in making use of existing earthworks. Even here, however, there is no mistaking the regular angles and straight lines of a British fortification when encountered in the field.

The second European fortification type was the stockade. This relied for defence on close-set posts loopholed for defensive fire. Usually a ditch encircled the stockade to add strength.

At the outset of the First Taranaki War Pakeha settlers built strong stockades to protect farming districts north and south of New Plymouth. The remains of Bell Block Stockade were destroyed by a hotel development in the early 1970s, but the Omata Stockade has survived as an important archaeological site and is now safe in an historic reserve. Excavations carried out at Omata in 1977 revealed the outline of stockade defences. Accommodation and guard rooms lined the small interior yard. Artifacts found included glass bottles and jars, broken china, clay tobacco pipes, buttons and other uniform pieces, ammunition, tin cans and building materials. Almost everything originated from outside New Zealand, mostly from Europe, to show that 20 years after New Plymouth was founded the settlement remained very much an outpost of the old world.

The Omata Stockade took the form of a rectangle 12.8 metres by 19.3 metres in size with two small bastions at opposite corners to cover all four sides. Many stockades, however, were of irregular plan to make use of available ground and local resources. A Taranaki example which can still be traced on the ground is at Mahoetahi near Waitara, where troops levelled off the top of an old lahar or volcanic mound, which was also the site of an abandoned pa, and fitted the stockade to the platform created.

The third form of Pakeha defensive work employed during the wars was the blockhouse. The term is sometimes used to describe a barrack or accommodation building situated within or near a redoubt or other military establishment. More importantly, it is used to describe an independently defensible roofed building, three to four metres square, typically garrisoned by eight or a dozen men. In New Zealand such blockhouses are characteristically of two storeys, the upper overhanging the lower so that trapdoors could be opened in the overhanging floor to reach any attacker at the walls. Upper and lower floors were loopholed for defence by small arms.

Small blockhouses took some weeks to build and thus could not be used on the battlefield or during the active phase of a campaign where earthwork redoubts, which could be thrown up in a day, were so important. In the later stages of the Waikato and Taranaki Wars, blockhouses were built along frontier lines to secure confiscated land for soldier settlers. At Onehunga, Auckland, there survives an unusual defensible blockhouse of one storey built in the form of a cross.

In 1978 excavations at Warea Redoubt in Taranaki (right) uncovered a stone hearth at one end of a well-built wooden hut which provided garrison accommodation just outside the earthwork fortification.

Soldiers dug the defensive ditch of Warea Redoubt (below right) to a depth of six feet (*c.* two metres). Long filled in, it was revealed in 1978 excavations when the fill of 120 years was removed.

A short length of General Pratt's 1861 sap (below) survives in the Pukerangiora Historic Reserve near Waitara in Taranaki. The sap allowed troops and guns to get close to defenders without too many casualties. Traverses can be seen jutting into the trench from alternate sides to prevent an enemy firing down the length.

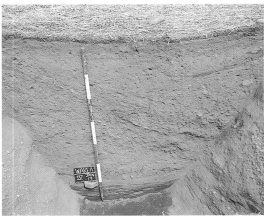

During 1861 British troops advanced up the left bank of the Waitara River, and eight redoubts were thrown up to protect the advance against Maori positions at Huirangi and Te Arei (Pukerangiora). Most of these were on a line of sap, or defended trench, which for three months was dug towards the heart of the Maori defences. The total length of sap was 1.5 kilometres and it was dug to approximately one metre depth with gabions, or wicker baskets filled with earth, on each side to give a total protected depth of about two metres.

The crucial campaign of the New Zealand Wars was fought in the Waikato in 1863–64. Initially the Waikato and allied tribes barred the way into their territory by a series of defensive lines at Koheroa, Meremere and Rangiriri. These lay across a narrow neck of land between the river and the vast Whangamarino Swamp. The defences were easily passed by armoured steamers on the river and when troops landed upstream they became untenable.

An even larger fortification barred the way from the Waipa River to Te Awamutu in early 1864. Paterangi was the largest fortification employed by either side during the wars: six or more strongpoints were connected by lines of trenches and within the strongpoints a maze of rifle pits, underground bunkers and sharply angled ditches enabled defenders to contest every yard. It was just such a confusion of earthworks which proved so impenetrable at Gate Pa, Tauranga, where the attacking troops actually entered the pa but could not dislodge the well-hidden defenders and so were forced to retreat. Rangiriri too presented insurmountable problems to the attacking force. Yet at Paterangi the British troops simply marched past the immense pa at night and the defenders were forced to withdraw.

Little now remains of these vast Maori fortifications of the Waikato campaigns. At Rangiriri a small reserve includes the central part of the old earthwork but visible remains are not easy to interpret. There is almost nothing to be seen of Paterangi.

Much archaeological work remains to be done on the various campaigns which make up the New Zealand Wars. Many sites are unlocated, more are undescribed, and almost none has been excavated. Archaeological excavations of a systematic nature have been carried out at the Omata Stockade and Warea Redoubt, Taranaki, at Fort Galatea, inland Bay of Plenty, and Runanga Stockade on the Napier-Taupo Road. Much of what is recovered tells of the particular history of the site; there are, however, more general lessons to be learned — of the process of settlement and the practice of war, of the nineteenth-century colonial economy and of the Maoris' response to social, economic and military incursion. The scatter of Pakeha redoubts, stockades and blockhouses tell very directly of the advance of European settlement. Maori fortifications tell of the struggle put up to preserve land and a way of life.

Nigel Prickett

A 1975 aerial photograph (left) shows clearly the shape of Kaitake Redoubt. The holes on the slope in front mark hut sites and tent platforms.

Nicholl Album/ATL

This late 1863 photograph of Kaitake Redoubt, Taranaki, shows the defensive bank built up by alternate layers of earth and fern. Inside is a wooden barrack building and outside are bell tents and a thatched hut. Canvas-covered wicker balls were raised and lowered on the cross-arm of the signal mast to relay messages to New Plymouth.

FROM the earliest days of European settlement in New Zealand there have been industries. Naturally, these reflected both the development of the fledgling colony and the mainly extractive nature of its export economy. Most industries were small in scale, limited in human resources and disadvantaged by a lack of capital and plant, remoteness from overseas markets and technological development. Many were housed in individual buildings or small groups, and ranged from boot factories to brickworks, lime kilns to lighthouses and woolsheds to woollen mills. The study of their evidence, visual and excavated, is known as industrial archaeology and involves the various skills of archaeologist, architect, engineer, geographer and historian. Industrial archaeology focuses on an important part of our heritage, helping us appreciate the interaction between industrial technology and sociological development.

Sealing and whaling took place very early but even in shore whaling there were few buildings of substance and artifacts are generally rather limited, although one notable exception is a crude retaining wall at Fyffe House, Kaikoura, where in 1857 the whaler George Fyffe built a store against a bank. This is possibly the oldest surviving evidence of concrete construction in the country. Today the building has gone, exposing the wall.

The oldest industry is really shipbuilding and the first commercial shipyard was established in the early 1820s at Horeke on the Hokianga. Shipbuilding was remarkably widespread during the nineteenth century and was consummate in both design and craftsmanship of sailing vessels and later steamships in both wood and iron. However, there is little remaining evidence of these early shipyards, with the exception of Lane and Brown's yard at Totara North.

Industries developing around townships usually serviced the needs of the local market. The most widespread early industry was flour-milling and from 1834 many flourmills were built, mainly near rivers, using wood, stone, corrugated iron, brick and concrete, and culminating in large six-storey mills in the 1880s. Waterwheels, turbines and steam were used to drive the millstones and later rollers. One of the best examples of these nineteenth-century water-driven flourmills is at Maheno, North Otago, recently restored by the Historic Places Trust.

The need for building materials for the domestic market saw the advent of sawmills from as early as the 1830s, but their heyday was from 1875 to about 1905 when the number of mills in operation reached 414 as the indigenous timber industry expanded in response to increased demand and advances in technology. Pitsawing was replaced by water-powered and steam-driven circular saws usually housed in wooden, gable-roofed buildings with flat-top and breast benches. The other aspects of milling — breaking out and transportation — were also mechanised, particularly in the South Island, where Dispatch steam haulers were used to bring the timber to a point where it could be transported on bush tramways to the mill. Sadly, hardly any remnants of this important machinery remain: forest regrowth, a wet climate, lack of public interest and some persistent scrap metal collectors have destroyed much of the evidence.

By the 1860s bricks were also becoming popular as a building material: they were more fireproof than wood and gave a greater sense of permanence, especially in public buildings. There was a steady increase in the number of brickworks from the 1860s, but the earliest yards date from the 1840s. In Auckland, for example, the first bricks were made in October 1840, just

The Talisman stamp battery at Karangahake, Thames, 1901. Mining here was difficult and required sophisticated machinery to extract the gold from crushed quartz. In its heyday Karangahake township supported a population of over 2000, and by the time the last major mine, the Talisman, closed in 1918 over $6 million dollars worth of gold had been extracted from the locality.

Auckland Weekly News

nine months after the town was established. As it grew, so the brickworks moved outwards into what were at that time rural areas. In the 90 years between 1840 and 1930, when many of the brickworks were amalgamated, there were some 105 brick, tile and pottery works in Auckland alone. Initially, these were small, employing three to four people and equipment limited to a few shovels, barrows and brick moulds. When isolated pockets of fine-quality clay were exhausted, the brickmakers moved to another site. From the 1860s larger works were established using machinery at first driven by horses but later by steam engines. Pug mills were imported for churning the clay which was extruded in the shape of bars the length and breadth of bricks. Machines for making field tiles, roofing tiles and even domestic crockery were used. Methods for firing the bricks were developed and, with the introduction of the Hoffman continuous kiln, productivity and quality were improved.

Bricks needed mortar and mortar needed lime, so lime burning was an early industry supplying a forerunner of Portland cement. A few early lime kilns may still be seen. The discovery of good limestone and marl deposits led to the manufacture of Portland cement, with the first successful production being in 1884 at Warkworth, soon followed by several other cement works.

Industries ranging from rope making and furniture making to bicycle building, foundries, fruit canning, jam manufacture, paint production, saddlery and harness making, cooperage, brush making, ammunition manufacture and chicory production were all in evidence in the nineteenth century and reflect the diversity and increasing sophistication of the local market they satisfied. Many of these buildings and factories still exist, some are in use. Many more have been pulled down because of obsolescence or urban expansion; familiarity confers no special privilege and nowhere is this more obvious than with our industrial heritage.

The first really major industry, one which brought much-needed capital into the colony, was sheep farming, mainly for wool. This progressed steadily with renewed optimism after the 1880s when refrigeration gave a new use for the sheep carcass as frozen meat for export to Britain. Dairy factories soon followed, for the production of cheese and butter, with similar success. We have a splendid heritage of farm buildings with a quite definite indigenous contribution to their development. Woolsheds especially, but also stables, barns, men's quarters, cookshops, stores, blacksmith's shops, killing sheds, sheep dips, yards, scab boilers, boiling-down works and so on, all furnish ample evidence of vigorous industrial enterprise.

Of the great nineteenth-century industrial enterprises, it was gold-mining, however, which has evoked the most sentiment. There can be no denying its economic importance and, although alluvial mining captured the public's imagination and produced an influx of population, most of which remained, it was the later developments in quartz ore crushing and extraction that brought capital investment and produced steady revenue. Unfortunately, all of the large batteries and mills have disappeared along with their machinery, but some smaller stamper batteries remain and a great deal of ancillary equipment. Poppet heads, however, are rare and only a few cyanide tanks are left.

The many auxiliary industries mining supported were also important. The need for

Harker's brickworks in Mechanics Bay, Auckland, *c.* 1879. The kiln is on the left and the works area runs along the base of the cliff from which clay for brickmaking was obtained.

115

mining machinery and equipment provided the impetus for a rapid development in engineering. Foundries sprang up even in quite small towns and a number of these evolved into large firms, some of which are still in existence. In addition to meeting the demands of mining, these firms produced all manner of items for sawmills, flaxmills and flourmills; also locomotives, bridge girders and caissons, iron lighthouses, boilers and steam engines, gold dredges and steamships.

For a small colony New Zealand had a surprisingly varied range of industrial enterprise. Today there is still considerable visual evidence of this requiring detailed investigation, recording, stabilisation, conservation and, where appropriate, presentation of sites to the public. Below are more detailed descriptions of two such sites, both mining complexes, each representing a different scale of operation.

Mining on Kawau

The pumphouse, Kawau Island (right). Because the copper seam extended below the sea, the pumphouse was needed to keep the mine dry. Like the smelting house, it was made of Mahurangi sandstone.

Smelting house, Kawau Island (below). Only the shell remains of what was New Zealand's first smelter. Built of sandstone from Mahurangi, the smelting house was a rectangular building with a gable roof.

*T*HE earliest mining in New Zealand by Europeans was for manganese and copper. It was while prospecting for the former on Kawau Island in April 1844 that Alexander Kinghorne's party found copper deposits at Miners Point. In July 1844 Sydney-based James Forbes Beattie, on behalf of a Scottish concern, received a Crown grant enabling him to buy the island. He thereupon formed the Kawau Company to carry out mining and his Kawau agent, John Aberdein, engaged Isaac Merrick of Auckland to mine manganese and copper. Some copper ore was sent to England for trial smelting in December 1844 and six months later a party of Cornish miners with their families sailed from Falmouth for Kawau Island. For the next six years the company mined on the island, during which time the operations were managed by Captain Ninnis who lived in a ten-roomed house. ('Captain' was a Cornish mining term for the working manager.) His house is now Mansion House, purchased in 1862 by Sir George Grey and bequeathed by him to the State.

The primary copper ore was some 15 metres below sea level, being solid pyrite with some chalcopyrite but no quartz. However, the company was working with richer secondary material overlying it — an ore that became unstable while being transported by sea in January 1847, causing dangerous overheating. It was quickly decided to erect a smelting house in Smeltinghouse Bay and so a masonry structure was completed in 1848. The smelting operations were carried out by Welsh smelters brought from Swansea.

Reverbatory furnaces outside the smelting house provided preliminary roasting of the ore. They had a fireplace at one end and a chimney at the other with a sloping roof between to throw the heat down on to the ore. Today there are no visible remains of these furnaces. We do not even know what happened to them and archaeological excavation is needed to help identify their nature. Inside the smelting house reduction took place in a roasting hearth. British practice was to repeat the process to give a richer copper with the removed impurities forming slag. Usually the slag was treated again to provide a little more copper. After all sulphides had been treated the concentrated or 'blister' copper was refined in a different furnace.

The mine site at Miners Point had three whims or winches for hauling the ore up the shafts using a capstan-like winding drum drawn by horses treading a circle. On the rocky beach nearby, a pumphouse, to keep the mine dry, was built using sandstone from Mahurangi on the mainland. This took the form of the traditional Cornish engine house. Small in area, such buildings were invariably of stone, including the

Geoffrey Thornton

Geoffrey Thornton

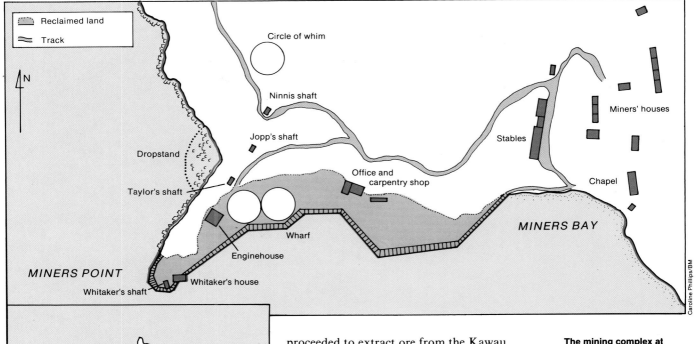

Reclaimed land
Track

Circle of whim

N

Ninnis shaft

Jopp's shaft

Dropstand

Miners' houses

Taylor's shaft

Stables

Office and
carpentry shop

Chapel

MINERS BAY

Wharf

Enginehouse

MINERS POINT

Whitaker's house

Whitaker's shaft

Caroline Phillips/BM

BON ACCORD
HARBOUR

Mansion
House

Miners Bay

The mining complex at Miners Bay, Kawau Island. Today, apart from the pumphouse and the mine shafts, there still remains the stone foundations of the wharf, part of one of the circles of whim, and terracing, where the stables and miners' dwellings stood. In its heyday in the 1840s Kawau supported a population of over 300 people from its mining operations.

chimney base, and had a substantial bob-wall to support the heavy rocker beam or 'bob', which worked the pump rods descending to the mine floor. The pumping machinery consisted of a steam-operated beam engine to create a vacuum in a cylinder filled with steam, thus drawing down the beam. Repetition of this movement produced the pumping action. A short distance away were the ancillary buildings: office, carpenter's shop and smithy, stables, miners' houses and a chapel. There was also the wharf for shipping out the ore.

Mining did not proceed smoothly, however. Trouble began when a rival group, headed by lawyer and speculator Frederick Whitaker and the surveyor Theophilus Heale, formed a company to mine copper on the island. By employing dubious methods they obtained rights to 11 hectares of sea bed to the south-west of the island with a boundary on Miners Point at high-water mark.

Towards the end of 1845 Whitaker and Heale sank a shaft at high-water mark and

proceeded to extract ore from the Kawau Company's rightful claim. By digging a drive towards their rivals the Kawau miners caught them redhanded. Having earlier protested about the Government's action in allowing the new mining rights, the Kawau Company then applied to the Supreme Court for an injunction. This was the start of a lengthy saga of legal argument and counterclaim involving the British Government, and it was June 1848 before Governor Grey was able to inform the Kawau Company that it had acquired the island legally and that Whitaker and Heale had lost their claim.

About the end of 1850 or early 1851 the sea broke into the mine. The rather scanty records indicate that most probably all mining ceased from this time. As much as £60,000 worth of copper had been produced between 1845-50, being the best return of this mineral in New Zealand to date. In 1900 the mine was dewatered but there does not seem to have been any actual mining as a consequence.

Today the pumphouse ruin stands roofless with broken walls and no machinery. It has been stabilised and repaired to arrest erosion of stone and brickwork. Similar work is to be undertaken on the ruins of the smelting house to complement the oldest visual evidence of mining ventures in the colony.

*O*F all the nineteenth-century coalfields the largest was in the Grey River gorge at Brunner. It developed into an industrial complex of nine mines, coke ovens and brickworks, employing 255 men and boys at its peak. Brunnerton township had 2231 people at the 1891 census.

The initial discovery of the coal seam 13 kilometres upstream from Greymouth was made by Thomas Brunner during his epic exploration

The Brunner Industrial Complex

of the region in 1848. After some sampling tests late in the 1850s and early 1860s Matthew Batty and party began commercial mining of this seam in 1864. Two years later the Nelson Coalmining Company had a lease of the mine and used six barges to carry coal to Greymouth for shipping, with horses hauling the empty craft upstream to the timber-built screens and loading chutes. Between 1868 and 1874 the mine was worked by the Nelson Provincial Council whose workmen were housed in a village alongside.

In 1874 Martin Kennedy, a Greymouth merchant, formed the Brunner Coalmining Company and from this time the Brunner coalfield rapidly expanded. In 1876 the Brunner-Greymouth railway opened, after which time all river transport of coal ceased.

The 1880s saw a peak when Brunner became the biggest producer of coal in the colony with 105,660 tonnes or 21 per cent of the country's total. A major calamity was the Brunner Mine explosion of 1896 with the loss of 65 lives; it was the colony's worst mining disaster.

The reputation of Brunnerton, as the site was called at this time, largely resulted from the high quality and large range of firebricks produced from the clay underlying the coal seams. Originally the Nelson Coalmining Company had built twin coke ovens on the riverbank in 1868 using Australian bricks, but these had been of poor quality. By August 1872, however, 500 Brunner firebricks had been produced; these were superior in quality and able to withstand the high temperatures needed in manufacturing coke, and with these the first two ovens were relined. In addition Martin Kennedy had three new beehive coke ovens made further upstream, which were in operation by August 1875 with three more early in the following year; meanwhile the older twin ovens continued in use.

In 1876-7 the six-year-old brickworks were moved a short distance and in 1883-4 were completely rebuilt with plant, grinding and pug

mill, a large drying shed and four kilns. The drying shed, with its part-brick walls, had underfloor heating carefully regulated to allow for changing requirements. With such technological improvements the company was able to advertise that it could produce any size or shape of firebrick that might be required and samples recovered from the site certainly support this claim.

Brunner's other major manufactured product was its coke which it supplied to foundries both in New Zealand and in New Caledonia, where it was used as a reducing agent for converting metal oxides into metals.

Coke itself is distilled from coal and the swelling properties of Brunner coal made it particularly suitable for coke production with slack coal being used — about 4 to 5 tonnes rendering 2 to 3 tonnes of coke.

Construction of the range of beehive coke ovens consisted of a base of large flat stones with vertical walls built of squared, coursed rubble with through stones all laid in lime mortar. The ovens with their characteristic beehive form had sloping floors and were lined with Brunner firebricks set in fire-clay. The six ovens built in 1875-6 were increased to 12 by 1884 with another bank of the same number completed by early 1890. They were built back to back to conserve heat and to use a common flue. An additional freestanding kiln was built either for experimental work or by-products.

Charging was done by means of small, hand-propelled 'tubs' running on rails above the

The twin coke ovens at Brunner (right) prior to restoration. It was necessary to carry out extensive drainage from the rear and replace the protective concrete capping. The former stone retaining wall also had to be reinstated.

Detail of the beehive coke ovens (below right) showing the firebrick lining inside the stone encasement.

Restoration work at the north end of the site (below). The beehive ovens have a full-length protective roof with a catwalk along the truss chords to facilitate public viewing. The foreground shows the archaeological excavations proceeding on the brickworks site. This view is looking upstream.

circular charging openings at the apexes. During firing the doorways were bricked up for the usual period of 72 hours. After this time quenching was done with water before drawing out the coke following the removal of the 'doors'.

From the turn of the century there was a decline in production and after all work on the site ceased in the 1930s a mantle of blackberry and scrub covered the remains of the various structures. Unfortunately, from this time much of the brickwork of the coke ovens was removed for pottery kilns. When in 1977 the New Zealand Historic Places Trust became aware of the coke ovens and classified them as historic structures it was quick to realise the need to become actively involved. The first priorities were in stabilising the twin coke ovens and erecting a permanent shelter over the beehive ovens to protect them

against the elements, especially frosts, and foot traffic. To provide viewing, a catwalk was built which runs along the bottom chord of the roof trusses.

Two archaeological excavations were carried out: the first to gain more information about the beehive ovens and to remove an overlay of debris, and the other was in the area of the brick drying shed remains. This required replacing the loosefill material so as to protect the brick floor and heating system after recording the archaeological evidence. Today the site has information shelters as well as noticeboards and signs along the paths giving public access to all parts of the site, including the massive brick portal of the Brunner Mine return airway. A 50-minute walkway through the bush reveals many mining relics.

Brunner at the turn of the century, showing the double range of beehive coke ovens with the tramway for top loading. The brick drying shed with its continuous lantern on the ridge and the kiln chimneys are behind. Bagged coke awaits loading into railway wagons. Beyond is the Brunnerton bridge leading to the Tyneside Mine.

Geoffrey Thornton

A view of the Brunner industrial complex (below) with the townships of Taylorville and Wallsend in the distance. On the opposite bank of the Grey River was the Tyneside Coalmine, opened in 1876. Today only the chimney still stands, and this requires some stabilisation.

Auckland Weekly News

CENTRAL Otago is dotted with remnants of former settlements and workings constructed by the Chinese, the largest minority among the many nationalities who came to New Zealand in quest of gold last century. This began in 1861 when Australian-born adventurer/prospector Gabriel Read discovered gold in Gabriel's Gully, a tributary of the Tuapeka River, near Lawrence. The exodus from Dunedin was slow at first but within a month, once the extent of the field had been proven, the Tuapeka rush was well under way. It was followed by rushes to the Dunstan (August 1862), the Arrow (September 1862) and the Shotover (October 1862). By the beginning of 1863 there were thousands of miners prospecting along the Molyneux (Clutha) River and its tributaries from the Tuapeka to the upper Shotover — 90 per cent having abandoned the Australian goldfields to try their luck in New Zealand. Among them were Americans, French, Italians, Germans and Scandinavians — forming a cosmopolitan element amid the predominantly British and Irish stock. The Chinese, later to become the most visible of all the nationalities on the goldfields, were not among this initial inrush.

By the end of 1864 declining fortunes and the advent of a new rush to the Wakamarina field in Marlborough hastened the exodus of 'Australians' from the Otago fields. The population of Otago began to decline rapidly which greatly concerned Otago business interests. Proposals to import cheap Chinese labour met immediate opposition from the remaining mining population but the business interests prevailed. In 1865 the Dunedin Chamber of Commerce announced it favoured Chinese immigration and a written statement conferring the right of protection (from harassment) was conveyed to the Chinese working on the Victorian goldfields. Initially few were interested but by the latter half of 1866 a steady stream were entering New Zealand, mostly through the Port of Otago. The

majority of the 15,000 Chinese who came to New Zealand during the nineteenth century spent their time on the Otago goldfields.

After kitting out, they wasted little time before heading inland to the goldfields. Despite language difficulties and harassment, the Chinese rapidly established themselves. By 1871, the peak year of Chinese immigration, there were over 4000 spread throughout Otago compared with 7000 European miners. Chinese settlements, both dispersed and nucleated, were established in all the main mining areas and towns in Central Otago. The settlements were supported by a supply network consisting of large Chinese merchant businesses in Dunedin, the most notable being that of Sew Hoy, which supplied an informal network of Chinese storekeepers throughout the goldfields.

The Chinese were remarkably adaptable. In the gorges they constructed shelters by walling up the front of rock overhangs with the readily available slabs of detrital schist rock. In areas where there were no natural overhangs, they built small huts of river cobbles or rock rubble, but the raw materials on hand were the chief determinants of construction techniques. Thus at Waipori and in the Nokomai, adobe and mudbricks were the principal construction materials. At Round Hill they employed wooden shingles, while in Westland, raupo, timber and

The layout (below) of the residential part of Cromwell's 'Chinatown', as revealed by excavation in 1980. The site has since been destroyed as part of the preparatory works for the Clyde dam.

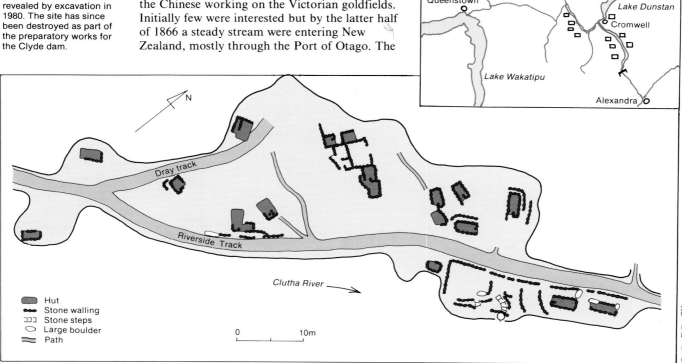

Hut
Stone walling
Stone steps
Large boulder
Path

0   10m

stone were used. In some areas, for example at Lawrence, weatherboards, rice sacks and flattened kerosene cans predominated. Fortunately for archaeologists, they shunned tents.

Cromwell's 'Chinatown', until its destruction during the preparations for the formation of Lake Dunstan, was the best preserved example of a Chinese settlement in Otago. The residential part also appears to have had the greatest longevity, existing as a recognised Chinese enclave for at least 50 years, from about 1870 until 1920. Its heyday was between 1870–85, after which it went into decline, hastened no doubt by the departure of the storekeepers before the turn of the century, and the increasing age and isolation of the remaining inhabitants. In its heyday, the little settlement was a thriving scene. About 40 Chinese miners lived in 30-odd huts surrounded by small garden plots, fruit trees, hen coops and pig pens. A small spring provided fresh water all year round. Other Chinese miners (over 400 in 1871) lived in the surrounding area. They regularly visited 'Chinatown', as it was known to the Europeans, where there were general stores, grog shops, gaming rooms and at least one, albeit shortlived, brothel (the proprietor was convicted and sentenced to two months' hard labour). A large market garden was across the street from the business area.

After the settlement's abandonment the buildings gradually decayed and became overgrown. Within a few short years the site had all but faded from memory, until an archaeological survey, undertaken as part of the mitigation work associated with the Clutha power scheme, noted its existence. Because of the density of Chinese occupation around Cromwell, many former Chinese sites are affected by the power scheme. They became a 'special focus' of the archaeological salvage programme conducted between 1977 and 1987. About 60 Chinese sites have been investigated, with complete excavations conducted on 20 including the site of Cromwell's Chinatown, Arrowtown's Chinese settlement and store, and scattered rock shelters, huts and workings in the Cromwell and Kawarau gorges and the Upper Clutha Valley.

Chinese sites are particularly amenable to archaeological research because they are easily identifiable by the presence of artifacts of Asian origin including ceramic food pots, cooking and eating utensils, embossed glass bottles, Chinese coins and many distinctive artifacts associated with gambling and opium smoking. As most of the Chinese miners were from humble peasant origins, they left few written records, so archaeology is able to make a very real contribution to knowledge of how they lived and worked.

Chinese alcohol (Ng Ka Py) and European black glass beer bottles (left) exposed in the base of a hut wall during the Chinatown excavation.

Excavation proceeds (below left) amid roots and collapsed walls in one of the schist-walled Chinese miners' huts at Chinatown.

The central group of huts in the Cromwell 'Chinatown' site (below). Their back-to-back construction is rare in New Zealand, but not uncommon in Guangdong, the province of origin of most of the Chinese miners.

Neville Ritchie

Compared with other groups of immigrant miners, the Chinese differed in several important respects. They did not readily acculturate with the dominant Anglo-European population of New Zealand and strongly maintained traditional lifestyles. This is reflected in their continuing reliance on products imported from China, such as foodstuffs, utensils, medicines and relaxants.

Although the range of traditional foods and other products is likely to have been considerably less than that available in China, nevertheless a wide range was imported by the Chinese merchants and stocked by the Chinese stores on the goldfields. Imported products included tea, rice, soya oil, preserved ginger, dried vegetables, herbs and spices, dried fish and fish sauces, alcoholic beverages, ceramic bowls, cups and spoons, brass and iron wok ladles, chopsticks, opium, traditional medicines, cloth and items associated with various games of chance. Judging from the volume of these items found around the former habitation sites, considerable quantities were imported or consumed. Archaeological evidence also indicates that the Chinese sojourners consumed large quantities of European preserved and manufactured foods such as jams, pickles, relishes, vinegar, canned fish and Worcestershire sauce. But, with the

possible exception of jams, these foods were largely substitutes for traditional foods.

Traditional forms of relaxation and opium and alcohol use persisted, but the adoption and predominant consumption of several European alcohols, notably brandy/cognac, gin and beer, is an example of a significant change.

The adoption of western-style clothing probably represents the most voluntary acculturative response of the Chinese miners in New Zealand. They quickly adopted European miners' working clothes and boots to combat the cold conditions, and employed similar tools for gold winning, such as picks, shovels, pans and cradles. Other items of western manufacture which are frequently uncovered during the excavation of Chinese sites include clay and briar pipes, bone-handled brushes, knives and combs, crockery and cutlery, enamelled and iron pots, alcohol bottles (particularly square case gin bottles), aerated water bottles, patent and prescribed medicine containers, sauce and pickle jars, ceramic toothpaste and ointment pots, many varieties of tinned products (such as fish, jams, condensed milk, tea, matches and tobacco), and a wide range of nails, spikes and clothing fittings.

Analysis of faunal remains indicates

Some examples of different types of European bottles (right) uncovered during the Chinatown excavation. The bottles are evidence that the Chinese miners acquired a taste for and purchased a wide range of European products and alcohols while retaining many traditional foods and beverages.

A reconstructed rare, brown-glazed, earthenware jar (far right) of Chinese origin uncovered during the excavation of a Chinese hut site near Queensberry, Upper Clutha Valley. More common green-glazed jars contained preserved ginger and other food products.

The Chinese store (below) beside the Arrowtown Chinese settlement in 1983 after excavation. Since the photograph was taken, the store, along with other Chinese hut sites, has been restored.

A team of archaeology students (below right) excavating Ah Wee's hut site near Luggate in the Upper Clutha Valley. Ah Wee, who abandoned the hut *c.* 1900, may have been the last of several Chinese miners who lived there.

consumption of cattle, pig and sheep meat. Although the Chinese are reputed to have had a marked preference for pig meats, cattle and sheep bones are well represented in the faunal assemblages, suggesting consumption of these meats in much higher proportions than they would have enjoyed in their home villages. The avian remains from the study sites indicate that many of the Chinese miners kept domestic poultry (fowls and to a lesser extent ducks) or were able to acquire their meat and eggs. They also supplemented their diet with wild birds. These included waterbirds such as swans, ducks and native quail during the earliest years of settlement. Exotic fish bones found in the midden deposits were probably derived from imported dried fish.

Both archaeological evidence and ethno-historic records indicate that the Chinese miners attempted to maintain their traditional material culture and lifestyle with as few changes as possible. Even when they adopted the trappings of the Anglo-European majority, they maintained their 'Chinese-ness' where it mattered most to them — in social behaviour, religious beliefs and philosophy. But they were nothing but practical and readily adopted European things they considered useful. Early writers have portrayed the Chinese as a frugal adaptive people who retained their customs as much as possible. Archaeological investigations support this impression and provide specific information on how the Chinese responded to their new situation.

The Rev. G. H. McNeur and three Chinese miners outside their hut at Macetown (about 12 kilometres upstream of Arrowtown on the Arrow River). The hut is similar to many of those built by Chinese miners in the Upper Clutha Valley.

McNeur Album/Otago Early Settlers Museum.

A *c.* **1895 view (below)** of the residential part of the Cromwell Chinatown on the banks of the Kawarau River. The stores associated with the settlement were sited on the river terrace above the huts.

McNeur Album/Otago Early Settlers Museum.

The Kauri Driving Dams

*Jack Diamond &
Bruce Hayward*

The gate of this 1920 stringer dam (right) has been tripped and the water surging through the gate has brought logs with it from above the dam while other logs will be picked up downstream.

A small rafter dam (below) with upright loose plank gate. The planks are hanging in an unset position. Dams were constructed to the builders' wishes as no plans or blue prints are known to have been used.

AT the end of the eighteenth century, the northern parts of the North Island were covered in vast stands of kauri forest. Kauri (*Agathis australis*) did not grow south of a line roughly joining Tauranga and Kawhia, close to the 38th south latitude, but north of this was 120,000 hectares of kauri forest. Today only 4000 hectares of this original forest remains, the vast bulk having been removed by the kauri timber industry and by land clearance for farming.

The first kauri to be cut in the late eighteenth and early nineteenth centuries were the tall young trees (rickers) that grew near the sea — highly valued as spars for sailing ships. From about 1830 teams of pitsawyers were also employed cutting kauri logs into boards for the local market and export; kauri timber was much preferred by carpenters and boat builders because the wood was straight and even-grained, remarkably free from knots and easy to work.

The first sawmills, powered initially by waterwheel and later by steam, were established in the late 1830s and soon there were numerous small mills cutting logs from the forests around the sheltered harbours of Northland and the Coromandel Peninsula. The demand for timber continued to increase, especially with the onset of the Coromandel gold rush in the late 1860s and 1870s. However, local consumption dropped off in the 1880s with the depression and a number of sawmills went bankrupt.

By 1900 over three-quarters of the kauri forests had been cut or destroyed by fire, but uncontrolled cutting continued. The peak year for production was 1907, after which the quantity of remaining kauri dwindled until now when felling kauri for timber has virtually ceased.

Kauri driving dams were used in northern New Zealand between 1850 and 1942. Written descriptions and photographs of these dams are almost entirely restricted to those built after 1900, so their archaeological remains provide the main source of information on their early design and architectural development. The sites of over 1000 kauri driving dams are still present in the stream beds of some of northern New Zealand's roughest country, and hold an enormous amount of valuable information about this spectacular aspect of the kauri timber industry, which is unobtainable from any other source.

For 90 years these driving dams were used as a means of transporting logs out of the bush-clad hills. A dam was built across streams and the water collecting behind was released in a flood to drive the logs downstream. Most dams had large built-in gates which could be completely opened by a strong pull of the trip wire — the logs either passed through the gate with the water or were picked up by the flood as it raced down the valley.

Typically, dams were constructed where the terrain prevented the economic use of other methods of transport such as bullock teams, rolling roads and tramways. As a result, dam sites are generally found in the roughest country, such as Omahutu Forest, the Waitakere Ranges and Coromandel Peninsula. They are not known to have been used in New Zealand outside the kauri region of the northern North Island.

The kauri driving dams were usually used for only a short period, three to five years, after which they were abandoned without being demolished. Over the years some have been burnt, others had their wood removed, but the

Jack Diamond Coll.

Jack Diar

124

majority have been rapidly disappearing under the attack of rot and floods. The best-preserved dam sites that remain today are those that were used most recently from 1910 to 1940. Several — for example, the Kauaeranga and Tairua valleys, Coromandel Peninsula — are in almost perfect structural condition, although the wood is badly rotted. The most interesting dam sites, however, are the earliest ones built when a wide variety of designs and innovations was being tested. Unfortunately, the remains of these 100 to 140-year-old structures are in a poor condition, with most or all woodwork gone, leaving only parts of the flume floor, holes in the rock bed or earthworks in the banks.

Written records indicate that the first reusable driving dams in New Zealand were constructed in the 1850s in the Waitakere Ranges, west of Auckland. Their remains in the Henderson Valley show that they were wooden rafter dams with low angle faces similar to those used in Nova Scotia, former home of their builder, John McLeod. The remains of other early driving dams (1850–1870), in the Huia and Whatipu areas of the Waitakere Ranges, are the only known examples in New Zealand made of rock and earth. These were built by the Gibbons family, who had just arrived from New Foundland where cribwork driving dams filled with rock were commonplace.

By studying the archaeological sites of these and other well-dated dams, it is possible to trace the architectural development of the unique New Zealand kauri driving dams that were widely used in the first half of this century. The earliest dams followed the familiar design of North America, where the driving streams were much larger and gentler and the broad, low dams banked up huge ponds. Their solid gates could be raised or lowered to maintain a steady flow of water over a long period to carry logs tens of kilometres downstream. It soon became obvious that these dams were unsuited to New Zealand conditions where a high flood of water was required for only a short time to flush the logs the small distances out of the forest. Thus the dams became higher and steeper and the gate

and trip mechanism evolved through a number of designs to perfect a rapid release of the water in one huge wave. Probably the most significant development was the change in the 1860s and 1870s from solid hinged gates to several designs with loose gate planks fitted together to close the gate opening. A pull on a tripwire was all that was needed to activate the trip mechanism to open the gate and release the water and logs in one rush. Originally the gate planks had been attached to the gate stringer by chains but by the 1890s rope wire was being used. A concurrent development was the reduction in the number of cills — the foundation slabs on which the dam was built — from 9 to 2-4. By the turn of the century such changes had resulted in two unique New Zealand designs — stringer dams and swinging rafter gate dams — adapted to the rugged terrain and widely used in the kauri forests.

Today, although such developments are significant when dating dams, evidence is rarely found. In many instances all the wood has gone and only the foundation holes cut in the stream bed remain. Often, though, in the banks by the dam, outlines can be traced, indicating the angle of its face and from that an assessment made of its age, as the trend from the low angle (30 to 45 degrees) to steeper faces (45 to 70 degrees) started to take place in the 1870s and 1880s, reaching the acme of development in the first years of this century.

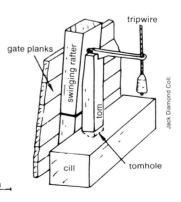

A wishbone-shaped hinged iron tom like those used in dams from the 1850s to the 1880s.

Site of c. 1910 dam (left). The only archaeological remains are the recesses for the cills cut in the solid rock on either side of the stream bed.

A variety of trip mechanisms were used to release the dam gates. Represented below are three such mechanisms, each activated by trip wire.

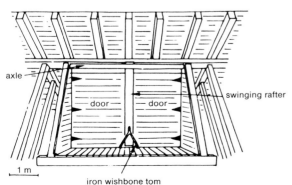

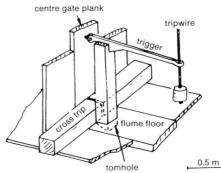

Further Reading

ANDERSON, A. J., *Prodigious Birds: Moas and Moa-hunting in Prehistoric New Zealand,* Cambridge University Press, (in press).

ANDERSON, A. J., *When All the Moa Ovens Grew Cold,* Otago Heritage Books, 1983.

BARRATT, G., *Queen Charlotte Sound, New Zealand: The Traditional and European Records, 1820.* Carleton University Press, Ottawa, 1987.

BEAGLEHOLE, J. C., *The Journals of Captain James Cook.* Four volumes published by the Hakluyt Society, Cambridge, 1955-1967.

BELLWOOD, P., *Man's Conquest of the Pacific: the Prehistory of Southeast Asia and Oceania,* Collins, 1978.

BRAILSFORD, B., *The Tattooed Land,* A. H. and A. W. Reed, Wellington, 1981.

BUCK, P., *The Coming of the Maori,* Whitcombe and Tombs, 1949.

DAVIDSON, J., *The Prehistory of New Zealand,* Longman Paul, Auckland, 1984.

DUFF, R. S., *The Moa Hunter Period of Maori Culture,* Government Printer, Wellington, 3rd Edition, 1977.

FOX, A., *Prehistoric Maori Fortifications in the North Island of New Zealand,* Longman Paul, Auckland, 1976.

GOLSON, J. (ed.), *Polynesian Navigation: Symposium on Andrew Sharp's Theory of Accidental Voyages,* A. H. and A. W. Reed, Wellington, 1963.

GREEN, R. C., Adaptation and Change in Maori Culture, in *Biogeography and Ecology in New Zealand,* (G. Kuschel, ed.), Dr W. Junk, The Hague, 1975.

HAAST, J. von, *Moas and Moa Hunters,* Times, Christchurch, 1871. Also published in *Transactions of the New Zealand Institute,* Vol. 4, 1872.

HOUGHTON, P., *The First New Zealanders,* Hodder and Stoughton, Auckland, 1980.

LEACH, B. F. and H. M. LEACH (eds.), *Prehistoric Man in Palliser Bay,* National Museum of New Zealand, Bulletin Number 21, 1979.

LEACH, H., *1,000 Years of Gardening in New Zealand,* A. H. and A. W. Reed, Wellington, 1984.

McCULLOCH, B., *No Moa,* Canterbury Museum, Christchurch, 1982.

MURRAY-OLIVER, A., *Captain Cook's Artists in the Pacific, 1769-1779,* Avon Fine Prints, 1969.

New Zealand Archaeological Association Newsletter (renamed *Archaeology in New Zealand* from March 1988). Published quarterly by the New Zealand Archaeological Association. 1957-

New Zealand Journal of Archaeology. Published annually by the New Zealand Archaeological Association. 1979-

PRICKETT, N. (ed.), *The First Thousand Years,* The Dunmore Press, Palmerston North, 1982.

SHARP, A., *Ancient Voyagers in Polynesia,* Longman Paul, Auckland, 1963.

SHARP, A., *The Voyages of Abel Janszoon Tasman.* Clarendon Press, Oxford, 1968.

SIMMONS, D. R., *The Great New Zealand Myth: A Study of the Discovery and Origin Traditions of the Maori,* A. H. and A. W. Reed, Wellington, 1976.

SKINNER, H. D., *Comparatively Speaking,* John McIndoe, Dunedin, 1974.

STEVENS, G. (principal author), *Prehistoric New Zealand,* Heinmann Reed, Auckland, 1988.

THORNTON, G. G., *New Zealand's Industrial Heritage,* A. H. and A. W. Reed, Wellington, 1982.

TROTTER, M. and B. McCULLOCH, 'Excavations at Takahanga Pa, Kaikoura, 1980-1982', in *Records of the Canterbury Museum,* Vol. 9 No. 10, 1984.

TROTTER, M. and B. McCULLOCH, *Prehistoric Rock Art of New Zealand* (second edition), Longman Paul, 1981.

TROTTER, M., 'A Prehistoric Back Pack from inland Canterbury' in *Records of the Canterbury Museum,* Vol. 10, No. 2, 1987.

WILSON, J. (ed.), *From the Beginning: The Archaeology of the Maori,* Penguin, 1987.

Index